T0300418

GARLAND STUDIES ON

INDUSTRIAL PRODUCTIVITY

edited by

STUART BRUCHEY
ALLAN NEVINS PROFESSOR EMERITUS
COLUMBIA UNIVERSITY

TECHNOLOGY TRANSFER

REJUVENATING MATURED INDUSTRIES

SHASTRI MOONAN

Routledge
Taylor & Francis Group
New York   London

First published by Garland Publishing, Inc.

This edition published 2012 by Routledge:

Routledge
Taylor & Francis Group
711 Third Avenue
New York, NY 10017

Routledge
Taylor & Francis Group
2 Park Square, Milton Park
Abingdon, Oxon OX14 4RN

Library of Congress Cataloging-in-Publication Data

Moonan, Shastri, 1946–
    Technology transfer : rejuvenating matured industries /
Shastri Moonan.
        p.   cm. — (Garland studies on industrial productivity)
    Includes bibliographical references and index.
    ISBN 0-8153-2997-0 (alk. paper)
    1. Steel industry and trade—Technological innovations.
2. Steel minimills—Technological innovations—Case studies.
3. Computer integrated manufacturing systems. 4. Technology
transfer—Japan—Case studies. 5. Technology transfer—Developing countries—Case studies. I. Title. II. Series.
TS307.M66 1997
338.4'7672—dc21

                                                          97-38585

Table of Contents

List of Figures		xi
List of Tables		xiii
List of Maps		xv
Foreword		xvii
Preface		xix
I	INTRODUCTION	3
	Resurgence of the Steel Industry	3
	Steelmaking and Technology Transfer	4
	Steel-Making Technology and Strategy	5
	Technology Outlook for the Future	7
II	AN OVERVIEW	11
	Central Technologies of Steel Minimills	12
	The Transfer of Steelmaking Technology	18
	Modern Steel Technology	31
III	THE SCRAP MARKET	39
IV	TECHNOLOGY TRANSFER—LITERATURE REVIEW	67
	The Market	67
	Technological Progress	71
	Models of Technology Transfer	76
	A Synthesis of the Three Approaches	78
	Toward a Dynamic Taxonomy of Technology Transfer	82
	Steel Minimill Technologies	87

V   A COMPARISON OF INTEGRATED STEEL
    MILLS WITH STEEL MINIMILLS   107
    Product Types   107
    Capacities of Mills   108
    Geographic Locations   109
    Raw Materials   111
    Technology   113
    Productivity   116
    Employment Costs   119
    Entry and Exit   120
    Technology Trends   122

VI   THE INTERNATIONAL TRANSFER OF
    TECHNOLOGY   129
    A Knowledge-Based Framework of Technology
        Transfer   129
    Knowledge Architecture   131
    Market Direction   144
    Inter Industry Technology Transfer   149
    The Technology Transfer Challenges   155
    Technology Transfer Opportunities to China   156
    The Technology Opportunities Generated in
        Europe and Latin America   157
    Conclusion   159

VII   JAPANESE CASE STUDY   165
    The Evolution and Unique Contribution of the
        Modern Japanese Steel Industry   165
    Steelmaking Locations in Japan   173
    Three Key Developmental Characteristics of
        the Japanese Steel Industry   181
    Lessons of Experience from Development of the
        Japanese Steel Industry   181

VIII THE DIRECTION OF TECHNOLOGY
TRANSFER WITHIN THE STEEL INDUSTRIES
IN NEWLY INDUSTRIALIZED AND
DEVELOPING COUNTRIES   199
Different Economic and Technological
Development Paradigms in NICs and LDCs   201
Options for Increasing Steel Capacity   207
Technological Prospects for NICs and LDCs   223
Conclusion   229

IX FUTURE RESEARCH   233
A Brief Review   233
A View to Future Studies   234
Stock and Flow Variables—an Interactive
Model of Technology Transfer   237
The Pathfinding Nature of this Study   238

Glossary   241

Bibliography   247

Index   277

List of Figures

2.1 Production sequence for steel products   14
2.2 Minimill based on direct reduction   15
2.3 The EOF process   16
2.4 Conventional minimill   17
2.5 Scrap pathways within the world steel industry   32

3.1 Summary of United States scrap in 1990   41
3.2 United States—scrap   42
3.3 Possible trend in United States scrap resources   43
3.4 Summary of scrap in Japan in 1990   44
3.5 Summary of scrap in the 12-member EC in 1990   45
3.6 United States scrap resources   54
3.7 Scrap resources in the European Community   55
3.8 Scrap resources in Japan   56
3.9 World scrap resources   57
3.10 Flow diagram of scrap recycling in production, processing and usage of iron and steel   60
3.11 Schematic comparison of the iron-ore and scrap systems   62
3.12 Iron ore, scrap and primary metals in steelmaking   63

4.1 Schematic representation of causal relationships   69
4.2 Apparent steel consumption of crude steel   73
4.3 World steel exports of finished steel   73
4.4 Production shift toward developing countries   74
4.5 Interdependent variables in the technology transfer process   83
4.6 The interaction of the main elements in the technology transfer process through stock and flow variables   84

7.1 The Purdue Model   169
7.2 Layered software architecture typically used
     in the modern Japanese steel industry   171
7.3 Energy consumption per ton of crude steel in
     Japan   184
7.4 Capacity of degassing (RH and DH) facilities
     in Japan   186
7.5 Change of average sulfur content in NKK's line
     pipe   187
7.6 Plans for NKK's diversification into the
     engineering and construction fields   189
7.7 NKK's sales by division   190

8.1 Per capita steel consumption vs. GNP   206
8.2 Steel production in Latin America   208
8.3 Scrap purchased/steel produced   213
8.4 Latin American DRI production   215
8.5 Usual ladle metallurgy processes   218
8.6 Ladle treatments (model reactor)   219
8.7 The NSR System (NSC) for producing clean
     steel   220
8.8 Reduction of impurities through combination of
     process   221
8.9 Steel plant productivity in tons of steel ingot
     produced per man-year   228

List of Tables

1   Residual alloying elements in carbon steel and
    cast iron: the United States case   30
2   Scrap consumption in Latin American countries   46
3   Possible change in resources of the main types of
    scrap in the Arab world   47
4   Total theoretical possibilities for scrap
    recovery in the main Arab countries   48
5   World trade in scrap: main exporting and
    importing countries in 1990   49
6   Average use of scrap in oxygen converter in
    selected countries in 1990   53
7   World trends in production or consumption of
    steelmaking primary metals   59
8   A knowledge asset-based view of technology
    transfer   130
9   Potential growth of electric furnaces in Europe   141
10   New ironmaking processes in commercial
    production   153
11   New ironmaking processes under development   154

List of Maps

1   Geographical Distribution and Industrial
    Development in Japan   175

2   The Inland Sea Coastline   178

3   The Tokyo Bay Area   179

4   Osaka District   180

Foreword

For more than a decade I served as the Director of the Alfred P. Sloan Fellows Program, at the Massachusetts Institute of Technology, and have had the privilege of getting to know many outstanding participants. Most of the participants have come from the more developed regions of the world. Rarely has there been participation from the Caribbean. And rarely has there been a participant like Dr. Shastri Moonan of Trinidad and Tobago.

I interviewed Shastri Moonan for the Program in the Spring of 1988. I learned that he had studied law in the United Kingdom and had been admitted to practice as an attorney, and ascertained his success as a businessman and entrepreneur in his native country. I was interested in his motivation to attend the Sloan Fellows Program. He had two primary reasons: his intellectual curiosity in the field of management, and his desire to prepare himself for service to the development of his country.

The Sloan Fellows Program is now in its 66th year and has a very distinguished list of graduates including the current Secretary General of the United Nations, the CEO's of many Corporations, including the Boeing Company, Caterpillar Corporation, Bell South Corporation, and other leaders in government and industry from throughout the world.

Shastri Moonan was an outstanding participant in MIT's Sloan Fellows Program, and went on to complete his Ph.D. at the prestigious Fletcher School of Law and Diplomacy.

Dr. Moonan placed primary emphasis in the study of technology transfer, and his research has led to the publication of this important book.

The author has brought a new perspective for readers to gain a more incisive understanding of how the processes of technology transfer have taken place and continue to take place. Within the matrix of competition enmeshed with globalization, the book offers three levels of analysis within which technology transfer at the intra-firm level, inter-firm level, and inter-industry level are examined. This approach provides value to the field of technology transfer, since in capturing these dynamic processes the reader can understand and even anticipate with measurable accuracy the effects of policies to facilitate technology transfer.

Throughout his career, Shastri Moonan has been an entrepreneur with a purpose. A primary objective has been to develop business that will provide employment for those from depressed areas in his country. He has also pursued advanced education in the United Kingdom and the United States with an orientation to learning that he can use in public service. This book is an outgrowth of Dr. Moonan's pursuit to communicate a new perspective on the process of technology transfer.

Professor Alan F. White, Senior Associate Dean of the M.I.T. Sloan School of Management, Massachusetts Institute of Technology, Cambridge, Massachusetts

Preface

Matured industries face incredible and, at times, intractable problems. If they are to stay alive, they must rejuvenate, they have to compete against the accelerating rate of change. These changes are in organization: at the micro-cosmic level, within the corporations as well as the macro-cosmic level, at the level of the industry. At the same time, there is technological change where the emphasis is on the quality of the product. Time is now a far more valuable commodity—time to market and just-in-time inventory. The steel industry has to assert its presence in the global economy: steel has to be used for more intricate functions and their customers have higher expectations from the products they purchase, as such, quality has become the central theme. Faced with these complex issues, the steel industry had to look for and find solutions. In the steel minimill industry, re-engineering the process and the management became the "answer." The ensuing chapters attempted with piercing agony, yet with excitement, to examine these issues.

THE STRUCTURE OF THE BOOK

Chapter 3, "The Scrap Market," discusses the increasing demand for steel, and hence for scrap, around the world, and examines the structure of the scrap market, scrap being the critical raw material that supplies the electric arc furnaces (EAFs), the ladle refining furnaces, and the continuous casters utilized in the minimill industry world-wide. The various implications of the trend are examined, including the minimill industry's various process routes for utilizing scrap, growing pressure on the volume, reliability, and quality of the world scrap supply and how new technologies (for example, thin-slab continuous casting, oxygen blowing, scrap preheating, and coal injection) are permitting greater penetration of minimill products into integrated product markets. The utilization of various scrap alternatives is briefly discussed, and the chapter concludes with an examination of the shifting economics of steelmaking using the blast furnace and EAF route.

Chapter 4, "Technology Transfer: Literature Review," focuses on the central questions that are being probed in the book. (However, it will limit itself to the analytical constructs which facilitate technology transfer, specifically, central questions 1 through 3 mentioned in Chapter 2.) The chapter will consider the economic underpinnings of technology transfer for both producer and consumer. The role of international competition and the effect of international cooperation on both globalization and capture of market share will be examined, as will steelmakers' responses to different geographic and strategic challenges inherent in the world steel market. With these constructs in place, the chapter will also treat models of technology transfer, and will go on to develop a new synthesis of the existing technology transfer models.

The foundation of this new synthesis lies in an examination of steelmaking in terms of dependent variables and independent variables, or the stock and flow variables that were developed by process engineering theory. The independent variables critical to this examination of the steel industry are the availability and quality of scrap and scrap substitutes. The dependent variables can be grouped into two major categories: organization of the steel firm and the environmental (societal) milieu in which the steel firm operates (including economic, cultural, political, administrative/legal, and infrastructure *issues*).

The chapter develops a dynamic taxonomy of technology transfer, examining the dependent and independent variables in the light of transfer risks, capital requirements, and market expansion and costs reduction. The chapter then concludes with an examination of steel minimill technologies and products in the light of this model of technology transfer.

Chapter 5, "A Comparison of Integrated Steel Mills and Steel Minimills," compares integrated steel mill and minimill technologies, and examines in detail the causative factors behind the technological migration from integrated steel mills to minimills. The chapter will examine such aspects of technological difference as product types, mill capacities, location criteria, use of raw materials, technologies in use, productivity figures and mill efficiencies, varying employment costs, entry and exit into the market, and technologies under development.

Chapter 6, "The International Transfer of Technology," examines how the three minimill technologies (the electric arc furnace, ladle technology, and continuous casting) are being constantly improved by developments in R&D (an intervening variable) and how the developments are being absorbed and assimilated into steelmaking technologies to improve steel minimill efficiency. I shall propose that these developments are inducing structural changes in the iron and steel industry with respect to the following:

1. The size of production facilities is becoming smaller while the efficiencies they achieve are becoming proportionally higher.
2. The market is trending toward achieving lower costs and economies of scale.
3. Firms around the world are rationalizing, relationships between management and labor are shifting, and relationships between manufacturers are often shifting along the competition-cooperation continuum.

The chapter concludes with a discussion of the effects of technology transfer on various regions around the world.

Chapter 7, "The Japanese Case Study," examines, within the context of a case study on the evolution of the Japanese steel industry, how technology transfer can be used to further the development of a national economy in particular and, by extension, the steel industry in general. The literature on technology transfer will now be examined with a market orientation. The following two general questions will be probed and answers offered:

1. How is the competition in this market organized?
2. What are the driving forces in the market?

The attitude toward the use of imported technologies, the *role* of geography, and the steel industry's relationships with other domestic industries will be examined, and six developmental measures of the evolution and performance of the Japanese steel industry will be thoroughly probed: the domestic market, the role of modernization, emphasis on particular product lines, market opportunities and business diversification, workforce loyalty, and governmental support, including the nature of domestic politics and financing arrangements. Further, the central questions set out in Chapter 2 will be examined against the structure of the Japanese steel industry. This examination should demonstrate how Japan has structured its steel industry to continually increase productivity while decreasing cost and price.

Chapter 8, "The Direction of Technology Transfer Within the Steel Industries in Newly Industrialized and Developing Countries," examines the special challenges the newly industrialized and developing countries have faced in developing their steel industries, stating whether the structure of technology transfer is changing and whether the new patterns which may be emerging are doing so within the context of globalization. Intuitively, I feel that the flexibility of the process of technology transfer will be a driving force behind the capture of market share. However, my approach will be scientific and will determine my findings.

Chapter 9, "Future Research," comments on the findings to the answers to the central questions I posed in the second chapter. My comments and suggestions for future R&D by the steel industry as well as for future research on the directions and trends taking place within the steel industry will address to issues:

1. The future direction of the system of industrial organization as it affects technology transfer and competitiveness in the steel minimill industry.

2. The future direction of the steel minimill industry with respect to the usage of scrap and scrap substitutes, operational processes, and development of the new product lines.

The technology transfer process is undergoing rapid change in the steel minimill industry. Corporations with the proprietary knowledge are collaborating with steel manufacturers to produce high quality products at affordable prices. The objective of the technology transfer process is to increase productivity and at the same time reduce costs per unit. Extensive publications over the years attempted to explain how the technology transfer process works. Essentially, this was done by isolating the variables with respect to organizational and societal structure as it impacted with the transfer mechanisms.

Part of the contribution to knowledge is the focus on the limitations of the transfer process dictated by the policies and needs of the host country. Also examined is the question: what are the levels of interaction with the possibilities for accessing capital and achieving market expansion and increased production? These are crucial issues which underline the need for an interactive model of technology transfer based on stock and flow variables.

Technology Transfer

I

Introduction

RESURGENCE OF THE STEEL INDUSTRY

Over the past twenty-five years there have been many changes in the technology of steelmaking, so that mills today are in many instances radically different from those of the 1970's. The 1970's is the beginning of the period of the refocusing of the steel minimill industry. By refocusing, expected and unexpected changes ensued. This book will demonstrate how every facet and every phase of ironmaking and steelmaking were revolutionized: from the preparation of raw materials to the delivery of finished products.

In the next twenty-five years there would still be two dominant types of mills that constitute the steel industry: the integrated mill and the minimill. I have devoted a chapter of this book and discussed the differences between the two types. Suffice it to say at this stage, that an integrated mill is large and based fundamentally on the blast furnace for the production of its metal, it is expected to undergo substantial changes. In contrast, we can expect incremental improvements in minimills. The minimills would continue to depend upon the scrap material for their metal. The sizing of the minimill is expected to remain the same with a capacity range from 500,000 to 1,000,000 tons annually. The focus of the minimill for its production capacity is now undergoing changes. Originally producing long products, a number of them have now turned to the production of flat-rolled steel. Most of the present minimills built in the recent past, those undergoing construction or being planned are designed to produce sheets rather than long products. For example, in the United States of America the total capacity of minimills to produce sheets is currently in the area of 7 to 8 million tons, and another 5 million tons of capacity is expected to produce flat-rolled products.

Integrated mills poles of growth shall be found mainly in developing countries. An example of this is in Taiwan by the Yien Loong Group. This integrated mill will be commissioned in the year 2002. It will be made up of three blast furnaces capable of producing 7.5 million tons of steel. In another example, an Australian Group is building a greenfield plant capable of producing 1.5 million tons of slabs for export. The steel for the slabs will be made in an electric furnace from direct reduced iron, so avoiding the limitation from the use of scrap.

STEELMAKING AND TECHNOLOGY TRANSFER

Technology transfer was the consequence in the steelmaking processes and the demand for steelmaking in near market conditions. In the 1950s, the open-hearth furnace produced ninety percent of the steel made in the established steelmaking countries in the world: the United States of America, the United Kingdom and Germany. In the late 1950s the basic-oxygen process (BOF) was introduced, and twenty years later it was the best available technology. In the 1970s the electric arc furnace (EAF) was introduced for minimills. Today, just over sixty percent (60%) of the world steel production employs the basic-oxygen process and about thirty percent (30%) use the electric-arc furnace; the remaining just under ten percent (10%) use the open-hearth process.

It is expected that the BOF and the EAF will remain the two main processes in operation for many years to come. The sizing of mills in the future will be to produce from 300,000 tons to 1,000,000 tons. The EAF will be considered to be the most appropriate technology because of the near-market conditions, and the environmental sensitivity.

Steel made by the EAF melts steel scrap and is dependent on scrap for its metal, which in most cases has tramp alloys, some of which remain in the finished steel. These alloys ordinarily operate as a constraint for some applications. However, with a supplemental charge of direct-reduced iron (DRI), iron carbide (IC) or pig iron (PI), these enhance the quality of steel, enabling it to be available for almost all applications.

STEEL-MAKING TECHNOLOGY AND STRATEGY

1. *The Electric Arc Furnace*

The Electric Arc Furnace (EAF) technology continues to evolve, with additional units being equipped for direct, rather than alternating current, and with the growing acceptance of such features as eccentric bottom tapping, water-cooled roofs and sidewall panels, oxygen injection, off-gas preheating, off-gas preheating of the furnace charge, and various charging systems.

The reasons for the anticipated increase in the electric arc furnace's share of steelmaking include the availability of electrical energy in industrialized countries; demand for steel in developing ones; low investment costs for EAF steelmaking compared with those for integrated mills; developments in EAF technology for better furnace performance, process control, product quality and costs; more use of scrap substitutes and hot metal in EAF steelmaking; and improvements in secondary metallurgical technologies, with higher output and quality.

Both the BOF and the electric furnace use ladle furnaces in the production of steel. This is a supplemental facility and, as such, refines the steel from the BOF and the scrap-melted steel form the electric furnace and increases the capacity of both the BOFs and the electric furnaces since it performs part of the function of steelmaking The BOF charge as it is poured into the ladle furnace has from 2.5 percent to 4.5 percent carbon. This is reduced in the ladle furnace to approximately 0.4 percent.

The furnace operates through electric power and the number of electrodes varies from one to three. The electric furnace is used to melt scrap, and the refining into acceptable steel is done for the most part in the ladle furnace. Thus, since less activity is performed in the BOF and electric furnace, the capacity of the units is increased. The amount of this increase depends on the size of the furnace as well as the amount of refining done in the ladle furnace. The addition of this facility to the steelmaking process is relatively recent. However, it has become widespread in the past few years and may well reach universal proportions in the next century.

The open hearth, which dominated steel production for so many decades, will probably disappear as a process on a worldwide basis early in the twenty-first century, leaving the field to the BOF and electric furnace. There will be modifications in these two processes. As indicated, the electric furnace will be charged with supplemental iron as well as scrap and the BOF will probably be charged with additional scrap.

2.   *Continuous Casting*

Continuous casting as an integral part of steel operations is a development of the last third of the twentieth century. Its acceptance has been rapid, so much so that many of the countries producing steel continuously cast more than 90 percent of their production. This is particularly true throughout the industrialized countries such as Japan and the USA and Western Europe. Some of the developing countries have been slower to adopt the process. Examples are China and India. However, in the past few years there has been a decided movement in these countries to increase the proportion of steel that is continuously cast. As the new century dawns, virtually every steel-producing country in the world will have 90 percent of its steel continuously cast.

A number of improvements have been made in this process with the aim of bringing the cast shape closer to that of the finished product. One of the significant advances has been made in producing thin slabs of two inches or less in thickness for sheet production. This requires much less reduction in the hot strip mill compared with the traditional slab of 8 inches to 10 inches thick, which constitutes most of the production from conventional continuous casters. The strip mill required to reduce the thin slab has a maximum of four to five stands, while that required for the 8 inch to 10 inch slabs uses 10 stands and represents a considerably higher investment.

The thin slab has been a great advantage for the minimill, since it operates with an electric furnace and a reduced-size strip mill. Thus the investment in an electric furnace plant with a thin slab caster and a shortened strip mill is far less than in the conventional integrated mill producing sheets with the 10-stand hot strip mill and a thick slab caster.

Unfortunately, at present the electric furnace cannot produce steel that is suitable for all applications. Consequently, sheets produced from the minimill are limited in use. However, as already indicated, there will be an improvement in electric furnace steel through the addition of supplemental iron units, and this, in conjunction with the thin slab caster and the truncated strip mill, will present a cost advantage.

Most of the sheets produced at present are from thick slabs rolled on conventional hot strip mills. However, it is possible that the integrated mills will install, in addition to their conventional slab casters and hot strip mills, thin slab casters along with electric furnaces and shortened hot strip mills. At present Pohang Iron and Steel Corporation in South Korea is installing such equipment at its Kwangyang plant. When the economics of this equipment are recognized, there will be an incentive for other integrated steel companies to follow suit and supplement their current production facilities by employing a thin slab caster.

Another development in continuous casting is the casting of near-net shapes for structural steel. This yields a product that requires far less work in the rolling mills and so reduces cost.

TECHNOLOGY OUTLOOK FOR THE FUTURE

Artificial neural networks were first developed as models of the biological neural networks. However, it was later realized that one kind of neural network, multilayer perceptrons, was useful as a function approximation technique. Multilayer perceptrons feed-forward neural networks can now be looked on as tools of non-linear multivariate data analysis, although they can perform several other tasks. There are various other kinds of neural network that have different sorts of application. Artificial neural networks consist of a number of neurons or nodes, which are simple computational elements directionally connected to other nodes in the network. The neurons collect a weighted sum of signals coming from the links to that neuron, and compute the output through an activation function, typically the logistic sigmoid.

The primary aim of alloy design is to ensure the required properties once the steel is in the direct forged component. This should be done so that the cost is minimized without risk of producing components that do not fulfil the required properties, and is best achieved by a mathematical model that can predict tensile and yield strengths from the chemical composition as well as the forging parameters.

Work is aimed at developing a neural-network-based system for supporting alloy design as well as to help in calculations of alloying additions during steelmaking. It also aids in controlling the required quality variables like mechanical properties after hardening. The system was developed for one low-carbon, hardenable steel grade. To achieve this, it was desirable to have a model that could reliably predict the mechanical properties of steel like the yield strength after hardening, which are the most important quality variables. Other quality variables like elongation at fracture, impact strength and hardness will be within the acceptable limits if the two more important variables are within specifications for the grade of steel considered. The quality variables depend on several factors. The most important of them are the chemical composition and austenitising temperatures, in addition to the dimensions of the component. The strength variables have a non-linear dependence on some concentrations as well as on temperature. Carbon content, for instance, has an almost parabolic effect on tensile strength. Boron has a complicated effect on hardenability, and the effect also depends on the concentration of other elements present in the steel.

Neural networks have been used for solving a variety of problems in steel industries. Among such problems, quality control systems are most common. Other categories of application are fault prevention, fault detection, fault diagnosis; pattern recognition and classification; process guidance, supervision and control; software sensors; process modelling; and prediction of important variables. Neural networks are particularly useful when the systems are non-linear. They are efficient tools of non-linear multivariate data analysis and can be programmed as learning systems. They have been applied in practically all parts of the iron and steel industries, including blast furnaces, desulphurisation, ladle furnaces, electric arc furnaces, continuous casting, hot rolling, cold rolling and annealing. One of the applications of neural networks in blast furnaces is that of predicting silicone content in pig iron. A guidance system can utilize the profiles of gas temperature distribution from the above-burden probes in blast furnaces—a typical pattern recognition problem.

Continuous casting diagnostic expert systems have been developed using neural networks. A Nippon steel technical report from 1991 describes a breakout prediction system in continuous steel casting. Takada et al of Nippon steel describe a special design environment for neural network applications. Cosipa steelworks in Brazil has benefited from neural network technology in the recent past, as revealed in one of the few public reports of Gorni. Vermeulen has reported four systems based on neural networks. Larkiola, Myllykoski and Nylander from Rautaruukki's thin-strip division have reported some experiences of neural network applications. They have also reported prediction of friction coefficient with neural networks. Another interesting application is a process guidance system for desulphurisation treatment in Kobe steel reported by Nakamura and Sagara. The system is expected to save about 10 percent of the reagent cost, in addition to the advantages gained by the automation of the system.

II

An Overview

This chapter first describes the central technologies employed in steel minimills producing high quality steel products from scrap iron. Second, it sets forth the central arguments of this study, focusing on the mechanisms facilitating transfer of steel minimill technology throughout world markets and the organizational systems found within the unit of the firm. Chapter 3 presents a fuller discussion of these behavioral issues. In addition, two salient questions are posed: How is capacity built? How is demand sustained? These central questions and the dependent and independent variables that are identified in Chapter 2 will be treated in detail later in this study.

The central questions posed in this chapter also lead me to formulate four hypotheses premised upon the special interests that exist within individual countries, the sensitivity of the industry to raw material costs and the effect of the reduction in size of the firms within the industry.

Finally, I embark upon a discussion of the scrap market, emphasizing the particular characteristics arising from its fragmentation and wide geographical dispersion. As part of this market discussion, I explain how the electric arc furnace, rather than processes associated with the basic oxygen converter or the open hearth furnace, can improve scrap utilization. This analysis provides a crucial link between discussion of the scrap market and the examination of the technology used in processing the scrap.

CENTRAL TECHNOLOGIES OF STEEL MINIMILLS

Central to the steel minimill are three technologies: the electric arc furnace, the ladling refining furnace and the continuous caster. [1]

The electric arc furnace (EAF) is normally an oval-bottom tapping furnace. The furnace is a high-power operation with high-density electrodes of a boxed girder construction, using copper-clad carbon steels. The boxed girder contains water used for cooling. In more conventional tubes there is no automatic cooling. It has been found that arcs using the water cooling process require fewer parts and have more rigid structures. The roof and sidewalls utilize a water-cooled pipe panel design. A monolithic working hearth is combined with carbon magnesite slaglime refractories, and the delta insert is a high alumina refractory. Oxygen provides meltdown assistance to decarbonize the scrap and produces a foamy slag as its waste. Carbon and lime are pneumatically injected through sidewall ports adjacent to the oxygen lance. Additional carbon is added with a forklift just prior to scrap charging. An interstop slide-gate with a nozzle and porous plug allow the heat to be tapped into a preheated ladle. Alloys and fluxes are automatically added via a lorry car type system.

The ladle refining furnace is powered by at least a 20 Mva transformer with a voltage of 290 volts and its electrode diameter is normally about 16 inches. The ladle heats rapidly at some 8 degrees Fahrenheit per minute. A side-draft fume evacuation system removes particulates. At the bottom of the ladle is a porous plug which injects carbon and calcium and stirs the metal. Measures of the uniformity of temperature and metallurgical samples are also obtained through the same porous plug. The ladle normally includes a vacuum degasser which permits alloying to be done under vacuum, strict temperature control, and wire feeding of calcium. When degassing is complete, the ladle is covered, lifted on an overhead crane, and transferred to the caster turret.

Continuous caster. The caster is designed with a dual radius of about 40 feet for the main radius and 70 feet for the second bending radius. The caster can produce any size product which it is suited to cut. At least two tundish cars equipped with load cells are required to carry the metals. The tundishes have a safety lining of clay brick and a working lining of 70 percent alumina and a magnesite veneer gunning mix is applied prior to each cast. A slide gate with a nozzle injects liquid into the tundishes. The metal streams are protected by argon-purged powering tubes as they travel between the ladle and tundish, and between the tundish and molds; six heat sequences per tundish are cast.

The molds are constructed of silver-bearing, copper-alloy plates that are normally about 30 inches in length. They have chamfered corners and are chrome plated. The roller support segments are located below the mold and footroll assembly. These segments are removable and changed when a mold size change is made. There are three air mist-type water spray zones.

The cast sections are supported by three withdrawal and straightening units per strand; these regulate the casting speed and straighten the product. The chain-link type starter bars are about 80 feet long. Three torch machines cut the product to pre-determined lengths. Blooms are transferred to a Telesis, pin-type stamper unit and by cutting torches, then transferred to skids for offloading via one of two cranes. The stamper identifies each bloom with the heat, strand, and piece number.

There are production sequences for steel products using the central technologies that were previously discussed. Generally the production sequence is represented diagrammatically in Figure 2.1.

Production sequences can be differentiated according to the specific types of processes. There are three main processes: the direct reduction process (DRP), the electric oxygen furnace (EOF) process, and the conventional minimill process. These processes illustrate how the three central technologies are combined to produce the finished steel. Diagrammatic representations of these three processes are given in Figures 2.2, 2.3 and 2.4.

Figure 2.1
Production sequence for steel products

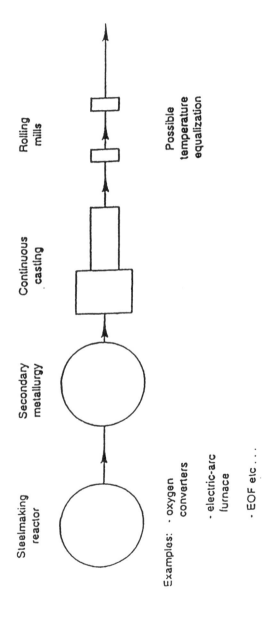

Source: Impact of Developments in Scrap Reclamation and Preparation on the World Steel Industry, ECE Steel Series 1993.

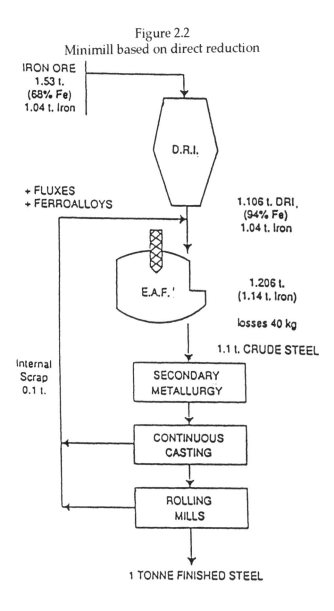

Figure 2.2
Minimill based on direct reduction

Source: International Iron and Steel
Institute (IISI).

Figure 2.3
The EOF process
(60% hot metal, 40% scrap)

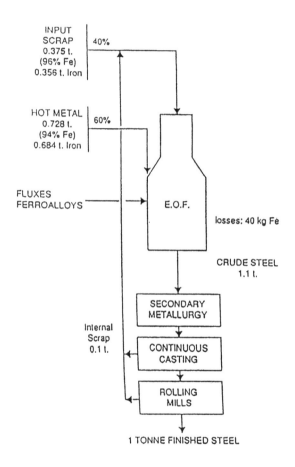

Source: International Iron and Steel
          Institute (IISI).

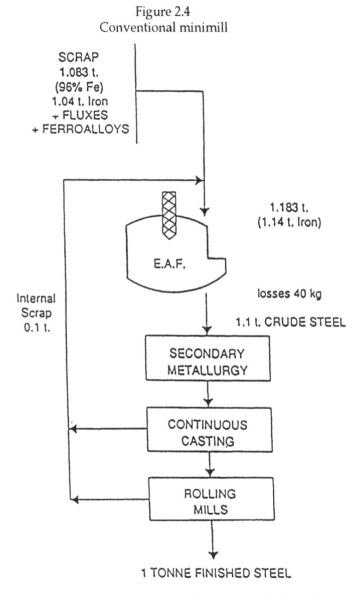

Figure 2.4
Conventional minimill

Source: International Iron and Steel
Institute (IISI).

THE TRANSFER OF STEELMAKING
TECHNOLOGY

The Central Arguments

The industrial environment of the steel industry inclusive of the minimill is characterized by markets and corporate hierarchies: these two core institutions of both capitalism and economic theory are but elements of larger systems of social-industrial order that also include, at a minimum, communities of shared cultural identity, associations representing common structurally-based interests, and state agencies protecting and creating socially-generated obligations and exercising public power backed by legitimate force. Environments of economic governance differ in the way in which these, and possibly other, elements are configured—in particular, the way in which market and corporate hierarchy relations are embedded in community structures; moderated by associational bargains; and protected, facilitated, promoted, subsidized, privileged, prescribed, or, for that matter, outlawed by the state. The resulting institutional configuration governs economic transactions by, among other things, generating and sanctioning motivations for gainful exchange, setting prices, standardizing products, providing and maintaining durable relations between traders, enforcing contracts, ensuring hierarchical compliance, arranging for cooperation in the face of competition, and extracting contributions for the generation and maintenance of collective resources without which the rational pursuit of self-interest would be self-defeating or yield unsatisfactory results.

Regimes of economic governance vary with spatial-territorial location and between functional-economic sectors. Variations by territory occur because social institutions are rooted in local, regional, or national political communities and their shared beliefs, experiences, and traditions. While localities and regions always were, and continue to be, important bases for distinctive institutional orders, comparative social research has focused primarily on the nation as its principal unit of analysis, because crucial resources for institution-building—

especially formal law and physical force—have come to be vested in the nation-state. Typically, as regimes of economic governance are configured and reconfigured, actors advance their interests by having recourse to "power resources" derived from their participation in national politics, from nationally shared cultural values, and from already existing nationally sanctioned institutional constraints and opportunities.

The Central Questions

The central questions for this assessment of technology transfer in the steel minimill industry with respect to market conditions and corporate hierarchies are:

1. What are the technologies being transferred?
2. Is the electric-arc furnace technology a tangible product, a process, or a combination of both product and process?
3. Is the steel mill technology emerging, relatively advanced, or old, and is it largely government-controlled or uncontrolled?
4. How are the raw materials obtained and what is the structure of supply?
5. Are there technological processes which can improve the condition of scrap, the essential feedstock for the steel minimill industry?
6. How is the ownership of this technology structured?
7. Does the structure of ownership make the technology accessible to others?
8. What are the policies of the governments of the technology providers toward the countries utilizing the technology?
9. How important is pricing of the technology in the negotiation process?
10. What weight is given in the negotiation process to the objectives for the acquisition of this technology?
11. What is the structure of the financing arrangements for acquiring the technology process and/or product?
12. If a country acquires proprietary technology, does the country offer the technology any legal protection?

13. When agreement is reached for the acquisition of the technology, what mechanisms will be used to facilitate the transfer?
14. How will the mutual expectations of the supplier and recipient be anchored to avoid misunderstandings and speed up the transfer?
15. What facilities are available in the recipient country with respect to manpower capability and the physical infrastructure to absorb advanced technology?

The ramifications and interlinkages of these fifteen questions will be probed throughout this study. Ultimately, the answers will help us to focus on two basic issues:

1. How is capacity built?
2. How is demand sustained?

The Dependent and Independent Variables

In order to formulate the hypotheses of this study, it is necessary to develop a model of the steel minimill industry. The focus will be on explaining the price of minimill technologies.

The steel minimill industry combines the three-step process of the electric arc furnace, the ladle process, and continuous casting to achieve efficiency.

The dependent variable of these three technologies is price. Sensitive pricing of technologies has resulted in productivity gains and the increasing use of these technologies.

The independent variables of steel minimill technology relate to either technological processes or feedstocks. There are three technological processes: the Mildrex process, the HYL process, and the Nucor continuous strip process.

The *Mildrex process* is applied to Direct Reduced Iron (DRI) and Hot Briquette Iron (HBI). DRI allows steelmakers and iron producers to maximize the value of their scrap resources in two ways:

1. DRI can be used along with scrap to make higher quality products. *Or*
2. It can be used along with lower-grade scrap to maintain the quality of output.

This technology has increased hot metal output, facilitated decreased coke consumption, and provided operational flexibility.

The main characteristics of the *HYL process* are:

1. It provides energy savings when DRI is produced and charged hot to the electric arc furnace (EAF).
2. It ensures high carbon deposition in the DRI or HCI (High Carbon Iron).
3. It assures higher productivity in the EAF with utilization of HCI, and even higher productivity with hot HCI.
4. HYL facilitates a higher yield in the EAF due to lower fines production and more so if pneumatic transport and direct injection to the furnace are used.
5. The product from the HYL process has been proven stable enough to be transported by land and sea, and is proving itself a candidate for long-term ocean transport.

The HYL process is making Hot Briquette Iron (HBI) a viable option for overseas merchant plants.

Entrepreneurs from Nucor, particularly Ken Iverson, have developed the *continuous strip production (CSP)* technology to allow the smaller and more efficient steel producers to penetrate the thin slab cast and flat rolled steelmaking market. It is not yet known, however, whether iron carbide can be effectively combined with scrap. Also, the Nucor process relies on high temperatures and requires a specific fuel—natural gas high in methane.

These three steel technological processes are statistically independent of the increase in scrap capacity as they are geographically dispersed in steel minimills throughout the world.

The Hypotheses for the Steel Minimill

1. Countries' transitions to open market economies will generate conflicts over international trade as special interests in individual countries seek to insulate themselves from competition.
2. The trend toward miniaturization of the steel industry— from integrated mills to minimills, thereby increasing the minimill product line—encourages global competition rather than hinders it.
3. This increase in global competition will gradually cause steel manufacturing technology to converge; the steel industry will be institutionally reconfigured, becoming path-dependent on prices of raw materials and on the corporate and political governance of countries.
4. Alternatively, global competition may create a greater thrust for specialization than for convergence.

Central to the theme of competition is the research and development (R&D) which both the minimills and the integrated mills have been undertaking. The extent of the R&D is reflected in the way in which the steel industry has been modernized and in particular the competitiveness of the minimills in reducing costs and increasing market share.

Markets will first be viewed as the generators of forces for institutional convergence indicated by performance requirements from the signals generated through market prices. Second, market forces will be examined as moving divergent sectoral-industrial orders toward convergence, thereby facilitating the process of technology transfer. Third, it is postulated that market direction could become more diversified, characterized by quality producers who can out-compete the mass producers. Alternatively, the market can produce more customized steel products at competitive prices.

Scrap Utilization

Having identified this study's goals, it is now possible to examine in detail the scrap industry upon which the steel minimill industry relies.

Product Quality

The user of a steel product requires it to be defect- and failure-free throughout its entire expected service life. This end-user requirement is usually termed "the fitness for purpose" of the product. The satisfactory fulfillment of this requirement depends on both the physical properties of steel itself and on the quality of the manufacturing and/or fabricating process the steel undergoes.[2] Corporations modify the processes to adapt to local conditions; as such, the market makes distinctions among Chinese steel, Korean steel, Indian steel, and steel originating from still other countries.

Obviously, if the end-user is to be satisfied, the steel must have all the physical properties required for a specific application. Since steel is the "raw material" of the production and construction process, the steel must also have the chemical and structural properties suited to the manufacture and/or fabrication of the product or construction.

In other words, the quality of a steel is not an abstract 'generic term' but it is rather the sum of a steel's chemical and structural properties. Control of the steel production process, and of the quality assurance process, which is currently undergoing exacting scrutiny in most production and manufacturing processes, necessarily begins with the specification of the steel's required chemical composition, as a steel's properties depend on its chemical composition. This dependence cannot be established explicitly for all properties, but if a steel's chemical composition cannot be adequately determined, its performance is in doubt and the steel will be worthless.

The steelmaker, of course, controls and fine-tunes steel's composition and is responsible for the internal structural homogeneity and surface quality of the cast steel. The specified microstructure of the finished steel, which governs all its useful properties, is produced in the course of shaping by rolling and forging, and by heat treatments and other finishing operations.

The current steel market is characterized by steadily increasing user demands for a product of higher and higher quality. For the steelmaking industry, these increasingly demanding requirements translate into tighter specifications of steel chemistry. Tremendous technological progress over the last few decades has allowed the iron and steel industries to keep pace with these increasingly stringent user demands. The replacement of open-hearth furnaces by oxygen converters and electric-arc furnaces, the development of ladle metallurgy, the substitution of continuous casting for ingot casting, and the recent introduction of computerized control of iron and steelmaking operations, as well as technological improvements in rolling, forging, and finishing have enabled the world's most advanced iron and steelworks to produce steels with chemical and structural properties tailored to the user's particular demands.

These improvements in the steelmaking process have been achieved through tight control of steel composition and through the reduction of harmful impurities to an extremely low level. Advances in rolling and forging technology and in finishing treatments have enabled the production of rolling and forging stock with tighter gauges, improved shape uniformity and dimensional accuracy, and much better surface finish. Particularly remarkable results in this respect have been achieved in the field of hot- and cold-rolled flat products.[3]

Several advances in the technology of steel production have worked together to produce these better quality products as well as the higher user expectations that fueled the manufacture of these products. In particular, the development of microchip-based CAD/CAM control systems linked to integrated design and manufacturing processes have raised and met user demands for consistent steel quality. A slight deviation during the steelmaking process from the programmed process designed for a particular heat can have an extremely adverse effect on the steel produced, but these sophisticated computerized systems offer strict, continual control over the steelmaking process and over steel chemistry within heats and from one heat to another, no matter how long the heat required. The most advanced iron and steel works are able to meet satisfactorily and consistently the most stringent demands for consistent steel quality.[4]

Product Quality: Clean Steels

The technological improvements and innovations enumerated above have enabled the iron and steel industry to achieve sharp improvements in steel cleanness. The cleanness of steel is determined by the presence or absence of impurities—the higher the cleanness, the higher the product quality. Any elements in steel which were not intentionally added to a heat to impart some specific chemical or structural property are accidents of the production process and are regarded as impurities in the final product. These impurities are usually called residual or tramp elements. The most important characteristic of these residual elements is that even in very low concentrations, they may exert a highly adverse effect on the physical and technological properties of a steel product.

The list of residual or tramp elements is long. A number of them—including sulphur, phosphorus, hydrogen, nitrogen, oxygen and all oxidizable alloying elements such as chromium, silicon and manganese—can be removed from steel during refining and ladle treatment. However, a number of elements—including copper, tin, antimony, arsenic, and non-oxidizable alloying elements such as nickel, molybdenum, and cobalt—cannot be removed from steel either during refining or ladle treatment. (Non-oxidizable elements, like lead and zinc, which have high vapor pressure at steelmaking temperatures, evaporate during the steelmaking process and do not pose serious problems for steel quality.)[5]

Many important and useful steel properties may be considerably improved by increasing the cleanness of steel.

Remarkable examples include the high upper shelf notch impact and fracture toughness of a series of high-strength, low-alloyed steels used for Arctic gas pipelines and North Sea offshore platforms. The achievement of extremely low levels of tramp elements has greatly decreased temper embrittlement in low-alloyed nickel-chromium-molybdenum steel used for fossil power plant turbine rotors. Improving the cleanness of steel has thus become a powerful alternative in modern steel metallurgy for producing steels with tailored properties. In this regard, it can replace traditional alloying methods, enabling substantial improvements in steel performance in a cost-effective way.

The Raw Materials

Two kinds of raw materials are used in steelmaking. The first is natural iron ore, and the second is man-made scrap.

In the modern iron and steel industries, both raw materials are used in approximately equal amounts in steelmaking, although iron ores are primarily used by integrated iron and steel plants while scrap is primarily consumed by non-integrated steel production facilities. However, before the advent of the large-scale bulk steelmaking technologies developed in the second half of the nineteenth century, scrap was not used very much for two basic reasons. First, it was not readily available in large enough quantities to justify development of methods for its industrial use. The second reason was purely technical: no furnaces of the day were capable of melting scrap. With the invention of the open-heart furnace, which coincided with the great accumulation of scrap in industrialized countries, scrap became more widely used.[6]

In modern steelmaking, scrap (both iron and steel) is primarily used in electric-arc furnaces, but its use in oxygen converters has been growing.

Scrap Quality: Definitions, Classifications and Cleanness of Scrap

Iron and steel scrap include:
- Any iron or steel scrap arising during the production and processing of iron or steel or recovered from old articles of iron or steel and which is suitable for remelting (including purchased scrap);
- Runners and other steel pouring-scrap (normal or bottom-poured), including funnels and gates, waste from delivery pipes in bottom pouring, etc., as well as rejected and defective ingots not included in production;
- Ladle skulls (except for those used in sand casting).

On the other hand, iron-bearing waste which is significantly contaminated with nonmetallic material and which arises during melting or heat or mechanical treatment is not considered scrap. Nonscrap waste includes:
- Blast-furnace runners;
- Launders from casting, splash, and other waste from pouring of iron, waste from casting pits;
- Steelworks slag;
- Scale from reheating furnaces and from rolling and forging;
- Spatter from convertors;
- Flue skull and lip skull;
- Skulls and remainders arising from sand casting.[7]

Scrap is usually graded either by origin or by quality. Iron and steel scrap graded by origin is either classified as scrap generated by the steel industry (including steel foundries and rerolling mills) or as scrap from sources outside the iron and steel industry.

Scrap generated by the steel industry is further classified as mill scrap and other scrap. The former is defined as *circulating scrap*, which comprises any iron and steel scrap arising during the production of iron and steel or during production in rolling mills or in any other steel finishing works. The latter is defined as *"old"* *(or capital) scrap* , collected in the steel industry, and *process scrap* , produced during the manufacturing process.

Scrap from sources outside the iron and steel industry may also be defined as *"old"* *(or capital) scrap* and as *process scrap* from processing and transforming industries. Scrap produced in another country is usually not utilized by a steel manufacturer.

Other classifications by scrap origin adhere essentially to the same scrap classes but utilize a slightly different classification system. Thus, "old" (or capital) and process scrap, which arise within the iron and steel industry, are frequently integrated into circulating scrap, which is also called *home or revert scrap*. On the other hand, scrap from sources outside the iron and steel industry is separated into old (capital or obsolete) and process (prompt industrial) scrap.

Both obsolete and process scrap are sometimes categorized as *purchased scrap*. This categorization is based on trade considerations, since obsolete and process scrap are, as a rule, traded, while circulating (home or reverted) scrap is typically consumed at the steelworks in which it was generated.

All classifications by origin or scrap are compatible with the current scrap statistics.

Over a decade ago home scrap made up on average, about 50 percent of the total scrap used; process scrap was about 20 percent and capital scrap was about 30 percent. Ten years later, in the middle and late 1980s, technological changes within the iron and steel industry, particularly the replacement of ingot by continuous casting, shifted the ratio of the three scrap types utilized. Throughout the world, the average use of process scrap has declined to about 15 percent and circulating scrap accounts for about 30 percent, while the use of capital scrap has increased to about 50 percent. Forecasts indicate that the ratio of capital scrap will increase further while that of circulating scrap will decrease.

Quality is perhaps an even more important method of grading scrap, and classification systems are legion. Most countries have their own classification systems which are particularly suited to that country's domestic scrap trade. In the international scrap trade, the classification of the exporting country is used. Since the United States and West European countries are the biggest world scrap exporters, their classification systems are most frequently used internationally.

Although one might expect that scrap quality classification systems used around the world might vary substantially, they are actually quite similar. They largely use the same quality criteria and they specify grades according to the material's physical and chemical properties.

Scrap is also classified quantitatively, by the physical properties of size and density. Upper limits on length, width, and height as well as lower limits on thickness are specified for large pieces of scrap called heavy melting and for bales of hydraulically compressed or hand-bundled scrap. A lower density limit is specified for fragmentized and briquetted scrap. These dimensional specifications are designed to prevent use of too-large or too-small charges of scrap: either will adversely affect performance of an electric-arc or oxygen converter furnace; for example, larger charges require longer heat times resulting in higher energy consumption.

Classification systems also take the scrap's original manufacture into consideration. Scrap may be classified by the manufacturing process from which it was generated (turnings, borlings, clippings), by the manufactured products from which it was produced (shipbreaking, railroad, dismantling scrap), by the scrap processing method (fragmentized or shredded, baled, briquetted scrap), or by two such designations used together, (e.g. shredded tin cans).

The steelmaker must also know the chemical composition of scrap to be used as a raw material in order to produce finished steel of a particular chemical composition. Although alloyed scrap was formerly listed in major classification systems, this is now no longer done. However, manufacturers must still be able to ascertain the presence of any major alloying elements before a reliable final product can be produced. The presence and quantities of any alloying elements can be determined with a portable spectroscopic analyzer, a tool which is now readily available. In addition to identifying scrap alloy content, these portable analyzers can also determine the presence of other specified, unspecified, and tramp elements.

The situation is much less satisfactory in the case of non-alloyed iron and steel scrap. Unlike alloyed scrap, the base chemical composition of carbon steel and cast iron scrap is not specified in any classification system. Some classifications do limit the content of alloying elements in carbon steel and cast iron scrap in order to differentiate them from alloyed scrap. Thus, for instance, in the United States scrap classification system, the content of residual alloying elements in carbon steel and cast iron scrap must not exceed the percentages shown in Table 1.[8]

Table 1
Residual alloying elements in carbon steel and cast iron: the
United States case

Residual elements in scrap	Percentage
Nickel	0
Chromium	0.20
Molybdenum	0.10
Manganese	0.65

(Other countries' classification systems may specify different contents.)

Instead of specifying the quality of nonalloyed scrap grades in terms of chemical composition, the traditional classification practice uses more general, descriptive terms. The internationally used United States classification system mentioned above refers to scrap cleanness, which is defined as freedom from dirt, nonferrous metals, or foreign matter of any kind as well as from excessive rust and corrosion. As previously mentioned, the presence of contaminants such as dirt and other nonmetallic foreign materials greatly affect the results of the steelmaking operations. The presence of such materials and dirt can be corrected—for example, sulfur and phosphorous in scrap can be transferred into the slag with a higher flux consumption, and a longer heat time—if the contaminants are known before the steelmaking process begins.

Scrap classifications address the content of tramp elements—which must be tightly controlled in order to produce clean, high-quality steels—in two ways. The first and more frequently used method is a descriptive specification regarding freedom of exogenous sources of tramp elements. Thus, a number of scrap grades are specified as being free of metal-coated materials, soldered joints, or pieces of nonferrous metals. The second, less frequently used method involves the specification of the upper permissible concentration of various tramp and unspecified residuals.[9]

A graphic view of the utilization of scrap used either by itself as feedstock or in combination with iron ore to produce finished steel is given in Figure 2.5.

MODERN STEEL TECHNOLOGY

The enhanced capabilities of the modern steelmaking process for producing high quality steels naturally impose quality requirements on scrap. One such requirement is the assurance of a scrap supply of consistent quality. As previously stated, the steelmaker cannot produce cost-effective, high-quality steel compatible with user demands if the raw scrap contains contaminants or unknown alloys. Consistency of scrap quality implies a uniform quality level of scrap, with minimum deviations from delivery to delivery.

Statistical scrap quality control is the most important means for the assurance of consistent scrap quality.[10] Quality control must be applied throughout the scrap handling process, from collection and sorting to every step of the scrap processing operation. Particularly important is stringent statistical scrap quality control at delivery. It has been shown that if statistical quality control is strictly applied, consistently satisfactory results can be achieved.

Figure 2.5
Scrap pathways within the world steel industry

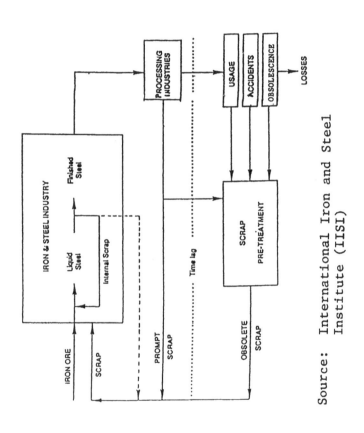

Source: International Iron and Steel
          Institute (IISI)

The fairly recent automation of the steelmaking process has imposed additional requirements on the scrap supply. Computer-controlled systems of refining in the primary vessel, of ladle treatment, and of continuous casting enable the production of higher quality steel grades at lower material and energy costs than could ever be achieved with traditional, operator-controlled steelmaking methods. However, automated systems cannot be relied upon to produce high-quality steel if a certain number of preconditions are not met. One of the most important preconditions is of course, exact knowledge of the chemical composition of all charge materials, including scrap. When supplied with this information, the computer controlling the steel production process can adjust the process as necessary to remove contaminants and to perform metallurgical treatments accurately.[11]

Maximizing Scrap Utilization

The steelmaking industry's high scrap consumption is cost-effective only as long as scrap prices are competitive with prices of iron-bearing charge materials produced from iron ores—either pig iron or direct-reduced iron. The iron and steel industry also uses scrap for environmental reasons: a high scrap to pig iron ratio in a charge means lower coke consumption during ironmaking, and consequent lessened environmental pollution form coke-producing plants.

Pressure to increase scrap consumption also arises from outside the iron and steel industries. First, the public is increasingly eager to protect the environment form accumulation of solid wastes, of which the amount of iron and steel waste may be small, but definite. This reason for higher scrap utilization has been growing sharply in importance over the last few years, particularly because of the growing shortfall of landfill sites for disposing of solid waste. The conservation of natural environmental equilibrium through reduced mining of iron ore is another important public requirement favoring higher scrap consumption in steelmaking. Although the iron and steel industry is not a major carbon dioxide producer, its share in industry's total carbon dioxide emission is not negligible. The higher the scrap rate in charge, the lower the carbon dioxide emissions, since the majority of the carbon dioxide generated during the steelmaking process arises during processing of iron ore and pig iron. [12]

However, there are several constraints on the increase of scrap consumption in steelmaking beyond current scrap levels. One is the availability of an increased amount of scrap. Another is technological limitations on the ability of the steelmaking industry to consume higher amounts of scrap; a possible decline in or leveling of demand by the steel market would also affect the industry's ability to consume scrap. A third constraint may be the existing capacity of the scrap recycling industry to process scrap from all available sources.

Since all circulating and process or prompt industrial scrap is usually consumed immediately, at least within industrialized countries, further sources of scrap than those currently available must be sought in capital scrap and in other, lower-quality scrap sources, such as steelmaking furnace dusts, muds and sludges, or machining discards in the form of swarf, solid municipal waste and various other types of industrial wastes.

The ferrous scrap reclamation industry stands in contrast to the iron and steel industry, for which there are comprehensive statistics. The ferrous scrap reclamation industry, as an upstream iron and steel servicing industry, has traditionally been fragmented into many small units. This far-reaching fragmentation characterizes the ferrous reclamation industry at both the collecting and processing stages, that is, at both its consecutive technological levels. The industry fragmentation is greater during collecting operations due to the large number of geographically dispersed scrap sources. Over the last decade there has been a trend toward integrating the large scrap reclamation companies even further into the processing level with an eye toward reclaiming over a million tons a year. But no matter how integrated the reclamation process becomes, in order to service widely dispersed sources of obsolete and process scrap, some degree of fragmentation must remain at the scrap processing stage. [13]

Fragmentation, geographical dispersion, and the lack of a more solid organizational framework makes the statistical coverage of the processing and throughput of the ferrous scrap reclamation industry difficult. Despite this lack of reliable statistical data, an estimate of the processing potential of the scrap reclamation industry will be attempted. This estimate should help to answer the question of whether the processing capacity of the ferrous scrap reclamation industry now limits, or will limit in the future, increased utilization of obsolete and process scrap as charge material in steelmaking.

The scrap reclamation industry in the industrialized countries makes frequent claims that running under available capacity is one of the profitability problems with which it contends. Unfortunately, such claims are not accompanied by any estimates of total capacities, and the question of how large a scrap processing margin there could be remains to be analyzed until a more extensive and representative set of statistical data on scrap processing facilities is collected. The establishment of a comprehensive statistical database on the scrap processing industry is necessary before a satisfactory and reliable scrap processing assessment can be done. Since the sites of scrap processing facilities are largely dispersed into many small units located over wide areas, this will not be an easy task. It will require special efforts on the part of the iron, steel and scrap reclamation industry statistical services as well as of the scrap reclamation industry itself.[14]

An approximate estimate as to whether scrap capacity could become a limiting factor for maximum scrap utilization in steelmaking may be done in the following way. The total number of shredders in the world is approximately 600. About one third are installed in the United States, one third in western Europe, and the remaining mostly in Japan. The importance of the shredders impacts upon the pricing of scrap. Beyond the quality of scrap is the capacity of the steel industry to utilize the scrap. Taking the number of shredders, and the lead time it takes to introduce new shredders of about two years, the steel industry has sufficient scrap to utilize the existing capacity of shredders.

The scrap reclamation industry of the United States is technologically the most advanced, and it controls just over half of the world shredding capacity. It is estimated that the share of shredders in the total scrap-processing capacity of other countries except Japan will be generally lower than one fifth. Increasing the world shredding capacity of a three-shift operation can be done by multiplying the one-shift operation capacity by a factor of between two and three. The final estimate of world scrap-processing capacity can be obtained by multiplying the estimated world shredder three-shift operation capacity by a numerical factor in the range of between six and ten. In this way, an estimate of the annual world scrap-processing capacity is obtained in the order of between 400 and 500 mt. Most shredders work on a three-shift operation.[15]

NOTES

[1]   Hess, G.W., "Minis move closer to maxi status," *Iron Age*, October 1992, p. 18. The author contends that if imitation is indeed the sincerest form of flattery, America's integrated producers are paying quite a compliment to minimills.

[2]   Cockerill, A., *The Steel Industry: International Comparison of Industrial Structure and Performance*, Cambridge: Cambridge University Press, 1974.

[3]   Fortune Magazine, "Steel: It's a brand new industry," December 1960, pp. 123-127

[4]   ibid. Fortune Magazine, pp. 130-137.

[5]   Zuckerman, A., "Mix reviews for ISO 9000." *New Steel*, Vol. 10, No. 2, February 1994, p. 41.

[6]   Nijhawan, B.R., "Global scenario of world steel industry growth particularly up to 1985," Paper presented in Paris, France, on the steel industry in the 1980s, OECD Publication, February 1980, document no. 5, pp. 113-126.

[7]   Ingham, J.N., "And the Earth Shifted: the revolutionary world of iron and steel, 1885-1920," in *Making Iron and Steel*, Ohio University Press, Columbus, Ohio, 1991, pp. 128-156.

8   Lankford, W.T., *The Making, Shaping and Treating of Steel*, *Herbick and Held Publication*, 10th Ed., 1985, pp. 632-639.

9   Schroter, L., "Steel Works Now!: The conflicting character of modernization," Paper presented to the International Institute of Management Conference, Berlin, Germany, 1982.

10 Pflaum, D.A., "Residual problems and the scrap industry," in Residual and Unspecified Elements in Steel, ASTM STP 1042, A.S. Melilli and E.G. Nisbett, Eds., *American Society for Testing and Materials*, Philadelphia 1989, pp. 11-25.
    Laycock, C., G. Winfield, "Scrap and the Consumer," *Ironmaking and Steelmaking* 3, 1976, No. 6, pp. 349-355.
    Zimmermann, W., K.-H. Heinen, H.G. Angenendt, "Statistische Einstazoptimierung bei einem Electrolichtbogenofen," *Stahl u. Eisen*, 103, 1983, no. 18, pp. 73-75.

11 Kuster, T., "Wanted: Low-residual scrap," *New Steel*, Vol. 10, No. 4, April 1994, pp. 48-51.

12 "Production, processing and usage of steel," *Evolution of the Specific Consumption of Steel*, Economic Commission for Europe, United Nations Publication, New York, 1984, pp. 53-91.

13 "Consumption of iron and steel products," *Evolution of the Specific Consumption of Steel*, Economic Commission for Europe, United Nations Publication, New York, 1984, pp. 92-122.

14 "Impact of the growing use of scrap in western industrialized countries," *Impact of Developments in Scrap Reclamation and Preparation on the World Steel Industry*, ECA Steel Series 1993, United Nations, Geneva, pp. 76-84.

15 Hogan, W.T., *Economic History of the Iron and Steel Industry in the United States*, Vols. 1-5, pp. 1442-1523, Lexington Books, 1971.

III

The Scrap Market

Scrap utilization in steelmaking could be increased in a number of ways. The most straightforward manner would be to increase steel production without attempting to modify current steelmaking technology.[16] Obviously, being closely coupled to demand for steel, the volume of steel production can hardly be influenced by the iron and steel industry.

Independent of the demand for steel, a purely technological method of increasing scrap utilization would be attempting to raise the rate of scrap in steel furnace charge. This method will now be discussed in detail in terms of electric-arc furnace technology.

The electric-arc furnace, the second in importance in the current steelmaking processes, is in the great majority of cases a completely scrap-based steelmaking route. As such, it does not possess any margin for a further increase of scrap share in the charge. However, the replacement of two currently important steelmaking processes—the oxygen converter and the open-hearth furnace which have lower capacities for scrap consumption—with electric-arc furnaces opens further avenues for higher scrap consumption.

It is well known that over the past few decades, the main thrust of restructuring and modernization within the steel industry was the replacement of open-hearth furnaces by oxygen converters and electric-arc furnaces. This replacement has now been almost entirely accomplished throughout the world, and a remarkable increase in the share of electric-arc furnaces in total steel production has been the end result. In particular, electric-arc furnace steelmaking expanded because oxygen converters were unable to consume all available scrap, as had been the case with open-hearth furnaces.

Obviously, further increases in scrap utilization could be achieved by installing greater numbers of electric-arc furnaces. In modernized, restructured iron and steel industries, this could be accomplished only by replacing oxygen converters. Reasons that could precipitate such changes in the current steel production process could be, on the one hand, an increased availability of high-quality and inexpensive scrap, and, on the other hand, technological changes that would enable electric-arc furnaces to compete against traditional products of oxygen converters.

Whether at present or in the near future, ferrous scrap availability will be increased depends, among other things, on further developments in the scrap reclamation sector. It is clear that a margin for increased scrap supply already exists in overall scrap arisings, without even mentioning the existing scrap supply. It is also clear that the existing scrap processing capacity of the scrap reclamation industry would not be a limitation. However, serious limitations may lie in increasingly higher production costs, which arise from environmental protection standards and from the necessity to use more sophisticated processing procedures compatible with customers' increasing demands for quality steel. Data on which to base a reliable forecast of a possible increase in scrap availability are limited. But as the scrap supply is closely related to the demand for steel, any available forecast for steel production in the near future should provide an outlook for the ferrous scrap market.

An international outlook for scrap is graphically represented in the following Figures and Tables.

Figure 3.1
Summary of United States scrap in 1990
(Kt)

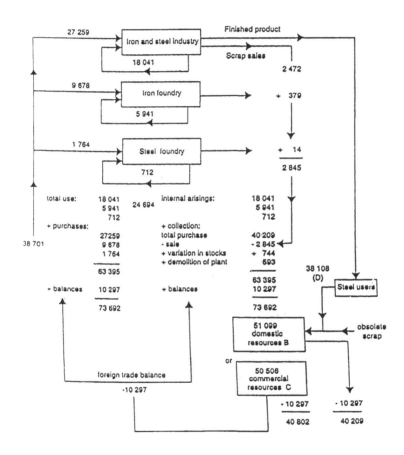

Source: International Iron and Steel
         Institute (IISI)

Figure 3.2
United States—scrap

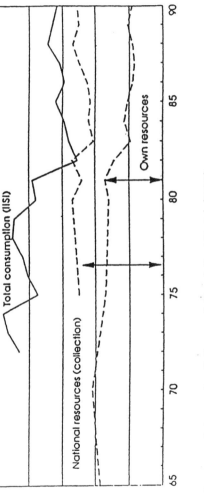

/yr

Total consumption (IISI)

National resources (collection)

Own resources

Source: International Iron and Steel Institute (IISI)

Figure 3.3
Possible trend in United States scrap resources

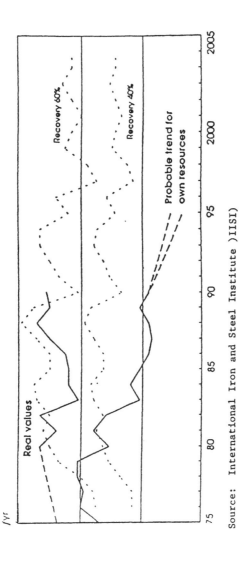

Source: International Iron and Steel Institute)IISI)

Figure 3.4
Summary of scrap in Japan in 1990
(Kt)

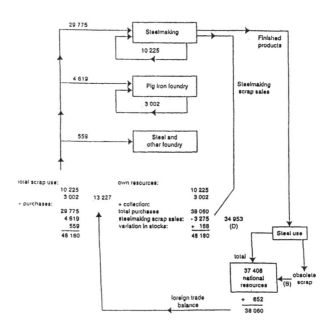

Source: International Iron and Steel
        Institute (IISI)

Figure 3.5
Summary of scrap in the 12-member EC in 1990

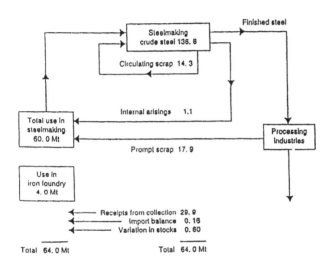

Source: International Iron and Steel
          Institute (IISI)

Table 2
Scrap consumption in Latin American countries
(By country, thousand metric tons)

Countries	1986	1987	1988	1989	1990*
Argentina	1.137	1.310	1.326	1.254	1.190
Brazil	7.198	7.319	7.676	8.032	6.505
Central America	138	137	124	110	88
Chile	138	219	290	279	256
Colombia	445	538	562	571	525
Ecuador	18	27	25	27	24
Mexico	2.951	2.580	3.422	3.010	3.613
Paraguay	0	...	...	...	4
Peru	265	311	276	175	174
Trinidad/Tobago	138	153	254	107	151
Uruguay	37	36	37	46	46
Venezuela	904	1.165	1.291	1.417	1.423
Total	13.369	13.795	15.283	15.283	13.999

Sources: ILAFA and IISI.

Table 3
Possible change in resources of the main types of scrap in the
Arab world
(Mt)

Year	1981	1989	1990
Circulating scrap	0.752	1.003	1.035
Process scrap	1.203	1.349	1.315
Capital scrap	0.855	2.651	2.277
Total	2.810	5.003	5.122

Source: Cavic and IISI.

Table 4
Total theoretical possibilities for scrap recovery in the main Arab
countries

Arab countries	Circulating + process + capital scrap, Kt/year		
	1981	1989	1990
1. Algeria	426	881	853
2, Bahrain	11	48	25
3. Egypt	633	1 138	1 333
4. Iraq	249	659	669
5. Jordan	79	74	88
6. Kuwait	157	112	95
7. Lebanon	142	177	105
8. Libya	184	300	282
9. Morocco	112	211	214
10. Oman	25	40	44
11. Qatar	106	121	116
12. Saudi Arabia	439	880	984
13. Syria	122	210	158
14. Tunisia	125	152	156
Total	2 810	5 003	5 122

Source: Cavic and IISI.

Table 5
World trade in scrap: main exporting and importing countries in
1990
(in Mt/year)

Exporters		Importers	
United States	11.580	Korea	3.885
USSR	2.700	Turkey	3.800
Australia	0.986	India	2.245
ECE (net)	0.467	Thailand	1.300
Austria	0.287	Taiwan	1.285
etc.		Indonesia	0.800
		China	0.500
		Mexico	0.300
		Singapore	0.221
		Philippines	0.150
		Brazil	0.103

Source: IISI.

Another possibility for increasing scrap utilization has emerged recently, that of increasing competitive penetration of electric-arc furnace products into the oxygen converter steel product market. Although a few electric steel plants regularly produced flat products with the conventional rolling technology,[17] they withstood the competition from oxygen converters because of convenient supplies of electrical energy and raw materials or because of favorable positions with the local steel market.

A new, more general approach to entering the flat product market consists in coupling electric-arc steelmaking with thin-slab continuous casting. A single heat of thin slabs are formed into hot-rolled strip, and a conventional cold-rolling mill forms the hot-rolled strip into cold-rolled strip and sheet. The German company Schloemann-Sieemag developed the new, thin-slab continuous casting and direct hot rolling technology, known as compact strip production or CSP technology, and the American company Nucor has pioneered the first industrial facilities of 800,000 tpy output, which have been in operation since 1989.[18] The first year of operation (1990) brought good technological and financial results, and it has been claimed that this process has cut the operating costs of hot-rolled strip production by US$50 per ton. The success of these new facilities has aroused much interest and provoked a series of forecasts regarding the prospects of the new technology for efficient competition in the flat steel products market.[19]

In view of possible implications for the minimill industry, this new process route merits some serious consideration. Assuming that the demand for flat products remains fairly constant, the assumption of an appreciable amount of production of flat-rolled products by the new process route would mean a proportional increase in scrap supply. But the high cleanness requirements of high quality flat steel products would naturally impose more stringent cleanness requirements on the steel scrap. The new flat product technology would require only the best scrap grades and this increased demand would stimulate the scrap reclamation industry to improve scrap preparation and processing procedures and to provide higher quality scrap.

Stricter requirements could also cause scrap prices to rise or, if the scrap became scarce, plants could be forced to use other, cleaner, iron-bearing charge materials for dilution purposes, such as pig iron and directly-reduced iron. In both cases, the cost advantage of the scrap-based flat product production would be lost. And it should be remembered that the lower price of scrap, compared with pig iron and directly-reduced iron, is what makes electric-arc steelmaking competitive. There is no technological reason that thin-slab continuous casting and compact strip production could not be coupled with the integrated blast furnace-oxygen converter steel route, as they are with electric-arc furnace in the Nucor plant; this configuration would enjoy the same cost advantages as the current continuous casting and hot-rolling procedures.

Finally, it can be concluded that the necessity of using only the highest quality scrap in electric-arc furnaces producing flat products may, on the one hand, stimulate higher scrap utilization and scrap quality improvement. On the other hand, it may conversely turn out to be a constraint on further expansion of scrap-based flat steel production. Future development will show which of these alternatives will prevail.

All measures that increase productivity of scrap-based electric-arc furnaces should also be considered as potential contributors to higher scrap utilization. Such measures are the application of oxygen blowing, oxy-fuel burners, scrap preheating by furnace off-gases, and, more recently, coal injection and the oxygen converter practice (K-ES process). All these new technologies are primarily aimed at saving electric energy by substituting lower cost energy sources, and at increasing furnace productivity by tap-to-tap time reduction.

An increased ratio of scrap used in the integrated steelmaking route may be another means by which the demand for scrap may increase. A survey of current oxygen converter scrap usage rates in different countries as well as the world scrap rate average shows that a leeway for increase exists. Assuming a 30 percent increase as a viable maximum, then a significant margin for a scrap rate increase at a worldwide level appears to be likely.[20]

The other side of this coin is the practicality of an increase of scrap consumption by the estimated amount. As with the previously discussed case of penetration of electric-furnace steel products into flat production markets, the constraint on higher scrap consumption in oxygen converters is again the problem of scrap quality. This point is illustrated by the Japanese preference for using iron ore instead of scrap for cooling in oxygen converters. Japanese integrated producers are reluctant to use more scrap for fear of uncontrollable steel contamination by tramp and unspecified residual elements. The higher the cleanness requirements of the finished steel—as for black plate; deep and extra deep drawing sheet; high strength, low-alloyed hot-rolled sheet; and plate for critical applications—the greater the fear and the stronger the reluctance to use scrap in charge. So the problem of higher scrap usage in oxygen converters, particularly as far as flat production is concerned, is reduced to the problem of scrap quality, or finally to the requirement for scrap upgrading. The particular sensitivity of integrated flat producers to scrap quality is illustrated by the case of Luxembourg which has the highest scrap rate, as can be seen in Table 6, and highest production of long products.

The major steel-producing regions of the world—the United States, European Community and Japan—have decreasing amounts of scrap available for their industries. This fact is depicted by a time series analysis for these three regions shown in Figures 3.6 to 3.8.

However with respect to Japan, there is a higher collection rate of scrap which is undoubtedly obtained from surrounding countries in the Far East, owing to the rapid industrialization of the region.[21]

There is a correlation between the increasing availability of scrap and the collection rate of scrap. World scrap resources have been increasing since 1980 and are expected to continue to increase.[22] However, at the same time, both direct reduced iron (DRI) and pig iron are being increasingly used. The available scrap resources are shown in Figure 3.9.

Table 6

Average use of scrap in oxygen converter in selected countries in
1990

Country	Scrap in charge, kg/t		
	Low rate	Intermediate rate	High rate
Japan	73	-	-
France	99	-	-
Germany	-	175	-
UK	-	174	-
USSR	-	-	283
Luxembourg	-	-	386

(a)   *Iron and Steel Scrap*, Fifth updating, UN/ECE, 1991,
        pp. 30-31.

Figure 3.6
United States scrap resources

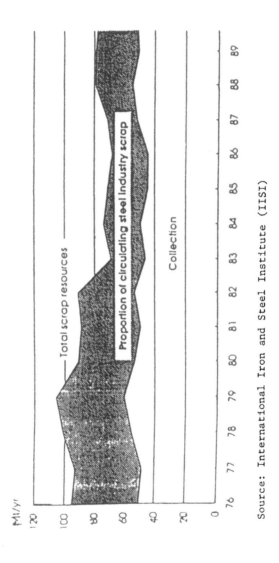

Source: International Iron and Steel Institute (IISI)

Figure 3.7
Scrap resources in the European Community

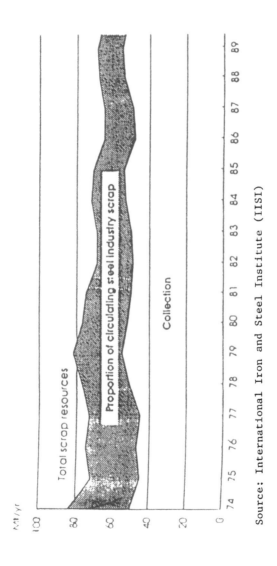

Source: International Iron and Steel Institute (IISI)

Figure 3.8
Scrap resources in Japan

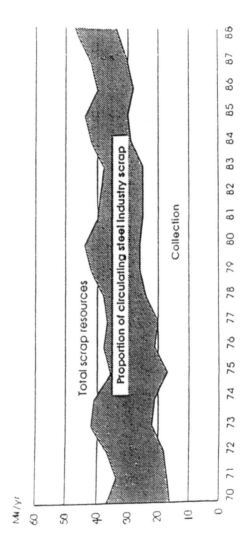

Source: International Iron and Steel Institute (IISI)

Figure 3.9
World scrap resources

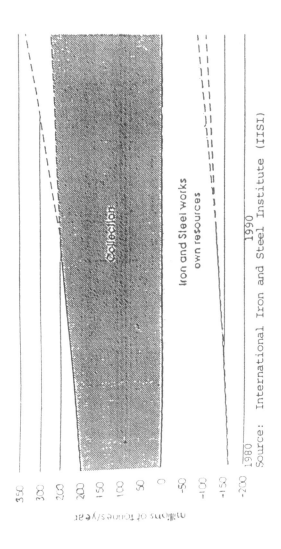

collection

Iron and Steel works
own resources

1980   1990

millions of tonnes/year

350
300
200
200
150
100
50
0
-50
-100
-150
-200

Source: International Iron and Steel Institute (IISI)

In addition, there is a direct relationship between the production and consumption of the three primary metals: pig iron, scrap, and DRI. These trends are represented in Table 7. The scrap resources discussed above include scrap which has been recycled. This secondary scrap material, particularly steel castings and forgings, is now becoming important to the scrap resources available. A flow diagram of scrap recycling in production, processing and usage in iron and steel is given in Figure 3.10.

Despite the restraining factors, which prevent existing oxygen converter scrap consumption capacity from being fully utilized, increasingly intensive research and development efforts to widen oxygen converter capacity for scrap use have been pursued. As a result of the growing number of research and development activities carried out by renowned steel producers, a series of innovative, scrap-based steelmaking technologies are emerging.[23]

All have been tested at a laboratory scale and the majority at a semi-industrial level, but only a few have been implemented on an industrial scale.

All the processes are based on the use of coal or coke for melting the scrap. In some processes, a portion of energy needed for the melting of scrap is supplied by the use of gaseous fuels. The processes may be categorized according to the reactor type used. Some use a conventional oxygen converter vessel (the K-OBM, K(M)S,[24] Tula, Kawasaki, Nippon Steel and ASLUC processes) and some are run in a specially designed reactor vessel (the EOF, KYS, SIFF, KVA,[25] Plasmascrap, Daido processes.[26] All can be operated with a completely scrap-based charge, with the exception of the K-OBM process,[27] which has only a slightly higher capacity for scrap in charge than the Q-BOF or LD processes. In processes using specially designed reactor vessels, scrap is preheated by off-gases in counter-current flow. In converters, scrap is preheated by solid or gaseous fuels. Apart from coal or coke, the additional energy sources, which are used alternatively or in combination in different processes, are either the post-combustion of CO to CO in off-gases in the vessel or the preheating of scrap.

Table 7
World trends in production or consumption of steelmaking primary metals

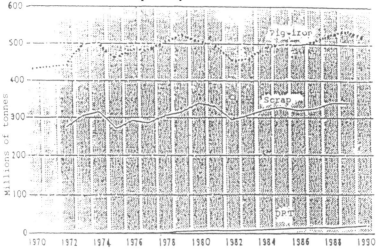

	DRI	SCRAP	PIG-IRON
1970	0.70		431.00
1971	0.80		435.00
1972	1.30	275.00	440.00
1973	1.90	305.00	495.00
1974	2.60	315.00	505.00
1975	2.70	270.00	460.00
1976	2.80	292.00	485.00
1977	3.30	285.00	484.00
1978	4.70	305.00	504.00
1979	6.90	315.00	525.00
1980	7.40	338.00	508.00
1981	8.10	328.00	497.00
1982	7.30	293.00	453.00
1983	7.80	306.00	458.00
1984	9.20	321.00	491.00
1985	11.20	327.00	499.00
1986	12.50	319.00	497.00
1987	13.70	323.00	510.00
1988	14.10	339.00	529.00
1989	16.00	339.00	539.00
1990	17.90		525.00

Sources: Annual Bulletin of Steel Statistics for Europe; International Iron and Steel Institute (IISI); Latin American Iron and Steel Institute (ILAFA); Secretariat estimates; and United Nations.

Figure 3.10
Flow diagram of scrap recycling in production, processing and usage of iron and steel

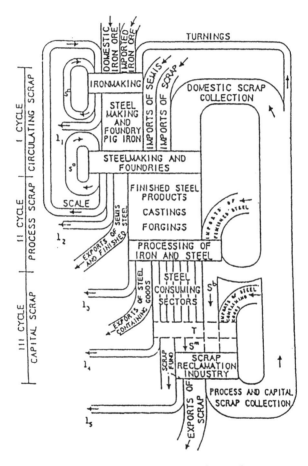

The market conditions, as we have seen, sustain two main technology types: "conventional" steelmaking, using blast furnace and oxygen converters, and the electric arc furnace using the ladle refining technology and continuous casting. Between 1980 and 1990 to produce one ton of finished steel using the blast furnace and oxygen converters there has been a reduction in the consumption of iron ore from 1,048 kg to approximately 690 kg, in contrast to the increase in the consumption of scrap from zero to approximately 350 kg. On the other hand, the electric arc furnace technology which used scrap exclusively is now employing prereduced iron and solid or liquid pig iron. To produce one ton of steel through the electric arc furnace, combinations of prereduced iron, solid or liquid pig iron and scrap are used. The scrap utilization to produce one ton of steel is based on 1,040 kg of scrap. A schematic comparison based on the interdependence between the iron ore and scrap systems is given in Figure 3.11.

A schematic combination of the use of iron ore, scrap and primary metals in steelmaking is given in Figure 3.12.

Both steelmaking processes are usually validated by their energy consumption, with the energy consumption of the totally scrap-based electric-arc furnace steelmaking being generally taken as a reference.[28] The economy of processes taking place in converter vessels is judged only by off-gas credit. If the high carbon monoxide and, depending on the coal used, some hydrogen content of the so-called steel gas were not utilized in the steelmaking process, the energy consumption would be unbearably high. This means that the off-gases must be captured, cleaned, and their chemical energy content utilized to produce power production purposes. The adjustment of post-combustion temperature is a means of controlling the process run and of managing the off-gas credit.

Figure 3.11
Schematic comparison of the iron-ore and scrap systems

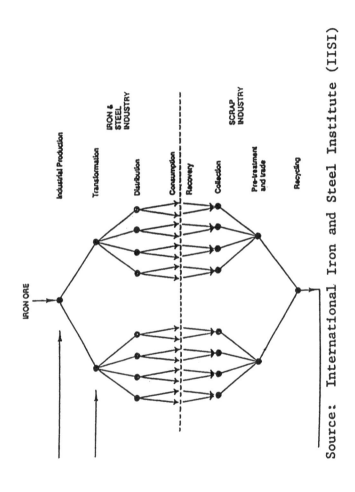

Figure 3.12
Iron ore, scrap and primary metals in steelmaking

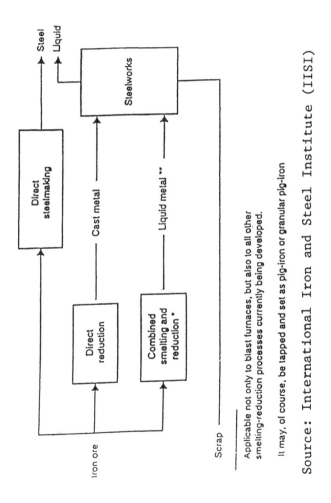

Applicable not only to blast furnaces, but also to all other
smelting-reduction processes currently being developed.

It may, of course, be tapped and set as pig-iron or granular pig-iron

Source: International Iron and Steel Institute (IISI)

The iron and steel industry is one of the major consumers of fuel and power in the national economies of industrially developed countries. This high energy intensity and the production of iron and steel impact upon the energy balances on any country which produces energy on a large scale. Because of the high energy intensity of the sector and relative high energy prices, direct energy costs account for between 20 to 60 percent of production costs at separate stages of iron and steel production. Combined energy costs of rolled-steel products using a multiplicity of technological systems reach 30 percent of total production costs in the former USSR and about 17 percent in the United States.[29] Although the price of energy has changed, over the previous decade, the higher temperatures gained in the furnaces have allowed the percentages of energy used in the production process to remain constant.

NOTES

[16]   *Impact of Developments in Scrap Reclamation and Preparation on the World Steel Industry*, ECA Steel Series 1993, United Nations, Geneva, pp. 71-75.

[17]   Birat, J.P., "Manufacture of flat products for 21st century," *Ironmaking and steelmaking*, 14, 1987, No. 2, pp. 84-92.

[18]   Lovatt, M., "United States mills play safe," *Metal Bulletin Monthly*, March 1991, pp. 41,43.

[19]   Lovatt, M., "United States mills play safe," *Metal Bulletin Monthly*, March 1991, pp. 41-43.
       Buchner, A.R., Das symposium "Endabmessungsnables Giessen" der AIME, *Stahl u. Eisen* 109, 1989, No. 24, pp. 1215-1217.
       Penson, S., In-line strip for Italian mini-mill, *Metal Bulletin Monthly*, March 1991, p. 59.
       Geneva Steel Installiert Stranggiessanlage, *Stahl u. Eisen* 110, 1990, p. 34.

[20]   Williams, Walter F., "The American steel industry in the 90s: Can it meet the challenges?" *Iron and Steel Engineer*, November 1991, pp. 21-23. Mr. Williams is Chairman and Chief Executive

Officer of Bethlehem Steel Corp., Bethlehem, PA.

[21] Summers, L.H.N. Birdall, et al, "Strategies for Rapid Accumulation," *The East Asian Miracle: Economic Growth and Public Policy*, Oxford University Press, pp. 191-258.

[22] International Iron and Steel Institute (IISI) Bulletin, 1993, p. 36.

[23] Mietz, J., M. Bruhl, F. Oeters, Stand der Verfahrenstechnik fur das Einschmelzen von Schrott mit fossiler Energie, *Stahl u. Eisen* 110, 1990, No. 7, pp. 109-116.

Hofer, F., F. Oeters, H.G. Geck, P. Patel, H.J. Selenz, Scrap melting with cost-effective energies, *Proceedings of the Sixth International Iron and Steel Congress*, 1990, Nagoya, Japan, ISIJ, Vol 4, pp. 1-10.

Patuzzi, A., K. Antlinger, H. Grabner, W. Krieger, Comparative study of modern scrap melting processes, *Proceedings of the Sixth Iron and Steel Congress*, pp. 49-57.

[24] Teoh, L.L., Electric arc furnace technology: Recent developments and future trends, *Ironmaking and steelmaking* 16, 1989, No. 5, pp. 303-313.

[25] Fritz, E., V. Pawliska, etc. "Scrap melting with effective use of fine coal in 5-ton test converter;"

Kondo, H., N. Tamura, etc, "Application of scrap melting practice to Q-BOP and K-BOP;"

Hirata, T., H. Ishida, etc, "Scrap melting process in steelmaking converter using initially charged coke;"

Ozawa, K., K. Umezawa, etc, "Development of scrap melting process and behavior of scrap melting;"

Demuki, N., S. Sugiura, "Development of reactor steelmaking process;"

All from *Proceedings of the Sixth International Iron and Steel Congress*, Nagoya, Japan, 1990, ISIJ, Vol. 4, pp. 18-64.

[26] Mietz, J., M. Brushl, F. Oeters, "Stand der Verfahrenstechnik fur das Einschmelzen von Schrott mit fossiler Energis," *Stahl u. Eissen 100, 1990, np. 7, pp. 109-116.*

[27] Steffen, R., 16. OBM/Q-BOP-Lizenznehmer-Konferenz, *Stahl u. Eisen* 110, 1990, No. 5, pp. 113-115.

[28] Patuzzi, A., K. Antlinger, H. Grabner, W. Krieger, Comparative study of modern scrap melting processes, *Proceedings of the Sixth Iron and Steel Congress*, pp. 49-57.

[29] United Nations: "Strategy for energy use in the iron and steel industry," *Economic Commission for Europe*, ICE/STEEL/41, UN, Geneva, April 1984.

IV

Technology Transfer—Literature Review

THE MARKET

The utility and profitability of the steel industry are premised upon the three pillars of product quality, price, and market share. In reviewing the literature on technology transfer, I shall consider the motivations for transfer as being a corporation's achievement of greater market share and purchasers' need of products at a fair market price. These motivations are examined through the lens of international negotiations among corporations seeking market presence by establishing production facilities in third countries to achieve economies of scale and scope in order to gain market presence. The product of these negotiations is technology transfer, and these negotiations between supplier and recipient are relevant in the formulation of a dynamic taxonomy. This discussion shall be limited to the steel industry.

Entry Induction

Corporate entrepreneurs saw the need to produce high quality steel at affordable prices for the construction, shipbuilding, and automotive industries. Scrap became the feedstock to be used, and the electric arc furnace (EAF), the principal technology to be employed. The output from these EAF mills were sheets, both hot and cold rolled, and bars. The pre-condition for producing these products of the EAF mills is dependent upon the dynamics of entry into the steel industry.

With increasing international economic activities, corporate entrepreneurs, although induced to enter, saw competition over standards and technological dominance as affecting entry. However, the EAF was and is still undergoing technological improvements. It now handles both scrap and direct reduced iron. It is being enhanced to use oxygen which increases the mill's melting capability. Other new technologies are now flourishing and there is now an "era of ferment" during which multiple standards for product compatibility coexist and new types of products are flourishing.[30] During this period, entry should be made since incumbents may be competing over the share of product sales compatible to their proprietary standards if there is an advantage to being dominant in the market and newcomers may also be able to capture a share of product sales.[31] To seek entry by offering value through increased market possibilities, a corporate entrepreneur can secure the advantage of "network externalities." By network externalities, it is meant that there is a positive return to scale to an installed technology,[32] or positive consumption externalities among consumers who use complementary products.[33] The new entrants can be supportive of the incumbent technology, although the standard is widely diffused. It is for this very reason that the incumbent firm needs new entrants. The diffusion of standards induces uncertainty over standard operating costs and costs of updating or switching technologies. The new entrant becomes a player and can exert influence on the appropriateness of the technology. Networking takes place between incumbent and newcomer to facilitate the technology transfer process through technology-based relationships so as to form a network. As these networks are formed the central objective of both firms is to achieve continued dominance. The allurement to the would be entrant by joining the dominant standard will be to enjoy a large and growing installed base of customers. A schematic representation of these causal relationships between the dominant players and would be entrant is given in Figure 4.1.

Figure 4.1
Schematic representation of causal relationships

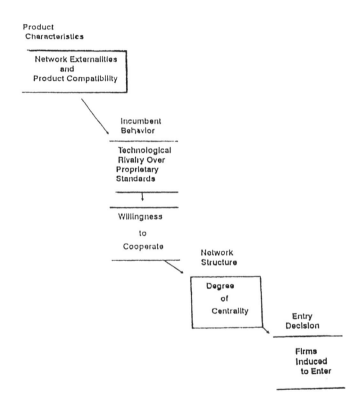

Dominant Players

The use of the EAF technology continues to increase in the global steel industry and EAF producers constantly seek to improve both their technologies and their market share. As previously stated, this technology is being modified to use oxygen; the capital cost is substantially lower than that of the basic oxygen furnace (BOF). The reduced cost makes a capital investment decision possible within a shorter time horizon. In turn, the dominant players compete in three market segments:

1. A global segment, in which industry forces span national boundaries, thereby requiring the firm to "integrate its activities on a world-wide basis."[34]
2. A multi-domestic segment which allows for differentiated strategic approaches across country locations.
3. A multi-focal segment in which the firms simultaneously respond to local market conditions in each country while integrating activities worldwide.

The steel industry and in particular the products from the minimills, such as sheets and bars, experienced greater difficulty in operating in multi-domestic and multi-focal segments and is more attuned to global configurations. This has implications for technology transfer through the force of competition which arises from different international firms competing in the same market. But perhaps surprisingly, given the global market context, a steel firm's activity is influenced by its geographic position. (Oceangoing vessels which transport steel help lessen the effects of geography, although steel is a bulky commodity to transport.) The global configuration also affects the strategic variety pursued.

Central to technology transfer is the geographic and strategic variety pursued by the firm to ensure market share. Geographic variety is determined by the degree of market differences across geographic locations.[35] Competing in a global segment is based on the identification and cultivation of common intermarket segments, defined as "the presence of well-defined and similar clusters of customers across international boundaries."[36] Hence, technology will be easily transferred in the global segment since business units will be competing in relatively homogeneous market conditions that span country locations. Strategic variety is defined by the degree to which business units within the firm pursue different international strategies.[37] Competing in a global segment implies that a unitary strategy underlies the firm's activities across locations, whereas in multi-domestic and multi-focal segments, business units must have considerable strategic autonomy so as to respond effectively to local conditions. Technology transfer is dependent on the business unit and less on modern technology and the purchasing of seconds on the market. It is not that the technology being transferred is "outdated" or that it doesn't give the supplier a competitive edge, but it is not leading edge technology.

The implication for technology transfer is that a larger portion of the value-adding process must reside in each country location, as compared to firms competing in global segments. For example, Minebea produces precision ball bearings standardized to global specifications. These bearings are sold off the shelf without any regard to location production requirements, as highly automated and dedicated production facilities are required for the production. In contrast, SKF custom-designs the "optimal bearing" to particular needs and this "customization" demands local production.[38]

TECHNOLOGICAL PROGRESS

The steel industry is an important user of high technology in its operations in process and quality control, in research and development, in planning and administration. The question is however, to what extent further advance in science and technology will influence the demand for steel in terms of quality as well as volume. D.F. Anderson, director at the Department of Economic Affairs of the International Iron and Steel Institute (IISI), states that the steel industry is facing an "S" curve-type development and that for a number of years to come, there will be only a moderate decrease in both the specific consumption of steel per unit of the main sectors' output and in the steel intensity of general economic growth.[39]

Effect of Globalization

Until recently, the steel industry did not operate globally. It is inherently unlike the automotive, electronics, paper tissue, and food industries, which are stable industries. But the economic advantages of moving toward world-wide operations are evident: low wages, low taxes, low land prices, and low land cost.

In recent times, steel enterprises—mainly from Japan— have entered into joint ventures, cooperation agreements, or outright participation with companies in different countries. European companies are forming strategic alliances with companies in the fast-growing regions of Asia or Latin America, and also in Eastern and Central Europe. This results in an increase in the international steel trade, as particular locational advantages favor production in the host countries for export to the parent companies' markets.

Three factors have influenced world-wide economic development:

1. political and economic changes in Eastern Europe and the former USSR,
2. globalization of industrial production,
3. regionalization of the world economy.

With the propulsion of the above three factors, the IISI forecasts that apparent steel consumption to the year 2000 will be as shown in Figures 4.2 and 4.3.

A transposition of these three factors to the world-wide steel industry creates a volatile market for steel. The demand for steel moves like a roller caster. World-wide steel production should grow at a rate of 1.5 percent per year over the next ten years.[40] Most of this steel market growth is shifting toward developing economies and away from non-free-market producers. The two pie charts (Figure 4.4) demonstrate this production shift.

Figure 4.2
Apparent steel consumption of crude steel
(million metric tons)

	1970	1980	1990	2000
Industrialized countries	375	363	374	374
Developing Countries	44	100	134	187
Western World	419	463	508	561
CIS and Eastern Europe	152	209	187	135
China and other CPEs	23	50	80	94
World	594	722	775	790

Figure 4.3
World steel exports of finished steel
(million metric tons)

Exporters	1970	1980	1990
Industrialized countries	73	112	114
Developing Countries	3	10	27
Western World	76	122	141
CPEs	14	20	24
World	90	142	165

Figure 4.4
Production shift toward developing countries

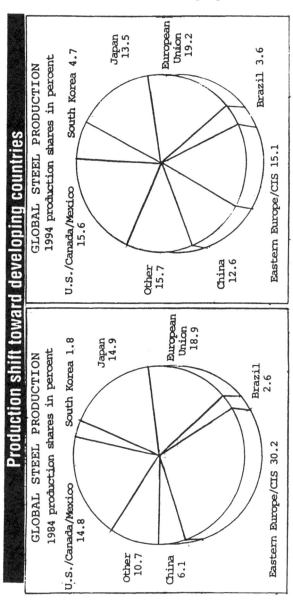

China, for example, is amidst phenomenal growth. The steel industries in Korea and more recently in some smaller Asian economies also are growing rapidly. Japan, however, is entering the latter stages of a substantial shift away from steel and steel-intensive industries.

Elsewhere, steel production in Eastern Europe and the Commonwealth of Independent States is close to hitting rock bottom after 4 to 5 years of free fall. Growth in Mexico and Brazil will be strong because of privatization and eventual economic recovery.

Meanwhile, the US steel industry has just passed its cyclical peak. Steel production in the US will be in a sustained decline for at least the next three years, 1996-1998.

As in other regions, the steel industry in the US is highly cyclical. Capacity utilization of US steelmakers changed either up or down by an average of 13 percent per year between 1980 and 1993. In six of the fourteen years, capacity utilization decreased; in the remaining eight, it increased. This constantly shifting market makes it extremely difficult for steel producers to plan volumes.

Before 1985, steelmakers based their strategy on simply being able to serve peak demand. As part of this traditional strategy, integrated producers invested in electric furnaces; production from these could be raised or lowered to meet current peak market demand more easily than it could at blast furnaces and basic oxygen furnaces. But since 1985, steel producers have shifted their strategy, trying instead to achieve profitability throughout the cycle. For example, the US steel industry structurally improved its operations to make more steel and more money from a given investment in plant and equipment.

From 1980 to 1986, the steel industry's operating rate averaged 65 percent of capacity. But from 1987 to 1993, the average operating rate was 84 percent of capacity. The operating rate has been at almost 90 percent of capacity for the past two years through February 1995.

The cyclical nature of the steel business causes substantial changes in price form one year to the next, especially spot prices. Nucor and Nucor-like low-cost producers inevitably will continue to be the bellwethers on price, particularly spot prices. Given the renewed strength of existing flat-rolled producers and the many new competitors jumping into the market, look for a colossal battle for market share to ensue.

MODELS OF TECHNOLOGY TRANSFER

The broad but specific patterns of technology transfer have their theoretical foundation in three interrelated models of technology transfer:
   a)   early appropriability models,
   b)   later dissemination models,
   c)   an anecdotal normative approach.

a)   *Early "Appropriability Models"*

        Early models of technology transfer emphasized quality R&D efforts as the primary impetus in the transfer process. Termed "appropriability models,"[41] these models rested on the assumption that if R&D results were of premium quality, the market would naturally adopt them as a function of normal competitive pressures. Appropriability models reflected a passive approach to the transfer process. In these models, scientists were presumed to be in contact with information users on an open and regular basis. As needs for or sources of new technology arose, the transfer process would utilize existing information linkages between suppliers and recipients.

b)   *Later Models: Dissemination Models*

        The shift to a more active perception of the transfer process began with the dissemination models developed between 1960 and 1980.[42] In these models, the researcher is portrayed as championing a particular technology and seeking market applications while the user is portrayed as pursuing innovation in order to satisfy specific needs.

Dissemination models also introduced the concept of intermediaries or agents who use market mechanisms to link research producers and users when network linkages were not already established.

These market transactions posited technology as a combination of tangible and intangible commercial assets required for production purposes. Consequently, the rate of technology dissemination became market dependent. Suppliers made their technology available through the market, and the recipients likewise utilized the technology through the market.

The success of this process depends upon both suppliers and recipients affirming mutual dependence upon one another.[43] Mutual dependence is even more evident in the more recent knowledge utilization models of technology transfer. Like dissemination, knowledge utilization involves both suppliers and recipients of information actively networking with one another to explore commercial applications. The focus of the new approach, however, is on the structure of interpersonal communications designed to reproduce technical knowledge in the mind of the receiver.[44] The interaction between researchers and recipients can lead to new applications for existing technology and to ideas for new technology.[45]

c)   *An Anecdotal Normative Approach*

Notwithstanding the above models, Jolly and Creighton (1975), Bell and Hill (1978), and Park (1982) contended that technology transfer and "innovation studies" in general, lacked an acceptable taxonomy. Talaysum in 1985 concluded that the literature had not been well analyzed from a managerial perspective. Following a survey of the literature concerning technology transfer between universities and industry, Boyle[46] concluded that the majority of the papers are anecdotal and normative, and that there is a lack of empirical and, particularly, analytical research in the field. A number of "universal modeling" approaches to technology transfer are commonly used but these do not apply to specific circumstances.

Few in-depth case studies have been done, making it difficult to account for nuances in each operating environment. Godkin's survey categorizes the literature into two main components: factors fostering technology transfer and factors constraining technology transfer.[47] Although this categorization supports the knowledge utilization perspective in an organization, it is non-linear. Further, it is contended, the linear process does not adequately account for feedback or provide for an orderly transfer process.[48]

A SYNTHESIS OF THE THREE APPROACHES

From the examination of all three approaches, four sets or clusters of interdependent variables emerge: technology, transfer, organizational, and environmental. Both technology and transfer have been dealt with at the beginning of this chapter. Definition of the remaining two interdependent variables will help to structure the development of a conceptual framework and will aid in the progression toward a dynamic taxonomy. Organizational variables define the supplier and recipient firms, their technological capabilities, relative bargaining power, and other characteristics of the two firms' "organizational profile." Environmental variables exist in the supplying and receiving firms' home and host countries and are, most notably, the host country's level of development and its capacity to absorb technology. The interaction of these four clusters of variables helps us to understand whether transfer will take place, the mode of transfer (arm's length or externalized vs. a wholly-owned subsidiary or another internalized form), price and other details of the transaction, and the impact of the transfer on the host and home countries as well as on the supplying and receiving firms.

The Technology Variables

What is the nature of the technology being transferred? How complex is it? How knowledge-intensive is it? Is the technology protected by patent law? Does the product have an expected life cycle? These are key questions in any transfer since certain technologies are more easily transferred, adopted, and diffused than others. The answer to these questions form the technology variables, which define technologies and differentiate them from one another through such criteria as industry, complexity, life cycle, or R&D intensity. Further, the answers to these questions are relevant to the three transfer models developed in the technology literature, that is, the appropriability theory, the dissemination model, and the anecdotal normative approach. These three models converge to illustrate how competition among firms and nations is embedded in the differences in the amount of know-how and information each possesses.

The Transfer Variables

The transfer variables define the mode and method of transfer and the contractual relationship between the technology supplier and recipient. Some modes of transfer are turnkey projects, wholly-owned subsidiaries, joint ventures with managerial control, joint ventures with minority participation and no control, and arm's-length licensing. Methods of transfer include planning and feasibility studies, product designs, machinery and equipment, personnel exchange, and on-the-job training.

Essentially, the transfer variables are the constraints, conditions, and parameters that are contained and set out in the contractual agreement between the supplier and the recipient.

The Organizational Variables

Technological knowledge may be coded in explicit form or held in a tacit mode, part of the informal knowledge derived from experience with particular activities. This organizational character of technology transfer suggests to encourage and enable it will need to be wide-ranging, yet many formal processes and policies for technology transfer make narrow assumptions about the nature of what is being transferred and the channels along which it may flow.

Another dimension of the organization variables is that they are not instantaneous events, but a time based process involving several stages. These range from initial recognition of opportunity or need, through search, comparison, selection, acquisition, implementation and long-term use involving learning and development. These are complex activities involving multiple actors and elements and various patterns of interrelationships, evolving from a relatively simple version relating the interactions between a supplier and recipient of technology to more complex variants involving actors and influences.

The Environmental (Societal) Variables

Essentially, environmental variables include all the host country's infrastructure-related capabilities, including its level of technological development and the capacity of its people to understand the technology being transferred. Various studies[49] have distilled the salient environmental variables which are classified as follows:

1. *Economic*
    GNP size and growth rate;
    GNP per capita and growth rate;
    Rate and size of savings and capital formation;
    Market size (demand);
    Relative size of manufacturing sector;

Price mechanisms—factor proportions and factor distortions;
Labor force—size and quality.

2. *Cultural*

Cultural propensity toward innovation;
Individuals' attitudes toward science and technology;
Attitudes toward foreign investment and technology;
Achievement orientation, motivation, and risk-taking propensity;
Attitude toward work, authority, and discipline;
Rising expectations and management of social tension in different cultures.

3. *Political*

Structure of the political system;
Existence of a political elite;
Policy toward foreign investment (political risk factors).

4. *Administrative—legal*

Explicit science and technology policies;
Developmental institutions and mechanism;
Administrative organs for policy-making and policy implementation;
Laws and regulations on foreign investment, science, and technology;
Patent and industrial property laws;
Social legislation (labor laws, welfare measures, and environmental regulations).

5. *Infrastructural*

Scientific and technological centers;
Manpower training institutions;
Institutions for promotion of transfer and/or development of technology;
Financial institutions.

TOWARD A DYNAMIC TAXONOMY OF TECHNOLOGY TRANSFER

The four technology transfer variables—technology, transfer mode, organizational, and environmental—constitute the conceptual framework of technology transfer. Identification of these variables helps us to recognize that technology is not value-neutral, and many studies have confirmed this fact.

But while many researchers have analyzed and defined these four interdependent variables over the past decade or more, the next step to be taken in an analysis of technology transfer is to show the systemic relationships among these variables. The methodology for this newest contribution to the literature is an analysis of stock and flow variables. The technology to be transferred is a stock variable, and the process of transfer is a flow variable. Thus, while the organization and environmental variables are essentially stock variables, it is important to realize that when the organization interacts with other inter-dependent variables, these become flow variables. Further, the societal variables are stock variables in that they reside in the host country's infrastructure and can be measured both qualitatively or quantitatively at any point in time.

Figures 4.5 and 4.6 show the interrelationships of these four variables. These diagrams reveal that, at any given time, a disposition exists either to facilitate or to hinder technology transfer into a host country. However, decisions to facilitate or to hinder technology transfer are premised on three flow variables identified as:

1. transfer risks
2. capital requirements
3. market expansion and costs reduction

Figure 4.5
Interdependent variables in the technology transfer process

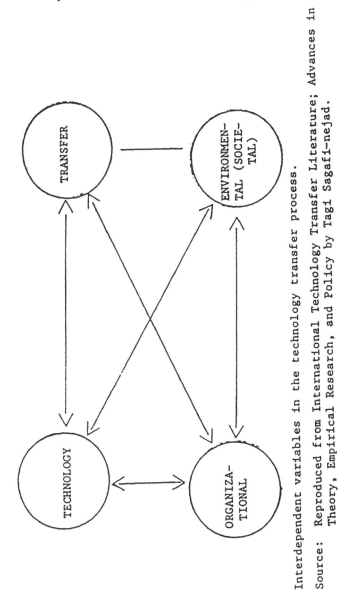

Interdependent variables in the technology transfer process.

Source: Reproduced from International Technology Transfer Literature; Advances in Theory, Empirical Research, and Policy by Tagi Sagafi-nejad.

Figure 4.6
The interaction of the main elements in the technology transfer
process through stock and flow variables

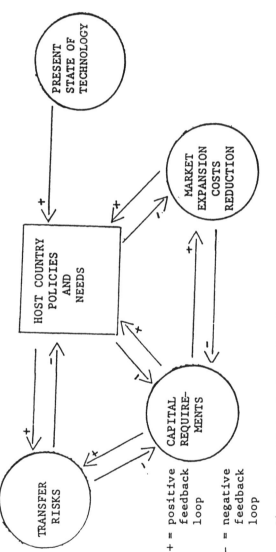

The interaction of the main elements in the technology transfer process
through stock and flow variables.

Source: Adapted from Systems Dynamics

+ = positive
feedback
loop

= negative
feedback
loop

Transfer risks:

Corporations assess the status of the host country's regulatory environment to ensure that patent laws will protect the technology that is being transferred. Any transfer risks inherent in the host country's environment affect the accessibility of capital for building a plant, thereby affecting market possibilities for the products from the minimill. The essence of this interactive process is the fact that these interdependent variables generate both positive and negative feedback. For example, the greater the transfer risks posed by any country, the less capital there will be available and the lower the likelihood of market expansion. Conversely, the lower the transfer risks posed by any country, the greater the amount of capital there will be available and the greater the likelihood of market expansion. Hence, the four interdependent variables of technology transfer create both a feed-forward and a feedback which dynamically affect the main elements in the technology transfer process.

Capital requirement and market expansion:

Each feedback loop thus has both a positive and a negative impact on other variables. This interactive process can constrain or contribute to market expansion, cost reduction, and technology transfer. With access to capital, technology can be transferred into a host country. Spatial and locational characteristics of technology development and transfer have been extensively dealt with in a previous doctoral dissertation.[50] However, to date, no systemic linkages have been made demonstrating the interdependence among these variables and showing how these factors affect one another.

Systems dynamics utilize stocks and flows to measure interactions. The stock for technology transfer is the host country's policies and needs. The flows depicted from Figure 4.6 originate from the present state of technology, and the stock of the country's policies and needs are affected by and interact with the transfer risks, capital requirements, market expansion and costs reduction. As these flow variables interact with the country's policy and needs, the manufacturer is responsive to ensure that its product is demanded in the market. The manufacturer is the unit which determines capacity. These are the two fundamental questions in this study: How is capacity created? and How is demand sustained? It is through this systemic approach of stock and flows that the interactive process of technology transfer takes place.

Public Sector Initiatives

At the microcosmic level, we have identified the variables which have affected technology transfer as the transfer risks, capital requirements, market expansion and cost reduction. Countries and corporations were cooperating to ensure these were variables which facilitated the process of technology transfer, and the development of the steel minimill technologies. The four countries with production capacities of over 50 mt/y (the former USSR, the United States, Japan and Germany) have greatly contributed to the development of this industry. Considerable and even decisive advances have been achieved in countries with smaller outputs such as Austria (the LD process), Mexico (direct reduction), Italy (miniplants), France (the OLP, LWS and Perrin processes and the Heroult furnace), Belgium and Luxembourg (the LD-AC process and the Wurth furnace throat), Sweden (the Wiberg and Hoganas processes and the Kaldo and Asea furnaces), Bulgaria (electrode coating), Romania (the ICEM process), and many others.

The next stage of technological development in the iron and steel industry will undoubtedly be marked by the substitution of hydrogen for carbon in iron ore reduction and by the use of nuclear energy. Again, these developments will be more of an evolution than a revolution, since a process of direct reduction by hydrogen in a fluidized bed was already at the pilot stage in 1958 and at the semi-industrial stage ten years later. Also, the direct application of nuclear energy to the preparation of the reducing gas (by electrolysis or thermal decomposition of water) raises important problems, and is even now occupying R&D laboratories.

STEEL MINIMILL TECHNOLOGIES

Raw Materials for the Steel Minimill

Scrap was for a long time the only source of feedstock for electric furnaces, but it has now been joined by pre-reduced products.

A scarcity of high-quality scrap, an unstable demand/supply situation, and the resulting price fluctuations have turned the attention of steel producers, particularly independent steelworks, to pre-reduced materials. The uniform and well-defined chemical composition of pre-reduced materials is an important factor when producing steel grades of high purity, and high quality; the quality of pre-reduced materials is not always matched by steel scrap which is often purchased from a variety of sources.

Also, provided certain standards (regarding gangue content and degree of metallization) are observed, pre-reduced ore is particularly suitable for use in electric-arc furnaces because it can be continuously charged at regulated speed; this practice does not have detrimental effect on refractory lining life and helps to utilize all the thermal energy available.

Development of the use of pre-reduced products in electric furnaces, which has long been a feature of steelmaking at Monterrey (Mexico), is now leading to increased use of pre-reduced products in UHP furnaces (for example, at Oregon Steel at Portland, and Korf at Hamburg).

The supply of raw materials and energy has helped to expand the use of direct reduced iron ore, which has become a very important technique of steel production. For example, test heats using 40 percent pre-reduced iron ore (continuously charged) were successfully executed at the 70 ton-45 MVA furnace at Daido's Chita works.

Technological Processing of the Raw Materials

The main objectives here are to control the metal's composition, to improve its homogeneity, and to remove gases from it, thus lowering the level of inclusions. When conducting metallurgical processing, emphasis is placed on the degree of efficiency with which a given composition can be produced rather than on its cleanliness. These practices are based on the ideas that it is best to:
- Use the production furnace to perform the tasks it is capable of fulfilling quickly and well (i.e., decarbonization of a bath of liquid pig and in the case of an electric furnace, melting of solid scrap) in order to obtain "primary" metal economically;
- Carry out in appropriate auxiliary equipment a small number of operations, including:
  * decarbonization, dephosphorization and desulphurization;
  * degassing;
  * deoxidation, elimination of inclusions;
  * refining;
  * temperature control.

These concepts behind and processes developed for metallurgical processing have led to the development of a number of new techniques, including the two extremely important techniques of vacuum remelting in arc or induction furnaces and remelting under conducting slag. These techniques have become widespread and are capable of producing ingots up to 2,300 mm in diameter and 165 tons in weight. Great advances in both these consumable electrode processes have been made in the last ten years. Vacuum-arc furnaces have seen reduction of idle time, regulation of the arc current and length, automation, bath agitation, and continuous weighing of the electrode: Electroslag remelting (ESR) furnaces have undergone improvements in multiple ingot melting, improved knowledge of the properties of fluoride slag and in the inception of the liquid slag process.

Comparison of the vacuum-arc and electroslag remelting processes seems to indicate that the electroslag remelting process has the technical edge since it offers the following advantages for a product of quality comparable to that produced by a vacuum arc-furnace:
- lower capital cost (i.e., no extra equipment to create a vacuum is required);
- greater flexibility with respect to its power supply and its capability of operating on monophase or polyphase alternating current;
- less stringent requirements regarding electrode geometry and the possibility of using several electrodes;
- simpler productivity, no shrinkage cavities, and no scalping;
- a wider range of metallurgical options, and slag selection and the possibility of introducing additions.

On the other hand, the process requires a thorough knowledge and complete mastery of its technological and physico-chemical parameters.

The vacuum processes:
The number of vacuum processes is large, and it is beyond the scope of this study to describe each one's developments. Suffice it to say that the originality of these processes resides in the way they solve the triple problems of:
- the method of exposure to the vacuum: in a single mass, in an unbroken flow, or by successive fractions;
- the application of the heat: superheating in the production furnace, arc induction heating, or simple preheating;
- the circulation of the metal: mechanical, by inductive heating, or by injection of gas.

Processes employing synthetic slags:
Synthetic slags may be used in a liquid state (after prior melting in an electric furnace) or in a solid state (with the addition of exothermic products that transform them to a liquid state on contact with the steel).

Stirring:

In addition to stirring by means of electromagnetic inductors, a process which may have had its heyday but which still has its supporters, there have emerged newer, simpler techniques involving bubbling with argon, nitrogen, or even compressed air as well as indicative agitation in a tunnel-type furnace.

Injection:

Injection may be carried out through a porous plug, through the stopper rod, or by means of a lance or submerged tuyeres. The substances to be injected may be gases, finely grained metallics, or fluxes in suspension in a vector gas.

Decarburization:

All these processes and auxiliary operations offer a wide range of possibilities, notably decarburization. In addition to the normal decarburization resulting from traditional melting or oxidizing processes, new methods of decarburizaiton have been developed based on reduction of the partial pressure of the carbon monoxide that results from oxygen injection. This reduction is accomplished either by dilution in an inert gas or by operation in a vacuum. Both versions of these techniques are rapidly becoming more popular in the production of stainless steels. Further, operation in a vacuum entails agitating the metal by blowing oxygen through it via injection of an inert gas through a porous plug; carbon concentrations of less than 0.01 percent are obtained.

A major impetus underlying the developments in decarburization was the need to improve steelmaking efficiency in the production of high-chromium steels, especially of extra-low carbon austenitic grades. Both dilution and vacuum techniques have revolutionized the production of these steels as regards:

- operational economy through the use of carburized raw materials;
- increased output by means of a huge increase in furnace productivity;

- increased quality by attainment of low carbon concentrations (on the order of 0.02 to 0.03 or even 0.01 percent), low gas content, and excellent micrographic texture;
- the use of dephosphorizing slags (of a lime base, rich ore, and spar) in the ladle have made dephosphorization rates of 40 to 60 percent possible.

Desulphurization:

In addition to processes such as using liquid slag with a lime alumina base that attack the evil of desulphurization at its root by desulphurizing the pig, new processes have been developed which employ either:
- synthetic slags in the form of self-melting alumina-lime powders, ignition being triggered by an alumina-thermal reaction;
- lancing of calcium and silica, using argon as the transporter fluid, and sometimes adding lime and spar resulting in 60 to 80 percent desulphurization.

Degassing:

Vacuum degassing became possible with the development of steam injectors, and its primary objective was the elimination of hydrogen. Assuming equal pumping power, ladle-to-ladle degassing is probably the fastest way to obtain the lowest concentrations of hydrogen, and it offers greater opportunities for metallurgical processing.

Deoxidation and control of inclusions:

Vacuum processes can not only achieve decarburization through the use of oxygen, they can also achieve deoxidation through the use of carbon. The popularity of the latter technique, which was very high a decade ago, has now declined because of the uncertainty of its results, the reoxidation of the metal by the refractors, and the advances made in the use of aluminium to "kill" steel.

The ladle techniques of vacuum stirring by induction, bubbling or simple agitation of the metal under deoxidized slag (which protects the metal from the air), makes it possible to coalesce and decant aluminates or silico-aluminates.

The use of other deoxidizers (to which reference has already been made) also enables the operator to control the size, morphology, plasticity and distribution of inclusions. For example, calcium acts on aluminates while cerium, zirconium, or titanium act on sulphides.

Refining:
Some vacuum processes permit the addition of large quantities of alloying elements without disrupting the homogeneity of the metal.

The introduction of solid electrolyte batteries has permitted great strides in the fine control of aluminium concentrations; this fine control presupposes very precise knowledge of the degree of the metal's oxidation.

Lastly, stirring ensures the chemical homogeneity of the bath.

Temperature control:
The achievement and maintenance of the correct temperature, which is vitally important for success in continuous casting, is facilitated by stirring in the ladle and the use of the slab "sucker." Results of trials using the tunnel-type induction furnace in more difficult situations when it is necessary to increase the temperature are promising. However, not all of the problems associated with this type of furnace, which was developed in connection with the continuous refining technique, have been solved. In particular, grading problems still exist with regard to the need to maintain a minimum quantity of metal in the bath.

To conclude this review of metallurgical processing outside the furnace, it should be noted that such processing has been particularly associated with electric furnaces throughout its development. Metallurgical processing has made possible substantial improvements in the steelmaking equipment's productivity of the and in the quality of the steels produced. It has also opened the way to new technologies which have

affected fields beyond those immediately concerned with steelmaking. In addition, metallurgical processing has proven extremely valuable in continuous casting processes, including:
- the use of submerged rods to take samples for analysis;
- electrochemical batteries;
- ladle preheating devices;
- new refractories of high-alumina or zircon brick and ramming mixes;
- replacement of the system of stopping casting ladles, stoppers, stopper rods, and sleeve bricks, with nozzle slide gates.

Shaping the Metal

The technological development of rolling mills has been influenced both by the increasing stringency of customers' requirements for both quantity and quality of steel and by the development of solid-phase steel production at the steelworks. The rapid advance of continuous casting has also played an essential part in this process.

Continuous Casting

The principal reason for the technological developments in continuous casting processes is that, after several decades of technical difficulties, the process became highly reliable at an industrial scale. In fact, the utilization rate (output/production-capacity ratio) around the world rose from 38 percent in 1970 to 64 percent in 1974 and 70 percent in 1994.

However, the development of continuous casting in individual countries has been very unequal. In 1990, continuous casting accounted for 70 percent of Japan's output; approximately 60 percent of the steel output in Italy, Spain, and the Federal Republic of Germany; 45 percent of the steel output in France; and less than 40 percent of the steel output in the United States and the former USSR. Used initially for square sections and to make the most of the metal saving achieved in the manufacture of special steels, continuous casting has accounted for a significant portion of output since large slab casters came into use. In 1976, there were 651 continuous casting machines in 54 countries; by the end of 1990, there were 7,000 machines in 66 countries.

Intensive research over the last decade has particularly affected the development of the following:

Type of machine:

Purely vertical machines, which required buildings of very great height, were succeeded by vertical machines that bent and straightened the product, and, later, by curved-mold machines. Although the latter are currently the most widely used, machines with straight ingot molds are sometimes preferred as they permit greater metallurgical "health" and greater symmetry when decanting inclusions.

Speed of withdrawal:

Speed of withdrawal has risen to 1.5 m/min for slabbing machines, 2 m/min for the most recent models, and from 2 to 4 m/min, depending on size, for square sections. Possible hourly outputs per strand reach 200 for slabs and 15 to 36 depending on their size, for square sections.

Reliability of operation:

The "drawer" type closing system and improvements in transfer form the ingot mold to the first set of withdrawing rolls, in secondary cooling control, and in regulation of withdrawal speed have helped to reduce the incident rate per line to less than 5 percent and the breakout rate to less than 1 percent.

Rate of utilization:

The use of ladle-changing devices, improvements in tundish refractories (such as exothermic plates that eliminate preheating), rapid changeover systems for closing mechanisms, and highly synchronized processing furnaces and casting machines have led to the development of sequence casting.

Quality products:
While the current state of continuous casting of very high carbon grades and heavy sections still leaves room for improvement, the use of improved coating powders, protection of the jet plunging nozzles, and argon protection atmospheres has produced steels equivalent to those produced by conventional rolling mills. One of the long-standing problems with continuous casting, the impossibility of casting rimmed steels due to difficulties in adjusting the effervescence, has been solved by the development of substitution grades.

The flexibility of the continuous casting process is characterized by:

- the use of adjustable-width ingot molds that permit rapid section changes;
- the ability to cast "dog's bone" blooms in beams or rounds, which are sometimes produced through centrifugal casting for the seamless tube industry;
- the use of reducing mills in series with the continuous casting machine.

The latter techniques are used in the manufacture of flat products and, perhaps more interestingly, in the manufacture of billets produced a "sizing mill" or by swing or continuous forging. With these techniques, the productivity of the continuous casting machine and the quality of semi-finished products for any final section can be improved.

Machine technology:
Continuous casting machines must meet two conditions:

- perfect geometry, established at the preassembly stage and conserved throughout manufacture, between the ingot mold and the various units in the process;
- the ability to replace various units when performing planned maintenance (in case of wear) or when extracting a trapped bar and repairing the machine (in case of accident).

These two requirements are sometimes at odds, and different designers adopted different solutions. Some solutions have focused on the connections between the ingot mold and the first secondary cooling unit, the one-string stand, or the pivoting of one to the other; other solutions have focused on the cooler itself, whether there are individual rollers in a single housing or rollers grouped in successive segments.

Whatever the solution, considerable progress has been made with regard to the rigidity and alignment of the sections in the continuous casting line, the ease of dismantling and reassembly, and lessening of wear by the use of cooling-off rollers.

The continuous casting process has by no means ceased to develop, as shown by recent research on, among other techniques, a mobile-rack withdrawal device at the head of the secondary-cooling system, electromagnetic mixing to improve the solidification pattern, and the resumption of research on horizontal machines.

To conclude this account, it is worth noting briefly the principal features that have led to the continual improvements in continuous casting: the technology's lower investment costs and its significantly higher metal yield.

Rolling Mills

The increased demand for steel products and the development of new techniques (coupled with improvements in rolling techniques during the sixties) have influenced development of rolling mill design and operation. However, changing market demands have influenced development of design and operation according to mill types; For example, market demands:

- sometimes favored increased production capacity by certain types of rolling mills (such as wide-strip mills and light-section mills) but not necessarily by other types of rolling mills;
- tended to decrease manufacture of certain products due to problems with technologies (such as heat exchange among the rolls and plastic deformation);
- affected requirements for product quality, regularity of dimensions, tolerances, and surface conditions.

The principal types of rolling mills discussed below are:
- Blooming and slabbing mills
- Continuous billet mills
- Heavy-, medium-, and small-section mills
- Wire rod mills
- Four-high heavy plate mills
- Wide-strip mills
- Tandem mills for cold-rolling strip
- Reversing mills for cold-rolled strip
- Coated sheets and plates
- Auxiliary equipment.

Blooming and slabbing mills:
Except for their heavy-beam blanks, blooming and slabbing mill products faced stiff competition from products of the continuous casting process. The only blooming and slabbing technologies that have developed appreciable are ingot weight installed capacity, twin motor drive, and in the case of slabbing mills, the use of universal stands. (It is interesting to note that the use of two stands in tandem can increase capacity without incurring significant technological changes.)

Continuous billet mills:
Continuous billet mill products are also facing stiff competition from continuous casting mill products. The use of diamond-square passes with successive vertical and horizontal stands has become the rule. Despite the limitations on output speed imposed flying shears technology and the lengths to be produced, continuous billet mill capacities amount to millions of tons per year. (It is interesting to note that the swing forge machine allows medium-capacity mills to change form blooms to billets.)

Heavy and medium section mills:
Although these mills can now be fed with continuously cast steel ("dog's bone"), the variety of sections needed generally entails the use of conventional feed system (blooms or section ingots). Heavy-section mill designs have remained relatively

static since the 1960s and the capacity of these mills exceeds 100,000 tons per month. Modern mills generally utilize a large reversing twin stand (of 5,000 to 7,000 KW) and a universal group (composed of a universal preparation stand and a universal finishing stand; the universal stand can be replaced by twin stands that allow rolling of sections with a low degree of symmetry, such as ancles, U-bars, sheet pilings, and rails).

Medium-section mills:

Medium-section mills can also be fed continuously cast steel, blooms, or section ingots. By comparison with cross-country mills, which may use universal stands for reversing, the development of a fully continuous medium-section mill that does not require looping has been an important innovation. All passes, whether utilizing universal or edging stands, are carried out in continuous sequence by eleven stands (grouped into one strand of five and one of six) with a bar throw-off device between them to facilitate speed synchronization. This expensive set-up is justified by the range of products that the mill can produce and by its train capacity, which can be as much as 140 thousand tons/month. Another unusual feature of this train is that storage is automatic, in vertical stockpiles.

Small-section mills:

Increasing the outlet speed of small-section mills to 20m/sec has led to increased cooler size. The use of horizontal or vertical rotating stands and dual finishing mills have now been replaced by the "multi-strand" train. The technique allows one-strand rolling at the top end of the range, and permits the preparation of the unutilized groups of stands for other assemblies. The technique also permits two-strand rolling on a single or mixed program at the bottom end of the range. Such mills are most common in Germany, the Netherlands, Belgium, and France.

Wire rod mills:

Increased demand for both quantity and quality of wire-rod products has given rise to numerous innovations. The most important have been:

(a) an increase in coil size, which now approaches two tons due to:
- enlargement of the initial section (from 80-100 mm to 125 mm) and addition of new roughing stands at the entry;
- increased billet length (now 19 or even 22m);
- a Soviet technique for the continuous welding of billets at the entry to the mill.

(b) design of finishing groups: two designs that have been available for quite some time were developed in the United States and Germany. The United States design employed three- or four- strand blocks in a combined drive, horizontal stands, twisting guides capable of high inputs despite a moderate output speed (35 m/sec), and average geometric characteristics and surface condition. The German technique utilized a single-strand finishing stand and alternating horizontal and vertical stands; this technique offers better quality, but at the price of higher investment costs and lower productivity. However, both designs became redundant with the appearance of single-strand blocks.

Single-strand blocks generally comprise 10 stands at an angle of 45 degrees to the horizontal, alternately crossed at 90 degrees and equipped with small-diameter tungsten carbide rolls cantilevered over single-drive stands; reducing groups can stagger the drives' speed.

The absence of guides and the compact arrangement of these groups allow output speeds of 60 to 75 m/sec and outputs per strand of 250 thousand tons/year of 5.5 mm rounds.

Four-high heavy plate mills:

Customers' requirements of heavy plate mills have developed in four main areas:

- increased plate width;
- regularity of longitudinal and transverse sections (with gauge tolerances of some tenths of a millimeter);
- precision of longitudinal and transverse dimensions (with tolerances on the order of 1 cm);
- physical properties of plates.

The steel industry has met these requirements with various improvements in the design and operation of heavy plate mills, such as:
- increasing the mills' load capacity: whether the mill is arranged as a single stand or as a two-high tandem stand depends on the desired output and the installed capacity; the constraints imposed by controlled rolling must be taken into account;
- roll counterbending devices;
- prestressing of columns to prevent yield;
- installing automatic gauge control (AGC) systems, generally hydraulic, which allow the roll adjustment to be modified with a very short response time; these adjustments counteract variations in rolling pressures due to differences in slab heating. These AGC devices are, of course, highly complex and can only be operated with the help of a process computer.

Wide-strip mills:
The requirements for finished products from wide-strip mills relate not so much to strip width as to regularity of size, to rolling and cooling conditions such as controlled rolling, and to increased weight per meter of coil width, which now exceeds 20 tons. It is worth noting a general increase in mill capacity. The 68" and 89" mills have now been succeeded by a third generation of 90"-width strip mills. The maximum gauge of hot-rolled wide strip reaches 20 mm, and trials with 22mm-gauge strip have been carried out. The output capacity of wide-strip mills now exceeds 4.6 million tons per year and expansion to 6 million tons is possible.
The most specific development has taken place:

(a) *at the roughing stage*—the use of edgers has allowed the widths of slabs supplied to mills to vary by 50 mm pitch. Strand arrangement has also varied. Besides the conventional arrangement of reversing edging stands and stands in series, the use of groups of stands in tandem and a bypass stand (Fukuyama, Mizushima, Solme) has reduced the number of installed stands while leaving more space.

(b) *at the finishing stage*—new techniques (i.e., process computers) at designers' disposal have facilitated the development of seven-stand finishing trains and created the possibility of installing an eighth stand despite the concomitant problems of cost and operational complexity, such as tension adjustment and speed synchronization.

(c) *at the coiler level*—to cope with increased rolling speed and much higher productivity levels, improvements in strip cooling and coiling (such as laminar-jet cooling and changes in cooler layout and design) have become necessary. Coiler development has kept pace with mill capacity and increased coil weight.

The growing complexity of wide-strip mills has been facilitated by computerization, particularly of the rate of furnace operation, adjustment and synchronization of finishing rains, gauge adjustment, spray control and temperature adjustment, coiler adjustment, and product tracking. Research is also being done on the automation of flatness and cross-section control.

Tandem mills for cold-rolling strip.
Market requirements for cold-rolled strip have grown particularly with regard to cleanliness, surface condition, size tolerance, and the availability of small-gauge strip.
The effect of these requirements is reflected in:
- increased rolling speeds (up to 1,000 m/min), which in turn give rise t lubrication and cooling problems;
- the number of stands in a train having increased to six in some recent installations;
- increased coil weight: to 25 tons per meter of strip width;

- use of devices for rapid change of rolls and for the hydraulic counterbending of rolls on the final stands.

Cold-rolling mills can now handle coils heavier than the slabs entering hot-strip mills, necessitating welding at the entry to the pickling line. This design is carried to its logical conclusion in Weirton's "continuous-continuous" train.

Reversing mills for cold-rolled strip .
Reversing mills for cold-rolled strip are generally reserved for rolling hard steels. The multi-roll sendzimir design predominates among cold-rolled strip mills, although the following innovations have emerged along sendzimir mills. The Hitachi Sexto stand permits the insertion of two intermediate rolls ensuring a redistribution of stresses that leads to improved flatness. In the "MKW" rolling mill, the working rolls, which are staggered in relation to the backup rolls, rest on lateral rollers; this setup eliminates roll bending, whatever the rolling direction, and permits considerable reductions with better flatness.

Coated sheets and plates.
The most outstanding advances with coated sheet and plate have been achieved by coating plate with nonmetallic paints or lacquers and by electrothinning, which has replaced hot-dip tinning in continuous galvanizing and electrogalvanizing lines. Tinplate has also been replaced by tin-free steels, i.e., steels that are electrolytically plated with chromium and chromium-oxide films.

Auxiliary equipment.
The spectacular development of rolling mills has been accompanied by numerous improvements in all types of ancillary devices that help to meet the strict requirements of end users. It is not possible to enumerate all the innovations introduced in bundling, dressing, and quality control of steel products. However, developments in heating or reheating of semi-finished products (both as regards furnace design—i.e., induction heating of slabs, conduction heating of billets, success of walking-beam furnaces, and the emergence of radiant dome

furnaces—and the actual heating process—development of rational heat-time curves and of controlled or "warm" rolling) deserves mention due to their effects on energy balance and lowering production costs.

While these technical developments have changed the face of the iron and steel industry in the past two decades, it should be noted that the two main developments, pure-oxygen oxidation and continuous casting, had already appeared in two Bessemer patents of 1851 and 1857. In addition, direct reduction has been practiced for fifty years or so. But this does not mean that new developments in the steelmaking industry are unlikely, only that the industry's problems are more difficult than those of other branches of metallurgy. Moreover, the tolerable margin of error in the iron and steel industry is narrower due to the extremely high costs of investment in facilities and research and of the slimness of the profit margin.

In the next Chapter, I will analyze the distinction between the minimill and the integrated mill.

NOTES

[30] Anderson, P., M.L. Tushman, "Technological discontinuities and dominant designs: A cyclical model of technological change." *Administrative Science Quarterly* 35, 1990, pp. 604-633.

[31] David, P.A., "Standards for the economics of standardization in the information age," in Dasgupta, P. and P. Stoneman, (eds) *Economic Policy and Technological Performance*, Cambridge, England: Cambridge University Press, 1987, pp. 206-239.

[32] Farrell, J., C. Shapiro, "Dynamic competition with switching costs," *Rand Journal of Economics*, 19, 1988, pp. 123-137.

[33] Katz, M.L., and C. Shapiro, "Network externalities, competition, and compatibility," *American Economic Review, 75, 1985, pp. 424-440.*

[34] Porter, H.E., (ed.) *Competition in Global Industries*, Harvard Business School Press, Boston, MA, 1986, p. 33.

35   Prahalad, G. and Y. Doz, *The Multinational Mission: Balancing Local Demands and Global Vision*, Free Press, New York, 1987, p. 145.

36   Samire, S. and K. Roth, "The influence of global marketing standardization on performance," *Journal of Marketing*, 56 (2), 1992, pp. 9-17.

37   Prahalad, G. and Y. Doz, *The Multinational Mission: Balancing Local Demands and Global Vision*, Free Press, New York, 1987, p. 145.

38   Collis, D.J., "A resource-based analysis of global competition: The case of the bearing industry," *Strategic Management Journal*, 12, Summer Special Issue, pp. 49-68.

39   Anderson, D.F., "World-wide political and economic change - Effect on the iron and steel industry," *Ironmaking Conference Proceedings*, 1992, p. 26.

40   Jacobson, J.E., "Staying alive in a volatile market," *New Steel*, Vol. 11, no. 7, July 1995, pp. 48-49.

41   Avery, C.M., *Organizational Communications in Technology Transfer between a Research and Development Consortium and its Shareholders*, Doctoral Dissertation, (1989) College of Communications, University of Texas, Austin.
     Devine, M., T. James, Jr. & T. Adams, "Government Supported Industry, University Research Centers: Issues for Successful Technology Transfer" *Journal of Technology Transfer* (1987) Vol. 12, pp. 27-37.

42   ibid.

43   McCardle, K.F., "Information Requisition and the Adoption of New Technology," *Management Science*, (1983) Vol. 31, No. 1, pp. 1372-1389.
     White, W., "Effective Transfer of Technology from research to Development," *Research Management*, (1990) Vol. 20, pp. 30-34.
     Cohen, H., S. Keller and D. Streeter, "The Transfer of Technology from Research to Development," (May 1979) *Research and Management*, Vol. 22, pp. 11-17.

44   Bailey, R.E., "The Development of a Practical Planning Framework for International Technology Transfer," (June 1990). In *Technology Transfer in a Global Economy*, Proceedings of the Technology Transfer Society's 15th Annual Meeting in Dayton, Ohio, pp. 7-19.

45   Avery, C. *Organizational Communication in Technology Transfer Between an R&D Consortium and its Shareholders*, College of Communication, University of Texas at Austin (1989).

46   Boyle, K., "Technology Transfer between Universities and the UK Offshore Industry," *IEEE Transactions on Engineering Management*, (February 1986), Vol. EM-33, No. 1, pp. 33-42.

47   Godkin, Lynn, "Problems and Practicalities of Technology Transfer: a Survey of the Literature," *International Journal of Technology Management*, Vol 3, No 5, 1988, pp. 590-598.

48   Dimancescu, D. and J. Botkin, *The New Alliance: America's R&D Consortia*, Cambridge, MA: Ballinger Publishing (1986).

49   Dahlman, C.J. and L.E. Westphal, "The meaning of technological mastery in relation to transfer of technology" in *The Annals of the American Academy of Political and Social Science*, 1981, pp. 12-16.

Lucas, B. and Freedman, S., *Technology Choice and Change in Developing Countries*, Dublin: Tycooly International Publishing, 1983.

OECD: *North/South Technology Transfer: The Adjustment Ahead*, Paris: OECD, 1986.

Office of Technology Assessment, "Technology Transfer to the Middle East," Washington, DC: US Congress, 1984.

50   Levonian, M., *Steel Minimills and the Spatial Characteristics of Steel Demand*, MIT Ph.D. thesis, December 1985.

V

A Comparison of Integrated Steel Mills with Steel Minimills

Both integrated mills and minimills are part of the same industry insofar as they produce and sell steel products. There are, however, a number of significant differences between the two types of mills: (1) the types of products that each produces; (2) mill size in terms of capacity; (3) geographic locations of mills; (4) raw materials; (5) technology; (6) productivity; (7) employment costs; (8) entry into and exit from the industry; and (9) mill technologies under development.

PRODUCT TYPES

Steel Minimills

The minimill's three basic operations are:

1. Scrap is melted in an electric furnace to produce liquid steel.
2. Liquid steel is poured through a continuous caster to produce semifinished steel, usually in the form of billets.
3. The billets are rolled hot on a bar mill to yield products such as reinforcing bars, small structural sections and rods which are then allowed to cool.

Integrated Mills

By their very nature, integrated plants perform many more operations than minimills. The integrated mill receives basic raw materials such as iron ore and coal or sinter, and it first turns the coal into coke. The iron ore and coke are charged into a blast furnace, along with limestone, to produce molten pig iron. (Of course, these preliminary steps are not necessary in minimill operations.) The molten pig iron is then charged with scrap into a basic-oxygen furnace, where it becomes liquid steel. The liquid steel is poured through a continuous caster and emerges in the form of a bloom, billet, or slab (or "sheet"). Sheets, which constitute the integrated mills' major product, are hot-rolled in continuous hot-strip mills, becoming hot-rolled sheets which can be further processed or sold as cold-rolled sheets.[51] The surface of the steel is cleaned through pickling, then the steel is cold-reduced and annealed to improve its physical qualities. Some steel is sold as cold-rolled sheets, some of which have been coated with zinc to create galvanized steel, or with tin to form tinplates.

CAPACITIES OF MILLS

An important difference between the two types of mills is size, that is, their capacity to produce steel. The steelmaking capacities of individual electric furnace minimills range from 150,000 tons to well over 1 million tons; capacities of the integrated plants range from about 1 million tons to as much as 6 or 7 million tons. The median annual production of a minimill is about 300,000 tons, while the median annual production for an integrated mill is 3.5 million tons.[52]

Minimills

The disparity in capacity was far greater when minimills first appeared in the early to mid 1960s. At that time, most minimills produced less than 150,000 tons, while the integrated mills at that time ranged from 1.5 million to as much as 8 to 9 million tons annually. Since then, the industry has seen a decided growth in minimill capacity and a concomitant reduction in many integrated mills' capacities. In a sense, the smaller minimills have been getting bigger, while the bigger integrated mills have become smaller. Outstanding examples of this trend are Chaparral of Midlothian, Texas, whose capacity grew from 400,000 tons to 1.5 million tons, and Inland Steel of Indiana Harbor, Indiana, whose capacity shrank from 9.1 million tons to 6.5 million tons. Based on the two types of mills' average capacities, *their proportion of output* is approximately 10 to 1 in favour of the integrated plant.

It is generally believed that minimills will continue to increase in capacity while integrated plants will continue to shrink, that the differences in capacity between the two types of plants will narrow substantially. Further, some integrated plants, which are described as "minimill-like-plants" have abandoned the coke-oven/blast-furnace/basic-oxygen complex in favor of electric furnaces. However, as long as some plants remain integrated and others remain electric-furnace operations, sizeable differences in capacity between the two types will remain. By their very nature, most electric plants are necessarily small when compared to the blast furnaces and BOF complexes of integrated mills.

GEOGRAPHIC LOCATIONS

The locations of integrated steel plants and minimills were determined by different forces. Most of the integrated mills have been in operation at their present locations for around 80 to 100 years, whereas the majority of the electric-furnace plants have come into operation during the past 25 years.

Integrated Mill Locations

Integrated mills were located in relation to raw materials as well as the market. The raw materials of integrated mills are basically iron ore and coal (which must be converted into coke for use with iron ore in the blast furnace). Areas in which iron ore and coal were found in close proximity were relatively few; when this co-location did occur, integrated plants were built.

In contrast, the "raw materials" of electric-furnace mills is scrap. Scrap can be found in any industrial area, and even when it must be transported, the distances are relatively short. Thus, the fundamental consideration for locating minimills was the market. In fact, minimills have been referred to in recent years as "market mills".[53]

No suitable new locations for integrated plants have been found, but many integrated steel plants continue in operation at their original locations despite increasing pressures from "market mills". Integrated plants were maintained as long as the market was strong enough to absorb their production. For example, the integrated steel market virtually collapsed in the United States in 1982, and its slow recovery has forced many integrated steel plants to close. Bethlehem Steel of Pennsylvania mirrors these events in the integrated steel industry.

The original Bethlehem plant was founded at its present location in Pennsylvania in 1860. In 1916, Bethlehem acquired the plant at Sparrows Point, near Baltimore, Maryland, which had been built in the 1880s by the Maryland Steel Company. Bethlehem acquired Lackawanna, near Buffalo, New York, (built by the Lackawanna Steel Company in 1902), in 1922 and operated the plant until shutting it down in 1984. Bethlehem built the fully integrated plant at Burns Harbor, Indiana, in the 1960s. (This is the most recently built integrated plant in the United States, and it was built at a new location.) Likewise, Johnstown and Steelton, Pennsylvania, were both integrated plants but have been transformed into electric-furnace operations. The Johnstown plant, which has been at that location since the mid-1950s, was acquired in 1922 from the Cambria Steel Company. The Steelton plant, acquired in 1916 from the Pennsylvania Steel Company, was originally built in 1867 by the Pennsylvania Railroad Company to provide rails.

Minimill Location

In contrast to the long-lived integrated plants operating at their original locations for decades, the minimills, which sprang up in the 1960s and 1970s, were established in areas where there was a growing market for their products, usually in areas removed from the integrated mills. As previously mentioned, scrap is found in large quantities in all industrialized areas of the world, so a minimill can be established in any industrial location with relative ease. Like the integrated mills, minimills have remained at their original locations.

Minimill location has been influenced by the needs of housing and service industries. For example, the construction of shopping centers requires large quantities of reinforcing bar and small structural sections. Construction market conditions encouraged steel companies to establish minimills in growth areas. Even when markets have become saturated, very few minimills have had to close, although many have changed ownership—some minimills more than once. Minimills continued to thrive—almost despite market conditions—due to the relatively low investment required to purchase or to revive a minimill. Fox example, the Tennessee Forging operation which had been closed down, was revived recently, when it was purchased by David Smith Associates, a company in the US.

The investment required for a new minimill today is substantially higher than it was in the 1960s and 1970s. Nucor and Florida Steel have built the most recent plant at a cost of $55-60 million.[54]

RAW MATERIALS

Minimills

As previously stated, the "raw material" of minimill is scrap. Scrap arises in any industrialized population center, and the types of scrap that minimills can accept are either prompt industrial scrap or obsolete metal. Prompt industrial scrap is generated at steel mills during the fabrication of steel into finished products such as automobiles, refrigerators, or machinery. Obsolete metal scrap is comprised of discarded items that contain steel, ranging from automobiles to old machinery to multistory buildings that have been torn down.

However, a few minimills in the United States and Japan use direct-reduced iron. Direct reduction is a process whereby deoxidized iron pellets are produced without the use of a blast furnace. In this process, iron pellets of approximately 60 percent iron content are fed into a shaft furnace. Natural gas is introduced, and it removes much of the oxygen from the iron ore; the resultant pellets are approximately 90 per cent iron and are relatively free of contaminants. The pellets can then be charged into the electric furnace.[55]

Integrated Plants

In contrast, integrated plants required huge amounts of raw materials that are concentrated in a few locations throughout the world. The raw materials of integrated plants are iron ore (which must be converted into pellets or sinter before it can be used) and coal (which must be converted to coke before it can be used). The materials, along with limestone, are charged into a blast furnace to produce molten pig iron. The molten pig iron is then charged into a basic-oxygen converter, along with scrap, to produce steel; the charging ratio is generally 70-75 percent molten pig iron to 25-30 percent scrap. Thus, while integrated mills use scrap in making steel, the integrated mill's scrap requirements are much lower than the minimill's.

As mentioned, iron ore must be converted into pellets or sinter before it can be used in an integrated mill's blast furnace. Pellets for use in integrated mills are produced by crushing and concentrating iron ore; the pellets have an iron content of 64 or 65 percent. The facilities required for this process are expensive, requiring an investment of approximately $90 per ton and an overall investment of $400 million.[56]

In addition to pellets, a considerable amount of sinter is usually charged into an integrated mill's blast furnace. Sinter is produced by mixing iron ore with coke breeze or anthracite coal fines. The final product is a clinker like substance that greatly facilitates blast-furnace operations.

Coal must also be treated before being charged into a blast furnace. Coal is converted into coke in ovens located at or near an integrated mill. There is an abundant supply of coal in the world, but many steel plants' coke ovens are old and need replacing.[7]

While integrated plants are often located close to raw material deposits, many must ship in their coal. Many steel-producing-countries, such as Japan, Korea and the United States, import iron ore, mainly from Venezuela, Canada, Brazil and Liberia. Naturally, integrated companies throughout the world have financial interests in ore deposits. For example, integrated companies in the US (including Bethlehem, National, Inland, and Acme) maintain significant interests in the Iron Ore Company of Canada and Wabush Mines, both located in the Quebec/Labrador area, while United States Steel's interests are confined to the Quebec-Cartier Mining Company. However, Brazilian, Venezuelan and Liberian ores are delivered predominantly to the East Coast of the United States and the Southern States, while Canadian ore is in use in plants in the Great Lakes area as well as the East Coast of the united States.[8]

TECHNOLOGY

The technologies of integrated mills and minimills vary widely, yet they are similar in some aspects. With few exceptions, the minimills have been built before 1980. These plants will need some updating if they are to remain modern and competitive. The integrated mills are older, most of them having been built prior to 1945. Integrated mills' facilities have been modernized using, in most cases, the most-up-to-date technology available at the time of their refurbishing.

Minimills

Steel minimills utilize electric furnaces. Improvements that have become available during these plants' lifetimes include water-coded side panels and roofs as well as high-powered transformers and the use of oxygen. A number of minimills have updated their electric furnaces to include these improvements.[59] Some have not. For example, the lower-powered transformers often found in some of the smaller, older minimills have not needed updating with water-cooled panels and roofs. However, many minimills have replaced furnaces with modern electric-arc furnaces.

Virtually without exception, minimills use continuos casting units through which steel is poured and formed into billets. While the age of the continuous casting machine tends to vary with the age of the minimill, all continuous casting equipment now in service functions reasonably well. However, older machinery often has higher operating costs.[60]

Minimills are also built as bar mills, rod mills and hot strip mills. Many bar mills were originally built as cross-country mills with looping devices. This mill design was later improved upon and gave way to straightaway mills with one stand after another in-line. While these in-line mills now lack the most modern equipment, their machinery is adequate for the production of minimill-type products. All rod mills now in service have been equipped with state of the art technology. Hot strip mills have adopted new technologies in order to produce flat-rolled products, and they represent a new approach to the production of steel sheets.[61] At these minimills, the slab to be cast is much thinner than that normally cast for the production of steel sheets. Furthermore, the hot-strip mill has only four stands.

Integrated Mills

On the other hand, there is the constant need to upgrade the technology in the integrated mills, which have been in operation for decades. Of particular significance is the installation of continuous-casting machines, which allow the molten steel being poured from the ladle to be cast through the equipment and come out in the form of a slab, billet or bloom. Integrated mills have been vigorously installing these continuos casting machines and, in this respect, they are technologically up to date.

As discussed in the previous section, significant advances have been made in the preparation of materials for use in the blast furnaces. The methods of sintering and of forming iron ore into pellets have upgraded the amount of iron in the burden from about 50 percent iron content in raw iron ore to about 66 percent iron content in the prepared pellet. With the improvement in furnace burden, the blast-furnace output has been increased significantly, and the use of coke to produce a ton of iron has been decreased by one half.[62]

Also, the integrated mills' steelmaking process has changed in the past 25 years from the open hearth to the basic-oxygen furnace, which provides a more efficient and less costly operations.

Significant advances have been made in the rolling and finishing mills. Perhaps the most important advance has been in the continuous hot-strip mill.[63] All forms of sheet products—and this accounts for over 50 percent of all steel products, including hot-rolled, cold-rolled, galvanized and various specialty sheets - must pass through the hot-strip mill. During the period from the early 1960s through the mid-1970s, 12 new hot-strip mills were installed in various plants throughout the United States. These newer hot-strip mills were called "second-generation" hot-strip mills because they are so far superior to the mills installed before that time.[64] The hot-strip mills in the US are currently being upgraded *to be competitive on a world-wide scale*.

One specific technological advance is the use of six rolls, instead of the conventional four-high mill, to produce sheets. United States Steel and Pohang Steel of South Korea have entered into joint ventures to utilize these six-roll mills in Pittsburgh and California. Other joint ventures between Inland Steel of the United States and Nippon Steel of Japan have led to successful cooperation in technological development and applications.

The Future of Mill Technologies

The integrated plant must invest heavily in coke ovens, blast furnaces, basic-oxygen steelmaking capacity, continuous casting, and an 80-inch wide hot-strip mill. On the other hand, a minimill relies essentially on electric furnaces, a caster to produce thin slabs, and a scaled down, 54-inch wide hot-strip mill, since thin slabs will require less reduction. But as H. Barnette, the chairman of Bethlehem Steel, recently said "I've stopped using the term 'minimills', I'm not sure what it means." Barnette went on to say that the cultures of the integrated and electric furnace producers are becoming more similar.[65]

Like integrated mills, minimills need to work closely with customers to get continuing feedback about the quality of their steelmaking practices; and they must continue to measure and improve quality statistically. Bob Garvey, the president of North Star Steel, told the minimill roundtable, "The definition of a minimill involved the manner in which you operate: maximum flexibility...You don't lock yourself into huge fixed assets that limit your flexibility—which blast furnaces, coke ovens, and basic-oxygen furnaces do... We don't marry technology."[66]

Some minimills now combine the use of electric furnaces with the use of blast oxygen furnaces. For example, Nucor in the US could find itself using a version of an oxygen furnace that would blow great amounts of oxygen into the furnace, then harness the post-combustion carbon monoxide to convert iron carbide directly to steel.[67] In addition, it is possible for the integrated steel industry to be as financially successful as Nucor. So said AK Steel's chairman Tom Graham, at the Paine Webber Annual Steel Conference.[68]

PRODUCTIVITY

The productivity of minimills and integrated mills is best measured through man-hours expended per ton of product shipped. For minimills, these figures vary from less than 2 hours to 4 hours; a good average would be 2 man-hours per ton. On the other hand, productivity figures for the integrated mills are greater, varying from 4 man-hours to 7 or 8 man-hours per ton shipped. At first sight, it appears that minimills are more efficient than integrated operations. However, one must examine their respective operations before reaching any conclusion.

Minimills

As mentioned in the first section of this chapter, minimills have three basic operations:

1. Scrap is melted in an electric furnace to produce liquid steel.
2. Liquid steel is poured through a continuous caster to produce semifinished steel, usually in the form of billets.
3. The billets are rolled hot on a bar mill to produce products, such as reinforcing bars, small structural sections, and rods, which are then allowed to cool.

Integrated Mills

Integrated mills have five basic operations which can be performed in up to eight possible steps. (Steps 6 to 8 below are optional operations.)

1. The raw materials are prepared: Iron ore is transformed into pellets or sinter while coal is turned into coke.
2. Both the pellets or sinter and the coke are charged into a blast furnace, along with limestone, to produce molten pig iron.
3. The molten pig iron, along with scrap, becomes liquid steel in a basic-oxygen furnace.
4. The liquid steel is poured through a continuous caster and emerges in the form of bloom, billet or slab.
5. The bloom, billet or slab is then rolled hot into various products, such as sheets.
6. Sheets, which constitute the major product of integrated mills, are hot-rolled on the continuous hot-strip mill, emerging as hot-rolled sheets.

7. The sheets can be sold as final products or further processed into cold-rolled sheets (this conversion required a pickling operation which cleans the surface of the steel). The cold-reduced steel can be annealed to improved its physical qualities.
8. Some sheets are further processed with zinc coating to form galvanized steel, or they are coated with tin to form tinplate.

An integrated mill goes through twice as many operations as does a minimill, and these extra operations account for the higher man-hours per ton of product shipped. In that case, what should be the basis of comparison between the productivity of a minimill and that of an integrated mill? The operations that best bear comparison are steelmaking, continuous casting, and hot-rolling. The operations preceding steelmaking should not be compared, nor should those that follow the hot-rolling process, since the minimill engages in none of these processes. For these three functions that offer the best comparison, the man-hours per ton of product shipped by integrated mills range from 1 to 2.5 man-hours.

For minimills, man-hours per ton vary according to the size of the product rolled. For example, when size 8 reinforcing bar, or rebar (which is about an inch in diameter), is rolled, man-hours total 1.1 per ton of steel shipped; when size 3 rebar (which is about three-eights of an inch in diameter) is rolled, man-hours increase to 1.7 per ton of steel shipped.

On the other hand, integrated plants require fewer man-hours to perform the three production phases that best bear comparison, largely because their economies of scale spread the labor input over a considerably greater output. For example, for the single step of steelmaking, a minimill's electric-furnace can melt an average of 330,000 net tons per year, while an integrated mill's basic-oxygen furnace can produce an average output of 2.8 million net tons per year. Both types of plants evince similar disparities for continuous casting output. However, minimills are improving their productivity rates, often resulting from an increased throughput due to changes in the product mix.

EMPLOYMENT COSTS

Integrated Mills

Workers at integrated mills worldwide are represented by strong unions. For example, most steelworkers in the US are represented by the United Steelworkers of America. The only US workers not so represented are at the Armco and Weston Steel plants (both of which are located in Middletown, Ohio); the employees at these plants are represented by independent unions.

Integrated mills are now making concessions in union negotiations to achieve partnership status. Further, recent changes in the work rules are enabling the mills' work forces to be employed more flexibly, which will permit an increase in productivity. Integrated mill companies have also agreed to profit-sharing plans and concessions involving stock.[69]

Minimills

In contrast to the heavily unionized integrated mills, more than 50 percent of all minimill companies throughout the US (consisting of more than 60 percent of production capacity) are non-union. Where minimill workers are organized, *those plants have other unions in addition to* the United Steelworkers of America. Employment costs at unionized minimill plants are considerably lower than at integrated plants. While costs vary among unionized integrated mills, their average costs run above $20 per hour. The unionized minimills' basic employment costs, in contrast, range from $8 to $10 less per hour.

Minimills worldwide operate on profit-sharing and incentive systems, so while the basic hourly employment rate may be low, the employees are able to earn almost as much as the unionized steelworkers in the integrated plants. The profit-sharing and incentive plans usually entail pooling a certain number of dollars per ton over and above a stipulated tonnage; these pooled profits are divided among the workers in the unit.[70] When a worker retires at one of these plants, the other workers will often petition management not to replace the retiree; in this way, fewer workers can divide the pool. Minimills also typically have a minimum of work rules, which provides for an effective use of the labor force.

ENTRY AND EXIT

The term entry simply means a firm's beginning to operate within a particular industry. Exit from an industry occurs when a firm cannot operate profitably within its industry, whether this inability arises from a lack of demand, an increase in operating costs, or an increase in materials (in the case of a steel plant, feedstock) costs.

Minimills

The entry of minimills into the steel industry was directly related to the capital investment requirements and price paid for energy. In short, the relatively low amount of investment capital required facilitated entry into the minimill business. For example, when minimills experienced their early growth in the 1960s, the cost of a minimill in the US, with an electric furnace, a continuous caster, or a breakdown mill for ingots, as well as a bar mill, ranged from about $7 to $12 million (in historic dollars). In 1964 the Tennessee Forging Company at Harriman, Tennessee, built its plant with an annual capacity of 60,000 tons of finished steel products for $4.2 million. Of this amount, $2.8 million was spent on land, buildings and equipment. The equipment included a 20-ton electric furnace with the capacity to melt 100,000 net tons of steel per year, a continuous-casting machine, and a relatively small bar mill.[71] Since minimills are situated at demand centers and their products are readily sold, the market promotes their continued growth.

During the 1960s, several minimills were built throughout the world at a cost of $10 to $11 million each. Although several integrated mills closed during this period, investment in minimills continued to increase the availability of these electric furnace and bar mills. Minimills made it easy to enter the steel business with a minimum investment in this period, and by the close of the decade of the 1970s there were many minimills throughout the world.[72] (In addition, the capacities of minimills built in the late 1970s were larger than those of earlier minimills; minimills built around this time averaged 300,000 tons of raw steel capacity.) By the late 1970s, when inflation rose worldwide, the cost of constructing minimills rose accordingly, to around $40 to $45 million. By 1981, the cost of entry had increased to about $60 million. In fact, this was the cost of a minimill built by Florida Steel at Jackson, West Tennessee, in the US. Today, the average cost of a minimill is between $90 to $110 million.[73]

Minimills have now become a permanent feature of the world steel industry. Their priorities are to gain market share from integrated mills and to respond to increasing needs for steel products. In the US, many minimill corporations, such as Steel Dynamics, Gallatin, Nucor, and Chaparal are among minimills responding quickly to high steel demand.[74] No minimill now in operation appears to be at risk of failing and exiting the market.

Integrated Mills

An integrated steel mill's entry into the steel industry is predicated on massive capital investment. An integrated steel plant requires coke ovens, possibly a sinter plant, a large blast furnace, a basic-oxygen steel shop, a continuous caster, and a rolling mill for either sheet or plates. For a small integrated mill with a capacity of 1.0 to 1.5 million tons, these costs are currently well in excess of $1 billion.

Greenfield sites have been identified throughout the world, although it is expected that no new steel mills will be built on these sites. However, existing integrated mills have been making substantial investments in equipment that permits them to produce light, flat-rolled steel products.

During the 1960s and early 1970s when the second generation of hot-strip mills (see section 5, above) was installed, the investment in this technology varied from $125 to $135 million. These mills were referred to as second generation since they were far superior to the mills installed before that time.[75] The latest hot-strip mill to have been installed is in the Qwanguang plant of Pohang Steel of South Korea, built in 1986 at a cost of $318 million. The output of these hot-strip mills consists mainly of light, flat-rolled steel, including hot-rolled sheets. However, these products can be produced by both integrated mills and minimills.

Other new technological developments permit higher yields from the slab to the finished coil as well as the ability to produce a sheet with a minimum of error, so that it has a consistent gauge from side to side. All companies operating second generation hot-strip mills are examining the possibilities of installing updated hot-strip mill technology. This newer technology includes roll bending, side shifting and hydraulic screw down, all intended to improve the quality of the sheet. Many integrated mills have undergone reorganization; during the market slowdowns in the 1970s, some plants were closed or, in some cases, mothballed. Today, earnings and profits are strong because of increased demand in the steel industry.[76]

TECHNOLOGY TRENDS

The strong demand for flat-rolled steel products has resulted in the emergence of new technologies. Mills are now juggling an alphabet soup of casting technologies: in-line strip production (ISP), compact strip production (CSP), and the Tippins/Samsung process (TSP). All three are being used in mills presently under construction as well as in integrated mills and minimills that are rebuilding or upgrading their facilities. It is expected that these technologies will offer world-class, low cost, high-quality strip production. Asjed Jalid, general manager, technical sales of Morgan Construction Co. of Worcester, Massachusetts, US, has stated "the common aim is to improve product quality in terms of tolerance and metallurgical properties". He further stated that to accomplish this "you also need a high-utilization mill with minimal downtime".

Different companies, naturally choose difference technologies to meet their differing needs. In the US, Ipsco will install ISP (in-line strip) production in the $360 million flat-rolled minimill it is building in Muscatine County, Iowa. Steel Dynamics is leaning toward CSP for its $354 million plant in Butler, Indiana. Gallatin Steel also favors CSP for its new mill near Carrollton, Kentucky. And WorldClass Steel will install TSP at the flat-rolled minimill it will build at Ambridge, Pennsylvania.

"Every plant has slightly different features," observes Shoun Kerbaugh, assistant vice president of sales at SMS Engineering in Pittsburgh. "Newer plants like Steel Dynamics, Gallatin, and Hylsa (in Monterrey, Mexico) are going after different products. They're going for thinner and thinner gauges off the hot mill."

In-Line Strip Mills

Ipsco.

Ipsco's minimill at Muscatine County, Iowa, will have an annual capacity of one million tons. It will include an electric-arc furnace, continuous slab casting, Steckel-mill rolling, and plate-finishing facilities. Ipsco will use a Mannesmann Demag Huttentechnik ISP line similar to the one that began service in 1993 at Acciaieria I.S.P. di Cremona SpA in Cremona, Italy. The caster will cast six-inch thick slabs as wide as 120 inches. Ipsco's Steckel mill will be a four-inch mill capable of producing two-inch-thick plates that is 120 inches wide, and it will be able to coil 96-inch wide material. The plate will be made in 30-to 40-ton slabs cut 250 feet long in finished thickness. The plate will pass over a cooling bed, be immediately cut to its final length, and be stacked.

"We want to make a light-gauge mill run plate at the same rate that the mill will make coil," says Roger Phillips, president and chief executive officer of Ipsco. 'This will be a very low-cost plate product with the flatness of universal-mill plate." Coil plate cools in coil form, then must be flattened, Phillips goes on to explain. Ipsco's plate will not cool except in flat condition.

Ipsco's sales will double once the mill is completed in March 1996, Phillips estimates. He expects the mill's productivity to be about 0.6 man-hours per ton, including support staff, sales people, and administration. "If we assume a static market, this mill will give us two times the market share we now have," Phillips says. The quantity of plate products from the rolling mill should increase by ten times, he says. "We've seen the electric-furnace producers go after the long-products market." Phillips says. "Nucor has made a run at hot-rolled coil with its thin-slab casting. This mill will take a third run at the integrated steelmakers; we'll be going after mass-produced plate for the first time."

Compact Strip Production (CSP) Mills

In the US, Nucor's plants at Hickman, Arkansas, and Crawfordsville, Indiana, use CSP. CSP is also the technology of choice at Steel Dynamics and Gallatin Steel, both of which are building new North American mills.

Acme Metals.
Acme Metals chose CSP for the $370 million continuous caster-hot-strip mill it recently began building at Riverdale. Acme, which produces a great deal of high-carbon steels, will be "the first mill that uses CSP and makes higher-carbon steels to feed to the caster from the BOF (basic oxygen furnace) instead of the electric-arc furnace," as Shoun Kerbaugh of SMS Engineering explains.

Steel Dynamics.
Steel Dynamics is reportedly installing a CSP line that includes minor changes from the lines in use at Nucor. The mill at Butler, Indiana, also will include a Fuchs melt shop, a twin-shell AC furnace, and two Fuchs ladle furnaces. Steel Dynamics is planning to produce between 700,000 and 2,000,000 tons of steel annually. Phase one of the project, which got under way in late Summer of 1994, is expected to be completed by January 1996. Phase two, a $160 million reversing cold mill and galvanizing line project, should begin in 1998 or 1999.

Gallatin Steel.

Gallatin Steel, a joint venture in Canada between Dofasco Inc. in Hamilton, Ontario, and Co-Steel in Toronto, has selected the CSP process. Gallatin will feature a twin-shell EAF supplied by NKK of Japan, a single-strand medium-slab caster to be supplied by SMS, a roller hearth reheat and homogenizing furnace supplied by Italimpiani of America Inc., and a five-stand high-speed hot-rolling mill supplied by SMS. Its CSP line will be similar to Nucor's though it will add several new features. (This steelmaker's building plans were delayed in late July 1994 when one of the mill's suppliers went into bankruptcy. That delay was expected to push the $350 million flat-rolled minimill project back anywhere from six weeks to eight weeks. Phase one of the project is expected to be on-line in the first quarter of 1995; annual capacity at the finished mill will be one million tons.)

"Intermediate-thickness slabs offer some short-term solutions," Gallatin president Milan Kosanovich said at the recent roundtable on improving operating efficiencies. Still, the future of thin-slab casting is bright, he says. "I believe that most of the problems we're facing [with] first-generation thin-slab casters will be worked on and that there will be a high degree of success," Kosanovich said.

Tippins/Samsung Process (TSP) Mills

The Tippins/Samsung process (TSP) offers smaller producers an economical entry into the flat-rolled market. Developed through a partnership formed in 1993, TSP combines Tippins' rolling-mill expertise with the caster technology of Samsung Heavy Industries of Korea. TSP includes steelmaking and ladle refining, continuous slab casting, slab equalizing/reheating, and hot rolling. In TSP, slabs that are 82.5 feet long are 4 inches (100 mm) thick. TSP produces a finished strip that is 0.06-1 inch thick and 35-120 inches wide. Maximum coil weight is 40 metric tons. The concept offers the economic benefits of a smaller building, leaner staff, and lower capital and operating costs than ISP or CSP, says Tippins president John Thomas.

WorldClass Steel.

WorldClass Steel will be the first to use the Tippins/Samsung process. The company will use TSP in its $340 million flat-rolled minimill, which will have an annual capacity of one million tons. Construction of the mill in Ambridge, Pennsylvania, should be completed by the end of 1996. Tippins president Thomas says another mill may be interested in announcing a TSP project soon.

"With TSP, you're looking at a price of about $200 million, which is about half the price of the other technologies," Thomas says. "The process takes advantage of the economy of thin-slab casting. But because it's an intermediate caster, there are not as many surface problems as there are with thin-slab casting." Thomas also states that "TSP can make building a one-million-ton per-year mill affordable." He points out that the trend has been to build minimills of that size. "Then people started looking at 2 million tons per year," Thomas explains. "A some point, when you increase the tonnage like that, you're no longer a market mill. You need a larger radius to get scrap, for example, and that will increase the cost of scrap."

Into the Future

As noted in this chapter, recent developments in the steel industry have begun to erode the basic distinctions between minimills and integrated mills. Minimills are beginning to gain entry in the cold-rolled products market by purchasing technology that is rapidly decreasing in price while increasing in quality. On the other hand, the integrated mills are seeking to maintain market share by reducing labor costs through good relations with labor unions. As a result, integrated mills are becoming aggressive, reliable suppliers once again.

NOTES

51   Russell, Clifford and William Vaughan, *Steel Production: Process products and Residuals*, Baltimore: The John Hopkins University Press, 1976.
      Peters, A.T., *Ferrous Production Metaliurgy*, New York: John Wiley and Sons, 1982.

52   Kredietbank "Mini Steelworks: Pygmies among Giants" *Weekly Bulletin*, March 27, 1981, pp. 1-5.

53   Kotch, J.A., "Neighborhood steelmaking: A look at the miniplants," *Iron and Steel Engineer Year Book* (1991), pp. 411-428.

54   Marcus, Peter and Karlis Kirsis, *Economics of the Minimill World Steel Dynamics Core Report*, New York: Paine Webber, June 1994.

55   Geiger, Gordon, "Minimills, technology and people", *ASM Metals Congress*, Detroit: September 19, 1984.

56   Cordero, Raymond, Serjeantson and Richard, (eds.) *Iron and Steel Works of the World*, 18th ed., London: Metal Bulletin Books Ltd., 1993.

57   Huettner, David, *Plant Size, Technological Change and Investment Requirements*, New York: Praeger Publishers, 1974.

58   *American Metal Market Co. Metal Statistics: The Purchasing Guide of the Metal Industries*, New York: AMM, various years.

59   Center for Metals production, "Electric Arc Furnace Steelmaking: The Energy Efficient Way to Melt Steel", *CMP Tech Commentary*, Vol. 1, No. 3, 1988.

60   Kotch, J.A., "Neighborhood Steelmaking: A Look at the Mini-plants", *Iron and Steel Engineer Tear Book 1971*, pp. 411-428.

61   Geiger, G.H., "Minimills, Technology and People", *ASM Metals Congress*, Detroit: September 19, 1984.

62   Huetlner, D., *Plant Size, Technological Change, and Investment Requirements*, New York: Praeger Publishers, 1974.

63   Ess, T.J., "The Hot Strip Mill Generation II", *Pittsburgh Association of Iron and Steel Engineers*, 1970.

64   ibid. *Pittsburgh Association of Iron and Steel Engineers*, 1970.

65   Barnette, H., *Address at the International Iron and Steel Institute Conference in October 1994.*

[66] Garvey, R., "Minimill round table discussion", *New Steel*, Vol. 10, No. 4, 1994, pp. 39-42.

[67] Berry, Bryan, "What is a minimill?" *New Steel*, Vol. 10, No. 11, p. 2.

[68] Graham, Tom, *Proceedings at the Annual Conference of Chief Executive Officers of the Steel Industry* held in New York by Paine Webber in June 1994.

[69] Berry, Bryan, "The Challenge of Union / Management Partnerships". *New Steel*, Vol. 10, No. 11, 1994, pp. 16-21.

[70] ibid. *New Steel*, vol. 10, No. 11, 1994, pp. 16-21.

[71] Marcus, P.F. and K.M. Kirsis, *Economics of the Minimill: World Steel Dynamics Core Report X*, New York: Paine Webber, 1984, pp. 35-67

[72] Marcus, P.F. and K.M. Kirsis, Economics of *the Minimill: World Steel Dynamics Core Report X*, New York: Paine Webber, 1984, pp. 68-97

[73] Conference held by Paine Webber in June 1994 at the Plaza Hotel, New York, U.S.A.

[74] Robertson, S., "Minimill priorities: Thin-slab steel DC furnaces, direct-reduced iron", *New Steel*, Vol. 10, No. 9, 1994, pp. 30-43.

[75] Ess, T.J., "The Hot Strip Mill Generation II", *Association of Iron and Steel Engineers*, Pittsburgh, 1970.

[76] Wriston, W.B., *The Twilight of Sovereignty*, MacMillan Publishing Company, New York, 1992, pp. 23-28.

VI

The International Transfer of Technology

A KNOWLEDGE-BASED FRAMEWORK OF TECHNOLOGY TRANSFER

The steel industry has been characterized by rapid technological developments with new processes such as strip casting, post-combustion of iron carbide, and coal-based production of liquid iron. It is this re-engineering of the steel industry which is making technology transfer possible. "What most companies are trying to do is cut the cycle time from when the customer decides he wants some steel to the time he gets it delivered,"[77] says Allan M. Rathbone, general manager of research at US Steel. He states that this goal sounds innocent enough, but it can involve drastic physical changes. In his capacity as the head of technology of the American Iron and Steel Institute (AISI), Rathbone is well positioned to spot broad trends. Rathbone points to the immediate future where "maybe what we need to do is put our computers in the customer's plant."

What should be a technology transfer framework? The fifteen questions which I posed in Chapter 2 in relation to capacity and demand can be structured in the following way.

Table 8
A knowledge asset-based view of technology transfer

Transfer Scope	Transfer Method	Knowledge Architecture	Organizational Adaptive Ability
General knowledge	Communications	Hardware	Staying flexible
Specific knowledge	Personnel transfers	Procedures	Production flexibility
Hardware	Roles	Experience base	
Behaviors	Bridges	Power structure	

Source: Robertisch, E.S. and Ferretti, M.
"A Knowledge Asset-Based View of Technology Transfer", WP No. 86-93, Massachusetts Institute of Technology, Cambridge, Massachusetts.

This framework is knowledge based. It describes the extent of the technology being transferred, the effort required for transfer, and the ability of the adopting organization to adapt to changes required by the new technology and to interact in the technology transfer process. The merit of this approach is that it provides a description of the interdependence between the categories and helps foster understanding of the technology transfer process as a whole.

Several relationships can be hypothesized using this logic. The first relationship is re-engineering of the industry in relation to the technology employed to realize the change in the industry. The expertise that is being brought together is as follows:
a) Current steel technology
b) Industrial gases technology
c) Steel equipment technology.

Transfer Scope

The above proposed framework is central to developing insight into the transfer of technology. This resource-based view of the firm holds that only assets that are not easily copied by competitors will provide long-term competitive advantage. These include so-called invisible assets such as reputation, management skill, knowledge gained through learning-by-doing, and distinctive organizational culture characteristics.[78] These assets are complex and involve large amounts of potentially tacit information. They represent a substantial transfer scope compared with technologies which embody only hardware or information. As the amount of embodied knowledge to be transferred increases, more intensive transfer methods with greater information-carrying capacity must be created.

Transfer Method

The transfer method itself has its own dynamics through the process of creative destruction. Schumpeter considered innovation both the creator and destroyer of corporations and entire industries and emphasized the role of entrepreneurs in seizing discontinuous opportunities to innovate. Innovations were taken in a broad sense of new "combinations" of producers and means of production, which include new products, new methods of production, opening up of new markets, utilization of new raw materials, or even the reorganization of a sector of the economy.[79]

KNOWLEDGE ARCHITECTURE

Three knowledge-based steel minimill technologies are capable of being transferred.

1) Placing of more scrap in the blast oxygen furnace (BOF)
2) Coal-based ironmaking
3) Post-combustion of iron carbide.

Placing More Scrap in the Blast Oxygen Furnace.
    In the oxygen steelmaking field, the techniques used in Russia for charging more scrap is being transferred through investigation by other steel companies. The Russian system permits scrap charges of 100 percent. US Steel's general manager of research, Mr. Rathbone, states "we are quite interested [in this technique]; we sent some people over to Russia to look at it. It's viable technology." Moreover, the technical director of US Steel, Michael Moore, states that such an approach is useful to determine ways to make limited increases in scrap use; "this research and subsequent transfer may allow us to melt more scrap in US Steel vessels by using some other fuel but not coal." However, Rathbone has stated that "the rising prices have cooled US Steel's interest in larger scrap charges". If oxygen steelmakers can devise a flexible system of using different scrap charges, the ratio of scrap to hot metal will be governed by economics. He says "we'd try to melt as much scrap when the price is low. We have no interest in the old open-hearth notion of using scrap as peaking capacity."[80]

Coal Based Ironmaking.
    The international technology transfer possibilities with respect to coal based ironmaking illustrate the Schumpeterian discontinuity for the development of heat-transfer technology.
    There is a joint venture between US Steel of the United States and Kobe Steel of Japan which has succeeded in employing coal instead of coke for making molten iron. The AISI is urging that a 400,000 ton demonstration plant be built. Many other steel companies are becoming interested in the process.
    Also, a process has been developed called Corex to use coal to produce molten iron. A 200,000 tons per year Corex plant is operating commercially at Iscor in South Africa. A Corex plant of 600,000 tons of steel production per year is being built at Pohang Iron and Steel Co. in South Korea. The challenge is through competition and cooperation to produce coal-based reduced iron. But different processes are converging on the coal-based technology which has given rise to the Corex process. Further developments are taking place, and already coal-based taconite pellets are being produced. US Steel is seeking strategic

partnering with companies in countries where there is demand for steel in addition to coal deposits. This would facilitate the use of coal injection into furnace.[81]

Knowledge Architecture.
Strategic partnership seem to create a large and flexible linkage between the organization, through which many types of technology can be transferred; the knowledge embodied in such a partnership is generally believed to be unique and unable to be duplicated or replicated. Common wisdom also states that the corporations engaged in these strategic partnerships have to be intensely engaged with one another. It is more likely that the intensiveness of the methods required to transfer the technology from one firm to another creates a barrier to transfer unless the participants are collaborating with one another. However, the theoretical underpinning of collaboration must be carefully examined.

Contingency theory holds that specific organizational structures are better suited than others to managing specific types of technology, and that organizations best suited to work with, for instance, incremental technological innovations, would not do well with radical innovations.[82] The use of coal based technology was based upon incremental technological innovations.

Post Combustion of Iron Carbide.
Knowledge architecture is the mechanism for the transfer of the technology of post-combustion of iron carbide. This transfer mechanism involves interdependencies among different technologies and organizational systems.

The making of iron carbide requires the use of technologies for the making of industrial gases and technologies associated with the production of steel. These technologies were effectively combined to produce iron carbide. The question is whether iron carbide will become available in commercial quantities. The first commercial carbide plant is being built at the Point Lisas Industrial Estate in Trinidad and Tobago. Iron carbide will be a substitute for scrap and can be used in combination with scrap.

Gordon Geiger, the inventor of a process specifically designed for the production of iron carbide, states that the technology ought to be used and sequenced in the following way:

1. Burning the carbon to produce carbon monoxide.
2. Converting the carbon monoxide to produce carbon dioxide.

These two processes produce considerable energy and promote secondary combustion. Rathbone of the AISI has indicated that, with a different reactor, it may be possible to produce the carbon dioxide without any additional energy.

These developments in the steel industry can be divided into four broad groups: (a) radical and major technologies, (b) incremental technological developments, (c) regulatory technology developments, (d) developments from other industries.[83] These developments can only occur when an organization has the necessary expertise as well as the ability to respond to new circumstances, beyond those the organization routinely encounters. Experts trained in multiple skills or functions are more likely to respond effectively to non-routine conditions than those with narrowly defined skills and responsibilities, and they would do this by using more intensive transfer methods. The development of new scrap treatment processes is a good example of this method of technology development.

Scrap has been found to have considerable amount of zinc. Scrap metal coated with zinc and scrap coated with tin present different problems and require different solutions. Zinc-coated (galvanized) scrap, is the more problematic today, even though its use is increasing steadily.[84] Although mills use zinc-bearing scrap in both basic oxygen furnaces (BOFs) and electric-arc furnaces (EAFs), Dr. Peter J. Koros states that "the sensitivity to zinc during steelmaking differs markedly for the two processes." BOFs generally use a much lower percentage of scrap per heat than do EAFs. This means that the knowledge architectures between BOFs and EAFs are different in hardware, procedures, and experience bases.

BOFs generally use a much lower percentage of scrap per heat than do EAFs. But heats in the BOF process are faster than in EAFs, so the zinc has considerably less time to vaporize out of the melt. Furthermore, Koros noted, because BOF vessels typically are deeper, zinc has a greater tendency to stay in the liquid steel. Zinc remains in the molten steel until and prior to casting or during ladle stirring.

Zinc poses emission problems. Zinc is removed from the steelmaking process almost totally by way of the dusts and sludges produced in the mill's environmental systems. Zinc directly impacts costs and recycling issues whenever galvanized scrap is used. In the event the BOF process is used for zinc separation, the dust cannot be recycled to a blast furnace. The iron oxide in the dust is lost; this is significant since 50-55 percent of the dust can be iron oxide. The mills also must dispose of the dust or sludge as landfill at a cost. The economic impact of this landfill-cost varies from mill to mill. For an EAF plant this cost approximates to about 50 cents per net ton of all steel produced at the plant's EAF shop. For a large, integrated mill, this cost might be more than $1 per ton of all steel produced at the BOF's plant. However, if the scrap content is more than 5 percent, the cost could be $20 per net ton.[85] And naturally, the higher the scrap's zinc content, the higher the cost of zinc removal.

Scrap Impurities.

The adaptability of a steel mill to respond to this problem creates technology transfer possibilities. In Japan, Toyota Motors and Toyokim Company are selling to companies in third-world countries a process called "thermal de-zincing". The recovered zinc offsets the cost of pretreatment. De-zincing costs about $10 per ton. Moreover, steel plants with EAFs have had less of a problem. For example, the United States' Environmental Protection Agency (EPA) has classified EAF plants' baghouse dust as hazardous waste, thus it cannot be used as landfill. Mills routinely send this dust to processors which remove the zinc and give the mill a credit for the recovered metal. The amount of zinc in the waste is the major factor in determining credit; credits as high as $30-$40 per ton have been reported.[86]

Dave Smith, melt-shop manager, Nucor Corp., Crawfordvill, Indiana, states that "the processors charge them to take the zinc away. However, the more zinc, the less are the processors' charges". A mill's use of zinc-coated scrap also depends in part on scrap-market economics. When such commodities as No. 1 bundles and No. 1 busheling climb to alpine levels, steelmakers—especially EAF mills—switch to lower-cost items and other materials, such as pig iron, direct-reduced iron (DRI), and hot-briquetted iron (HBI).

Some mills, as part of their organizational adaptive ability, are developing new technologies to offset the costs of disposing of baghouse dust. At its No. 1 electric furnace shop, Inland Steel Bar Co., part of Inland Steel, has tried a wet-briquetting extrusion process. This was development together with Laclede Steel, and Alton, Illinois, USA. The goal is to generate a greater concentration of zinc in baghouse dust so that the dust will be more valuable when sold to the processor. The system will recycle the briquettes back into the furnace as part of its charge, explains Darryl Miller, Inland Steel's director of quality and technology. Each time the briquettes are recycled the baghouse dust has a higher zinc content. Tests have shown how many times the briquettes can be used to build up zinc concentration before furnace performance is impaired. The objective is to arrive at steelmaking efficiency through minimizing energy consumption and to find out at what point the dust stabilizes.[8]

The inter-relationship in the analytical schema presented for technology transfer earlier in this chapter provides four pillars: transfer scope, transfer method, the knowledge architecture and organizational adaptability. When applied to the efficiency of the electric arc furnace (EAF), the improvement in technology substantially reduces hazardous waste. This involves the following:

1) Transfer of scrap is not possible from non-industrial sources since it is often very dirty and sometimes close to unusable.
2) The architecture of this type of scrap is its rapid contamination on the ground compared with other scrap, thus requiring quick handling.

3) Organizational adaptability by suppliers segregates clean material from dirty material as well as from other grades. Clean compressed scrap is not as dense as other scrap grades. This means that suppliers cannot load as much of it (by weight) on rail cars and trucks as they can other grades.

Even though some mills avoid using tin-coated scrap, it is becoming more popular in the scrap industry. Its usefulness is that tin-coated scrap increases the throughput of materials, enhances profit margins, and removes waste cans from the community. Burns Apfeld, ferrous marketing manager at Sadoff Iron and Metal, Fond du Lac, Wisconsin, states that tin-coated scrap is becoming an important commodity for scrap suppliers to foundries because of its low residuals. The supply of can scrap may dry up for suppliers like Sadoff if it is diverted into such high-priced grades as bundles and shredder scrap. Organizations have to keep adapting to the changing use of scrap and supply them in bundles, briquettes and shredder scrap.[88]

Adapting through Organizational Restructuring.
The transfer opportunities are created by the fight for markets and customers. Public opinion on subsidies to steel firms is at an all-time low, and the competition among steel companies for market share is fierce. The steel industry's history as a building block of economic and political growth created a sizable financial cushion that has been severely deflated during the past 15 years.

Major steel companies in the United States such as LTV Wheeling-Pittsburgh and Sharon Steel have responded to this downturn by reorganizing under Chapter 11, with varying success. Steel enterprises in Europe are slowly moving toward privatization and genuine rationalization: witness the privatized British Steel emerging as a low cost competitor. Privatized steelmaking enterprises in Latin America have increased the industry's efficiency.[89]

In the four areas of East Africa, Western Europe, the United States and Latin America, definite patterns are emerging. Steel production in China, South Korea, and other developing Asian regions such as Taiwan, is growing robustly. The Japanese steel industry, however, has peaked and is undergoing a period of rationalization. In 1992, combined steel production for China and South Korea surpassed production in Japan for the first time. Within three to four years, steel production in China alone will permanently surpass production in Japan. In fact, Japanese steel production has been supported by substantial exports to China. Recent financial results for the major Japanese steelmakers demonstrate the onset of difficult times; Japanese steel producers are now among steel companies with the highest costs in the world. Because of these high costs, Japanese steel companies are at a distinct competitive disadvantage and are likely to face financial hurdles in the ensuing years. [90]

Western Europe 's financial and competitive comfort level has deteriorated sharply. Lower government funding has reduced the financial buffer once available to many European steel companies. Privatization of steelmaking assets has been proceeding, resulting in increased pressure on steel companies to improve efficiency and profitability.

Trade barriers within Eastern Europe have eroded access to low cost steel. The combination of reduced aid, more pressure to perform and entry of low-cost competitors now burden West European steelmakers. In addition, minimill steel producers have begun to make bigger inroads into specific product markets within Europe. This places even more pressure on the traditional large integrated steel companies.

The financial results of major steel companies in Europe indicate that spot prices of steel have fallen. There is also the expectation that export prices will continue to fall. The effect of this change will increase the need for restructuring, yet such changes will be more difficult to realize. This is because there will be less consensus and motivation by management and labor to bring about these changes.

In Latin America, the steelmaking assets are out of the hands of government and in the hands of private enterprise. This shift is translating into rationalization of excess capacity, improved operating efficiency, and ultimately, better profitability. More privatization is also improving product quality, reliability, and pricing; all these encourage greater market growth. Greater steelmaking efficiency and improved overall economic prospects are fueling a resurgence in Latin America's steel industry. Combined steel production in Brazil and Mexico should increase more than 44 percent between 1990 and 2000. Finally, Latin American steel companies are now subject to the minimill philosophy of low capital costs, employee empowerment, and high productivity.[91]

In the United States, the traditional integrated steel producers are confronted with the quest of how to compete with minimill companies whose cost structures are between 25 to 50 percent lower. The biggest problem for traditional steel companies is that they have evolved into employment centers rather than project centers. A tremendous bureaucracy of vice presidents, administrators, and technical and other support staff have added a huge fixed-cost burden. In the mill, the union saw to it that as many people as possible were paid as much as possible to do as little as possible.[92]

In contrast, minimill steel producers, such as Nucor, Birmingham, and Mac Steel, have based their success on getting the most out of their people. Labor productivity at the best minimills is generally 200 to 300 percent better than at traditional integrated steel producers. This superior productivity translates into a $100 per ton cost advantage for minimills in comparison to traditional integrated steelmakers. Ten of the largest minimills have been outpacing the Big Six US Steel companies in other areas too. From 1987 to 1992:

- Sales grew 45 percent at the minimills and fell 6 percent at the Big Six, which are US Steel, Bethlehem, Inland, National, Armco, and LTV.
- Shipments increased 47 percent at the minimills and decreased 10 percent at the Big Six.
- Steelmaking capacity rose by 5.3 million tons per year (tpy) at the minimills and fell by 11.7 million tpy at the Big Six.[93]

Some companies have devised unique strategies to stave off the ups and downs of the steel cycle. Canada's three largest steel companies provide clear evidence of this trend. Dofasco has embraced some very promising market strategies, such as the continuous pickle cold mill (CPCM), and DNN galvanizing. Dofasco also has considerably improved labor productivity and customer focus. As a result, Dofasco is emerging as one of the more promising steel companies in North America. On the other hand, Stelco continues to writhe round with numerous identity problems and painful labor relations. Algoma seems to be in a very difficult situation with rather limited prospects. Canada's strong domestic economy and increased exports recently are facilitating a much improved performance of its steel industry. It is likely that this upturn will be sustained for the next few years.[94]

But the integrated steelmakers are merely responding to a current crisis. Integrated steelmakers face major decisions about technology that will shape their companies' futures. "The cokemaking, ironmaking and steelmaking facilities in many companies are approaching an age at which simple repairs and maintenance will not restore them to an efficient, competitive state," says Robert Darnall, chairman, president and CEO of Inland Steel. Steelmakers will have to undertake expensive, time-consuming refurbishing of current technologies—or use the "new technologies that can deliver significant benefits at about the same or less capital expenditure," Darnall points out.[95]

Steelmakers from France's Usinor Sacilor, Japan's Nippon Steel and NKK, and South Africa's Iscor Limited are proposing quite different responses to these issues. Like Darnall, executives of these companies discussed the future of steel at the conference of International Iron and Steel Institute (IISI). The conference, restricted to presidents and chairmen of the world's steel companies, gathered in Paris in October 1993. Mr. Shunkichi Miyoshi, president of NKK, stated that the introduction in the near future of the direct iron-ore smelting (DIOS) reduction process will provide much-needed flexibility in production and raw material selection. As part of this flexibility, the modern technologies such as pulverized coal injection (PCI) and pulverized ore injection (POI) are being used. However, the oxygen furnace, the conventional blast furnace process, will ensure the continuing role of integrated mills as a primary producer of iron.[96]

There were contrasting views at the conference. William van Wyk, CEO of Iscor Limited and Henri Faure, director of research and development at Usinor Sacilor stated they were witnessing the beginning of the end of coke ovens, blast furnaces and large integrated steelworks. Rebuilding the "obsolete equipment" of conventional steelmaking by revamping a blast furnace/basic oxygen furnace facility on an existing site requires $450 per annual metric ton of crude steel in investment; an electric furnace on a greenfield site costs $100 per annual ton. Electric steelmaking could claim up to 100 percent of the alloyed long products and 50 percent of the sheet and coil made in the European Community. An independent study conducted by IISI Committee on Statistics confirms this view.[97]

Table 9

Potential growth of electric furnaces in Europe

European Community: 1991	Production million metric tons	EAFs present share of market % million metric tons	EAFs metallurgical capacity % million metric tons
Stainless steel	3	100% = 3 MT	100% = 3 MT
Long products - alloyed	8	75% = 6 MT	100% = 8 MT
Long products - carbon	48	64% = 31 MT	80% = 39 MT
Plates	9	33% = 3 MT	80% = 7 MT
Sheets and coil	69	0% = 0 MT	50% = 35 MT
TOTAL	137	31% = 43 MT	67% = 92 MT

It is to be noted that the metallurgical capacity is increasing among European producers. Usinor Sacilor, the French steelmaker, produced 21.1 million metric tons of crude steel in 1992, making it number 2 in the world in production. Usinor Sacilor is now replacing some of its blast furnaces with electric arc furnaces.[98] Number 1 was Nippon Steel, with 25.4 million metric tons.

Scrap and Electric Furnaces.

Opinions differ widely about the future of scrap, its price, its supply, and the possibility of using lower quality scrap grades. Scrap supply and price will limit the growth and profitability of scrap-based minimills. On the other hand, minimill executives have disagreed with the argument. Their response is divided into the short-term and the long-term. In the short-term, the 9-10 million tons of scrap now exported from the US will feed the increasing number of electric furnaces. Over the long-term, the growing number of alternative ironmaking facilities—Mildrex, Corex, Fastmet, and iron carbide—will compete with scrap and put a cap on scrap prices.[99]

North Star's chief executive officer, Mr. Robert Garvey, states that iron made by alternative processes presently is less expensive than such premium scrap grades as No. 1 factory and dealer bundles. Moreover, scrap prices have dropped in real terms. There is no expectations of a shortage of scrap but some dislocations in scrap. Since steel is made and used it eventually is added to the supply of scrap. Government and industry on a world wide scale are getting serious about reclaiming metals that used to be put in landfills. Seventy percent of steel now produced is recycled instead of fifty percent earlier. For example, at the North Star mills scrap accounts for 90 percent of the charge. Direct reduced iron, hot briquetted iron, and iron made by the Midrex process account for the other 10 percent.[100] Kobe Steel of Japan produces 800,000 tons of iron by the Midrex process in Venezuela now and should add another million-ton plant there. Posco of Korea is constructing a Corex plant that will start shipping later this year from Venezuela. North Star itself has "a very active project" to make iron carbide by the same process Nucor is using in its plant at Point Lisas in Trinidad and Tobago.[101]

Scrap prices are stabilized by companies such as Co-Steel which help to control the flow of scrap by owning scrap yards. Co-Steel has a captive scrap yard in Toronto, it also is the part owner of Major Parry, a major scrap processor in Britain.

Scrap prices are high now partly because the integrated mills are using about 90 percent of their capacity and buying more scrap for their metallic charge to jack up scrap prices. High scrap prices, after all, hurt an electric furnace using a 90 percent scrap charge more than an oxygen furnace using a 10-20 percent scrap charge. Thomas Graham, president and CEO of Armco Steel, Inc., stated that economies of minimills are heavily dependent on low-cost scrap. Moreover, the minimills are investing more in substitute sources and the industry expects that this will stabilize or lower scrap prices. For example, Nucor plans to put iron carbide from its Trinidad plant onto a barge and send it to New Orleans at $100 per ton.[102]

Electric arc furnace (EAF) steelmaking offers lower capital costs, a smaller unit size, more flexibility, and fewer emissions than the coke oven/blast furnace route. An electric furnace can profitably produce 0.5 to 1 million tons per year; an integrated steelworks typically produces up to 4 million annual tons. The smaller scale of the EAFs gives minimills greater flexibility to economically target smaller market niches than is possible for the blast furnace/oxygen furnace configuration.[103]

Usinor Sacilor's director of research and development, Henri Faure, has declared that instead of complaining about newcomers, the industry itself should look at one of the newcomers. The integrated steelmakers should think about the electric arc furnace as a tool, which through progressive technological improvements, is becoming a process unit comparable in performance to the BOF. Brian S. Moffat, chairman and chief executive of British Steel, has emphasized that the common factor linking Corex, direct reduced iron, iron carbide, thin-slab casting, bean-blank casting, and compact strip production is the reduction of the optimum scale of production and capital intensity.[104]

MARKET DIRECTION

Lower Cost vs. Economies of Scale

Robert J. Darnall, chairman, president and CEO of Inland Steel Industries, has stated that the current steel market favors low-capital intensity technologies that offer significant operating cost advantages because of the over-capacity of steel production worldwide which is not expected to grow significantly in the next decade. The potential for recovery of capital expenditures for refurbishing and modernizing existing facilities through price increases seems unlikely. Smaller investments and smaller returns can look much better than huge investments and huge losses.[105]

NKK's president, Shunkichi Miyoshi, explained that integrated steelmaking is fundamentally a mass-production method that has significant benefits when steel demand is growing. But the maturing of demand has exposed the weaknesses of integrated steelmaking. The blast furnaces lack production flexibility; when demand for steel drops, the huge complexes of blast furnace/basic oxygen furnaces can be under-used and unprofitable.[106] However, Mr. Moffat of British Steel, speaking on the strategic views of world market on the growing internationalisation of steel, has stated that there is still a lot of life left in integrated steelmaking from a technical and economic point of view. Further, he opined a good blast furnace based operation can match a top-class minimill on cost and produce a wider range of products. There is the need for the organization to become smaller, reduce the administrative layers and become as streamlined as the minimill. On the other hand, the larger support staffs of the integrated steelmakers have enabled integrated mills to develop new steel products. These include improved coated sheets for autobodies, improved fire protection for structural steels, and improved tin plate for cans.[107]

NKK's president, Mr. Shunkichi Miyoshi stated that these new products, allied with improvements in blast furnace/basic oxygen steelmaking, are the hope for the future of the integrated steelmakers. Rather than abandoning their present facilities, integrated steelmakers must improve operating efficiencies by adopting new management techniques and new technologies. This is because the steel plant of the future would be a combination of the blast furnace/converter process, the direct iron ore smelting (DIOS) reduction process, and the cold-iron-source melting process.[108]

In Japan, the integrated steel works combine the benefits of production flexibility with those of economies of scale. The large converters, with a furnace capacity of more than 200 tons per heat, are able to handle smaller volume orders and make a greater variety of products. This is accompanied by Japanese steelmakers having developed such new technologies as divided tapping. In particular, NKK has simplified the processes of hot-metal preliminary treatment, blowing, and secondary refining, all of which are done separately. With respect to lade-refining technology, it operates separately by having tundish refining and electro-magnetic control that enable high speed casting of high quality steel.[109]

Through the development of new technologies the integrated steel mills are connecting multiple processes and developing an in-process material-handling system to better handle smaller lot orders of a greater variety of products. The entire process is now continuous, the effect of which is an increase in labor productivity per ton of steel produced. Many integrated mills have adopted this technology and have therefore moved from batch-type to continuous annealing.[110]

In Japan, most of the steel mills have adopted the continuous annealing process. In their mills 97 percent is continuously cast and the remaining 3 percent is for the customers who prefer ingots. In particular, NKK has introduced artificial intelligence for blast furnace and is using sensor technologies for inspection. In maintenance, NKK and many other steelmakers are now using devices that measure the vibrations of the equipment to forecast when maintenance will be needed. This enables steelmakers to know more accurately when parts need to be changed; it also reduces the number of spare parts that must be stockpiled.[111]

Mr. Leonard Halschuk, secretary general of the IISI, has stated that the steel industry has moved in the direction of preventative, time-based maintenance to conditional maintenance. Conditional maintenance involves consistent monitoring of each piece of equipment and only undertakes maintenance when indicated by its condition. This form of maintenance requires such sophisticated diagnostics as the vibration sensing equipment. The point of this adaptation of technology is that it originates from that which has been developed by minimills.[112] Through this process advantages also accrue to the minimills; for example, at Nucor, thin-slab casting had experienced surface-quality problems. However, by the further development of the vibration-sensing equipment, Nucor adapted this technology which led to be a defect-free surface. The integrated steel mills worldwide are now following the same Japanese philosophy and technologies that are used in Japan. Fox example, nearly all the major US Big Steel companies are refurbishing or rebuilding coke ovens, blast furnaces, and/or basic oxygen furnaces.[113]

The challenges facing the Big Steelmakers focus on improving their present facilities. In Japan, NKK's Fukuyama works produces hot-coiled and hot-band steel at 1.61 man-hours per short ton (industry average is about 4.50 man-hours). This is the direction in which the remaining integrated steelworks in Japan are moving. Nearly all these steel companies are refurbishing or rebuilding their coke ovens, blast furnaces and/or basic oxygen furnaces.

Likewise, US steelmakers are engaged in the same rebuilding; for example, US Steel made the decision to improve the drawing and surface quality of their thin-slab cast steel. This was achieved by using continuous casting technology adapted from the minimills. The president and chief executive officer of Inland Steel has stated that the integrated steel industry in the United States will have to modernize their plants since the upgrades and repairs of the coke ovens and blast furnaces would not be sufficient. Indeed, as a group, US steelmakers are faced with the following challenges:

1. Will US steelmakers build new plants with basically the same iron and steel making technologies?
2. Will they decide sooner than their counterparts in Asia and Europe?
3. Will the technology chosen be different?

The technologies affecting steel mills are still undergoing extensive changes; take for example, the Corex direct smelting process. This process entails replacement of coke ovens and smelting reduction which takes place in smaller-scale production units. By using coal rather than coke and fine ore rather than sinter or pellets, cost-intensive pretreatments are eliminated. Although the industry remains excited by the possibilities of these advanced smelting processes, a number of questions remain unanswered:

1. Will steelmakers decide the future of steel in response to their local conditions and particular customers?
2. How much scrap is available, and at what price?
3. How much does electricity cost? For example, in Japan, electricity is at a higher cost and as such electric steelmaking may be less economically attractive to the Japanese.
4. Is the work force skilled and flexible enough to handle new technologies?
5. How good can the drawing and surface quality of thin-slab-cast steel become?
6. How fragmented is the steelmakers' market?
7. What benefits are to be derived from economies of scale by adopting flexible production processes developed as part of other technologies?

These are questions which will be focused on the steel minimill industry.

The new steel paradigm of decentralized decision-making, problem solving, lavish communication, and investing in people and customers first[114] attitude demonstrates that there is more than a casual relationship between demand and quality.

Whenever demand for steel increases, assuring the quality of individual shipments of scrap becomes more difficult.

Good quality scrap, low in tramp elements, is becoming increasingly important in the steelmaking process. At the same time, good quality scrap is becoming harder to come by. Steel users are demanding higher quality steel from mills. Steelmakers are realizing that what used to be choices in the quality of production are now requirements.

Mr. Richard Issac, vice president of Issac Corporation from Ohio, USA, a scrap supplier, has stated that the demand for low-residual steel seems to be increasing significantly. Indeed, he says that part of the change corresponds to a natural maturing trend in the scrap-using industry, in that scrap gets recycled, more and more the residuals show up.[115]

The preoccupation with the increased prices of scrap prompted executives from some of the leading minimill companies to gather in Nappa, California, USA, for a round table discussion. It was a frank, free flowing discussion which focused on the supply of scrap metal and alternative sources of iron for the electric furnaces; issues in trade; the new technologies by which minimills are cutting costs; the relationship between steelmakers and equipment suppliers; and the differences between integrated and minimills. Mr. John Correnti, president of Nucor Corporation stated that despite the scrap price increase by about \$50 per ton for premium grades, his company was able to stay even in the long-products area: rebar, angle, channel and wide-flange beans. Moreover, in the flat rolled area, their sales price has more than exceeded the rise in the price of scrap. Mr. Correnti proceeded to make an incisive distinction by stating there are really two scrap markets. There are the dealer grades and secondly, there are the low residual No. 1 dealer bundles. The integrated competitors have bid up these dealer bundles to a point where many minimills no longer use No. 1 dealer bundles. Instead, use is made of pig iron and direct reduced iron.[116]

The ongoing discussions of minimills becoming more like integrated mills was met by disagreement. Mr. Correnti emphatically pointed out that iron carbide was not developed by an integrated steel company. Thin-slab casting was not developed by an integrated mill. The new direct current (DC) furnace was not developed by an integrated mill. They were developed by equipment manufacturers and suppliers. Manufacturers build and sell their equipment. However, minimills are in the business to make steel and sell it at a profit. There was general agreement by all the participants on making quality steel and selling it at a profit.

An off-shoot of Nucor, Steel Dynamics, as well as Nucor itself, Gallatin, Chaparal and Georgetown are among the minimills responding quickly to high steel demand. For example, Steel Dynamics Inc. raised the $370 million needed to build a new sheet plant in Butler, Indiana in about 10 months. Financial managers in the steel industry considered this speed of financing a minor miracle. This fast tempo is typical of current minimill activity. Technology is advancing greatly. Markets are changing abruptly. Steelmakers are starting up new mills in a little over one year after groundbreaking.[117]

Steel Dynamics and Gallatin are participating in an 8 million ton expansion of minimill steel capacity. Increases are expected if US Steel goes ahead with a minimill it is considering. Further, the effects of technology thrust now on the way at minimills are comparable in magnitude to the early application of electric furnaces and continuous casting, particularly if there is rapid development of small electrodes for DC furnaces. Voest-Alpine, an Austrian steel manufacturer, has developed a new DC furnace which employs four side-mounted electrodes. The electrodes are relatively small, reportedly about 10 inches in diameter and pointdown at a 45 degree angle. The new system allows mills to precharge and preheat scrap as gases go up a central shaft. It provides for symmetrical melting; with the four electrodes there are five melting pockets because all the gases are driven to one central point: one for each electrode and one in the center. Voest-Alpine is testing these features in a prototype furnace in Austria.[118]

INTER INDUSTRY TECHNOLOGY TRANSFER

The minimill industry has in some instances moved forward by linking the blast furnace to the electric arc furnace.[119]

Kawasaki's managing director in charge of steel sales, Mr. Reiji Nakatoh, has stated that mini and integrated mills can share their resources: electric power, water, land, security, and after-sale service networks. Kawasaki's blast furnaces feed molten iron to Daiwa's electric furnaces; the iron travels in torpedo cars. Kawasaki's blast-furnace mill operates side by side Daiwa's electric furnaces. Daiwa is a subsidiary of Kawasaki.

The combined operation has many advantages. Daiwa's electric arc furnaces use large amounts of mill scrap that Kawasaki Steel generates. This system is economical and improves steel quality at Daiwa. Feeding Daiwa's furnaces with hot metal from Kawasaki's blast furnaces saves energy. Kawasaki also supplies iron to Daiwa's EAFs for mixing with scrap iron; this ensures high uniform quality of production at Daiwa.

Kawasaki determines the mixture for the metallic charge according to the price of scrap and of pig iron and the quality requirements of the steel product. Scrap could be 50 percent—60 percent of the mix. The minimill can use Kawasaki's casting, rolling, finishing, shipping, distribution, marketing, and service facilities. Daiwa also has access to Kawasaki's steelmaking technology and expertise.

The trend of combining integrated and minimill operation initiated in Japan has spread to South Korea and China. Some European mills which earlier had planned to scrap blast furnaces in favour of EAFs are now rethinking their approach.[120]

The Kawasaki-Daiwa link was patterned after Tokyo Steel's manufacturing company, Japan's largest independent minimill which had gained a competitive edge through a link with Nippon Steel. Nippon Steel is the largest producer of steel in the world and has 8 ironmaking and steelmaking plants.

Nippon Steel has been able to maintain its position in the world because of its corporate strategy premised on multi-business management. It has streamlined its operations and emphasized its R&D capabilities. Steelmaking using cutting edge technologies is at the center of its operations. As part of the management strategy, Nippon emphasizes a linkage with engineering. To maintain its cutting edge status, Nippon Steel has entered into the dynamic field of electronic equipment, information and communication systems, and telecommunications, using computer applications and software development to meet the company's own needs.[121]

Equally, the Kawasaki-Daiwa link has combined its research capability to increase the thermal efficiency of the electric arc furnace. Daiwa's mill has only one operator in the central control room; he runs the mill by computers and industrial television. Automatic devices analyse chemicals in the hot metal. Radio controls automatically lift ladles containing scrap. Kawasaki engineers provided Daiwa with expertise on blast-furnace techniques, such as slopping, slag foaming, and handling hot metal.[122]

The American minimill market has gained great strides since the first big wave of minimill construction about 30 years ago. In September 1994 New Steel conducted a capital spending survey and found that all the minimills are engaged in improving their product and extending their product line.[123]

Electric furnace steelmakers hope that technical gains would make spending for replacement more rewarding. Continuing technical advances have been made in melting and casting, but there has been progress elsewhere, for example, minimills have invaded the high-quality bar market. This market was traditionally dominated by integrated mills. Minimills such as Birmingham Steel, which owns American Steel and Wire Corp. (AS&W) have captured much of the merchant bar and rebar sections. Further, minimills such as North-Stars at Monroe, Michigan, USA, are supplying 455,000 tons per year of special bar-quality (SBQ) for automakers. Other minimills are beginning to enter the North America market for value added rods and bars. AS&W will spend up to $85 million to build a new bar mill.[124] Mr. Walter Robertson, executive vice president of AS&W, states that they now produce 500,000-600,000 tons of bar per year.[125]

Minimills have improved quality, but they face barriers to making top quality, low cost products. Minimills would have to invest large sums of money to enter the SBQ market with force. This spending would lead minimills away from their mission to be high quality, low cost producers. Mr. M.O. Kessler of

Republic Engineered Steel, whose company currently supplies 30 percent of the SBQ products in the US, states that the competition in this market is very keen. For example, AS&W is currently expanding its plant for the SBQ market and its shipment would increase 100 percent after completion of the expansion by no later than January 1996. This is another aspect of technology transfer, in which the minimill has adapted its organization to compete directly with the integrated mill products. It is known by both integrated and minimills what new ironmaking processes are in commercial production and what new ironmaking processes are under development. Tables 10 and 11 are diagrammatic representations of both.

Table 10
New ironmaking processes in commercial production

Process	Direct Reduction (Shaft type)	Direct Reduction (Retort type)	Direct Reduction (Kiln type)	Direct Reduction (Fluidized type)	Corex
Raw material ore	Ore pellet Coarse ore	Ore pellet Coarse ore	Coarse ore	Fine ore	Ore pellet Coarse ore
Fuel	Natural gas	Natural gas	Non-coking coal	Natural gas	Non-coking coal
Product	Sponge iron (92-96% metal)	Sponge iron (85-92% metal)	Sponge iron (90-93% metal)	Iron briquette	Molten iron (Carbon = 4%)
Production (1992) (Million metric tons per year)	13.3	5.3			0.3

Source: International Iron and Steel Institute (IISI)

Table 11
New ironmaking processes under development

Process	Hismelt	American Iron & Steel Institute	Direct Iron Ore Smelting (DIOS)	Iron carbide
Raw material ore	Fine ore	Ore pellet	Fine ore	Fine ore
Fuel	Non-coking coal	Non-coking coal	Non-coking coal	Natural gas
Product	Molten iron (Carbon = 4%)	Molten steel (Carbon = 0.1%)	Molten iron (Carbon = 4%)	Iron carbide (Carbon = 6-7%)
Present status	Demonstration plant being erected: 0.1 million metric tons per year	Pilot plant: 5 tons/hour	Pilot plant: 500 tons/day	Plant design

Source: International Iron and Steel Institute (IISI)

THE TECHNOLOGY TRANSFER CHALLENGES

The minimills' need to expand was caused by the structural changes in the demand for steel in China, Europe, and Latin America. This topic was covered under management strategies in a Paine Webber conference cosponsored by the American metal market.[126] There was also a revolution with respect to the float rolled instrip production process (ISP), the integrated compact mill (ICM), and the Tippins/Samsung process (TSP).

The ISP process is a "wholly new process, starting from the submerged nozzle and mold system integrated with the cast-rolling right up to the downcoiler," said Giovanni Gosio, managing director of Italian steelmaker Finarvedi's ISP plant in Cremona, Italy. Finarvedi and Mannesmann Demag, in Germany, patented ISP. The goal of ISP is to make thin-gauge, high-quality steel at low cost.[127]

The plant produces steel 0.048-0.06 inch thick; 0.04 is a goal. "At the Cremona Works, we are producing hot-rolled coils with dimensional tolerances similar to those of cold-rolled products and with extraordinary internal properties," said Gosio. "We believe with the ISP, it is possible to produce a million tons per caster strand of almost all grades," said Gerd Moellers, board member and executive vice president of Mannesmann Demag. Automotive and stainless steel are among possible grades. "For normal applications, plate can be sold off the caster."

The developers are trying to improve the mold, the nozzle, mold powders, induction furnace, and descaler. A thicker slab in the mold improves surface appearance, Moellers said. Korea's Posco purchased an ISP mill on June 21, 1994.

The integrated compact mill (ICM) combines the best aspect of ore-based integrated mills and scrap-based minimills, said Dr. Karl Schwaha, senior vice president, steelmaking division at Voest-Alpine. An ICM will use hot metal from a direct-smelting process like Corex, scrap, and scrap substitutes. The ICM process directly links casting and rolling. Casting will be near to net shape. Benefits of the ICM include shorter production times and more flexibility in productivity, raw materials, and product mix Schwaha said.

The Tippins/Samsung process (TSP) "combines the efficiency of a medium-thickness slab caster of approximately 120-125mm with the economy of a reversing hot-rolling mill," said John Thomas, president and CEO of Tippins. Minimills with the TSP will be able to produce a wide range of products. The TSP will be able to use either a basic oxygen or an electric-arc furnace. The capital cost for the TSP is nearly $200 million.[128]

TECHNOLOGY TRANSFER OPPORTUNITIES TO CHINA

The Chinese steel industry will produce 100-120 million metric tons by the year 2000 as it modernizes facilities to reach world standards, says Wang Zhen Wu, president and senior research fellow of the China Metallurgical Information & Standardization Institute. China produced about 93 million metric tons in 1994, an increase of 5 percent over the total in 1993, he said. Imports totalled around 10 million metric tons in 1994.

The industry will focus on modernizing and expanding capacity at existing plants. By the end of the century, the Baoshan Iron and Steel Complex, Anshan Iron and Steel Co., Wuhan Iron and Steel Co., and Shougang Corp. each will have an annual capacity of more than 10 million tons.

Chinese steelmakers are phasing out open-hearth steelmaking. In 1980, the open-hearth method accounted for 32 percent of production; basic oxygen furnace, 41 percent, and electric-arc furnace, 19 percent. In 1993, open-hearth steelmaking dropped to 16 percent of production, basic oxygen furnaces produced 62 percent of total output and EAFs, 22 percent. "Continuous-casting technology is regarded as a key link to modernize the industry," Wang said. The ratio of continuously cast steel to raw steel increased from 6 percent in 1980 to 35 percent in 1993.

The industry will also use more pulverized coal injection. Chinese steel mills will inject nearly 3.7 million metric tons of coal into blast furnaces this year. "Obsolete technology and equipment are still used in may Chinese steel plants," Wang said. About 25 percent of the equipment in Chinese mills meets advanced world standards. The industry is trying to implement newer technologies. The Guangzhou Zhujiang Steel Plant will use thin-slab casting, Wang said. The Chinese government has lifted price controls on almost all steel products, but price reforms have a long way to go, he said.[129]

THE TECHNOLOGY OPPORTUNITIES GENERATED IN EUROPE AND LATIN AMERICA OUGHT TO BE FOCUSED ON INDUSTRY EFFICIENCY

The European Steel industry is somewhat healthier today, but capacity cuts are still needed, said Lenhard Holschuh, secretary general of the International Iron and Steel Institute. Steel consumption in Poland grew 4 percent and 1 percent in Romania in 1993. Hungary, the Czech Republic, and Eastern Germany also had higher steel consumption numbers.

Steel consumption in eastern and central Europe will grow through the end of the century, Holschuh predicted; annual growth rates for this region will be about 4 percent. The level of consumption, however, will be only half of what it was when these countries were centrally planned. Foreign consultants are helping central European steelmakers reduce capacity and modernize facilities. Western European companies generally are not forming joint ventures with Eastern European mills. "Most of the plants coming into consideration are of a size that frightens individual western companies," Holschuh said.

Europe still has overcapacity, and "state-owned companies are still being propped up by their governments," Holschuh said. But Western European mills and their governments are moving towards a free steel market. The European Union (EU) aimed to close about 20 million tons of capacity by September 1994.

Japan, the EU, Eastern Europe, Russia, and the Ukraine will look to export to China and Southeast Asia to pick up some slack in their surplus capacities. "But large-scale cuts in steelmaking capacity must continue" in these areas, Holschuh said. [130]

Elsewhere, steel demand in Mexico will grow, said Felipe Cortes, president of Mexican steelmaker Hylsa. Although demand dropped 5 percent in 1993, average growth before then had been about 8 percent a year. The country consumed about 7.2 million metric tons of steel last year. Hylsa will need to improve performance to compete with foreign mills for this growing market, Cortes said. Its productivity last year was 4.5 man-hours per ton; the average employee cost was $12 an hour. Fifty-three percent of Hylsa's metallics come from its three DRI plants at a cost of $106 per metric ton. The DRI allows the company to use lower-quality scrap and save money. The company is building a thin-slab caster. The DC furnace will melt hot scrap and hot DRI to save 15 percent in electricity consumption.

Two South American steelmakers report that their companies became more efficient after privatization. Acesita of Brazil, which went private in October 1992, has reduced its staff by 25 percent, said Wilson Nelio Brumer, CEO of Acesita. Levels of management decreased from 6 to 4. Production at Acesita rose 15 percent. This led to a rise in productivity of 50 percent. [131]

Siderar, an Argentinean producer, was privatized in 1992. Since then it has decreased man-hours per ton from more than 14 to 8, said Javier Tizado, Siderar CEO. During this time production at the hot-strip mill increased from 95,000 tons to 127,000 tons per month. Variable production costs, however, have dropped 35 per cent. [132]

International technology transfer is based on a system of close collaboration among equipment manufacturers, their suppliers, and mill operators. The entire industry recognizes that for products of the minimills to remain competitive, there must be close collaboration among the different organizations which comprise the industry. This is because the improvement in the products of the industry lies with proprietary technology. Hence the modality of transfer is based on neutral protection of proprietary technology.

CONCLUSION

This chapter has demonstrated that the technology transfer drive is to ensure that the minimill remains competitive. The central technology for the minimill, that is, the electric arc furnace, the ladle furnace and the continuous casters, is being constantly improved by equipment manufacturers. The manufacturers obtained their information from the minimill operators. This process of diffusion of information allows the minimills to have an adaptive organization ready to incorporate and use new technologies. For example, we have seen earlier in this chapter how, through the flowering of new technologies such as instrip production, the integrated compact mill and the Tippins/Samsung process, these processes have combined to revolutionize the making of thin-slab steel.

International technology transfer is also focused on finding substitutes for scrap. The mixture of direct reduced iron, hot briquette, as well as the very recent use of iron carbide, all to be mixed with scrap, is used to stabilize the price of the products from the minimill. Products such as thin-slab and rebars are produced by integrated mills. however, we have seen that prices of products from integrated mills have become extremely competitive and the minimills, in order to increase market share, have to continue to have competitive pricing.

An in-depth look at the structure of the steel industry in Japan as well as Latin America would contrast the way in which the industry has been organized in these different parts of the world. Notwithstanding the large geographic distances between these two areas of the world, it would be seen that the challenge to the industry is to ensure that it remains competitive. This implies the use of the best available technology and corporate strategies which focus on efficiency and product quality.

NOTES

[77] McManus, G.J., "Re-engineering the steel industry," *New Steel*, Vol. 10, No. 1, January 1994, p.17. The point of this article is that re-engineering is taking place through new product and process technologies, such as strip casting, post-combustion of iron carbide, and coal-based production of liquid iron.

[78] Itami, H., *Mobilizing Invisible Assets*, Cambridge, MA: Harvard University Press (1987). Itami maintains that changes to existing organizational architectures will probably still require transfer of additional information from the donor organization.

[79] Tyre, M.J., "Managing the introduction of new process technology: international differences in a multi-plant network," *Research Policy* 22, 1991, pp. 57-76

[80] McManus, G.J., "Re-engineering the steel industry," *New Steel*, Vol. 10, No. 1, January 1994, p. 18.

[81] ibid. *New Steel*.

[82] Burns, T. and G. Stalken, *The Management of Innovation*, London: Tavistock Publications (1966).
      Ettlie, J., W. Bridges and R. O'Keefe, "Organizational Strategy and Structural Differences for Radical versus Incremental Innovation," *Management Science*, Vol. 30, No. 6 (June 1984), pp. 682-695.
      Dewar, R and J. Dutton, "The Adoption of Radical and Incremental Innovations: An Empirical Analysis," *Management Science*, vol. 32, 1986, pp. 1422-1433.

[83] Utterback, J.M., "The Process of Innovation: A Study of the Organization and Development of Ideas for New Scientific Instruments," *IEEE Transactions on Engineering Management*, Vol. EM-18, No. 4, November 1971, pp. 124-131.

[84] Berry, B., "Scrap Magnet," *New Steel*, Vol. 10, No. 6 June 1994. p. 31.

[85] Hoeffer, E., "The ups and downs of recycling coated scrap," *New Steel*, Vol. 10. No. 9, September 1994, p. 53.

[86] Kuster, T., "Wanted: raw residual scrap." *New Steel*, Vol. 10, No. 4, April 1994, pp. 48-51.

[87] Hess, G.W., "Reclaiming zinc from electric-furnace dust," *New Steel*, Vol. 9, No. 12, December 1993, pp. 34-39.

88 Hoeffer, E., "The ups and downs of recycling coated scrap," *New Steel*, Vol. 10. No. 9, September 1994, p. 56.

89 Berry, B., "Future of Steel: Big Steel vs. Mini Steel," *New Steel*, Vol. 9, No. 12, December 1993, pp. 18-24.

90 Keeling, B., "The World Steel Industry," *The Economist Intelligence Unit (EIU): Structure and Prospects in the 1990s*, July 1992, p. 30

91 Jacobson, John E., "Future winners in world steel: minimills, Dofasco, China," *New Steel*, Vol. 10, No. 1, January 1994, p. 30.

92 Wriston, W.B., *The Twilight of Sovereignty*, Chapter 2 New York: Charles Scribner's Sons, 1992, pp. 18-39

93 Berry, B., "Future of Steel: Big Steel vs Mini Steel," *New Steel*, Vol. 9, No. 12, December 1993, pp. 18-29.

94 Jacobson, John E., "Future winners in world steel: minimills, Dofasco, China," *New Steel*, Vol. 10, No. 1, January 1994, p. 29.

95 Berry, B., "Future of Steel: Big Steel vs Mini Steel," *New Steel*, Vol. 9, No. 12, December 1993, p. 12.

96 *Proceedings of the European World Steel Conference of the International Iron and Steel Institute*, Paris, France, October 1993.

97 The limitation of these figures is the reference to the European Community in 1991.

98 *Annual Report of Usinor Sacilor*, 1994, Paris France, p. 17.

99 McKenna, M., "Steelmakers' focus on survival strategies," *Iron Age*, Vol. 9, No. 8, August 1993, pp. 29-30.

100 Garvey, R., "The 1993 Steel Survival Strategies (SSS) Forum" sponsored by *American Metal Market and Paine Webber's World Steel Dynamics*, June 1993.

101 Hess, G.W., "A new steelmaker built in the image of Nucor," *New Steel*, Vol. 9, No. 11, November 1992, pp. 38-40.

102 Berry, B., "Future of Steel: Big Steel vs Mini Steel," *New Steel*, Vol. 9, No. 12, December 1993, p. 23.

103 ibid. *New Steel*, p. 24.

104 Moffat, B.S., "The growing internationalization of Steel," *Financial Times Conference on the World Steel Industry*, London, England, March 6-7, 1995.

105 Darnall, R.J., "Prospects for the US Steel Industry," *Financial Times Conference on the World Steel Industry*, London, England, March 6-7, 1995.

106 Berry, B., "Future of Steel: Big Steel vs Mini Steel," *New Steel*, Vol. 9, No. 12, December 1993, p. 14.

[107]   Miyoshi, S., Address on the Japanese steel industry at the conference organized by the International Iron and Steel Institute held in Paris, France in October 1993.

[108]   Miyoshi, S., Address on the Japanese steel industry at the conference organized by the International Iron and Steel Institute held in Paris, France in October 1993.

[109]   ibid, Miyoshi.

[110]   Berry, B., "Future of Steel: Big Steel vs Mini Steel," *New Steel*, Vol. 9, No. 12, December 1993, p. 18-22.

[111]   *Annual Reports of NKK*, 1987-1993, Tokyo, Japan.

[112]   *International Iron and Steel Bulletin (IISI)*, 1993, pp. 9-18.

[113]   Hess, G.W., "Big Steel is still spending more than $1 billion a year," *Iron Age*, vol. 9, no. 9, September 1993, p. 39.

[114]   Jacobson, J., "Old Steel and New Steel," *Iron Age*, Vol. 9, No. 9 September 1993, p. 25.

[115]   Kuster, T., "Wanted: Low residual scrap," *New Steel*, Vol. 10, No. 4, April 1994.

[116]   Minimill Round Table Discussion held on February 16, 1994 in Nappa, California, attended by John Correnti, president of Nucor Corp., Thomas Boklund, president and CEO of Oregon Steel SMA, Bob Higgins, publisher of New Steel, and Bryan Berry, editor of New Steel, as the moderator.

[117]   McManus, G.J., "Thin slab steel, DC furnaces, direct-reduced iron," *New Steel*, Vol. 10, No. 9, September 1994, p. 30.

[118]   McManus, G.J., "A DC furnace with four electrodes," *New Steel*, Vol. 10, No. 9, September 1994, p. 31.

[119]   Furikawa, T., "Linking the blast furnace to the electric arc furnace," *New Steel*, Vol. 10, No. 7, p. 24.

[120]   Hogan, W.T., *Steel Capacities in Industrialized Countries*, Lexington, MA: Lexington Books, 1991, p. 57.

[121]   *Nippon Steel Annual Report 1993*.

[122]   Furikawa, T., "Linking the blast furnace to the electric-arc furnace," *New Steel*, Vol. 10, No. 7, July 1994, p. 26.

[123]   McManus, G. J., "Capital Spending Survey." *New Steel*, Vol. 10, No. 9, September 1994, pp. 33-36.

[124]   Robertson, S., "New minimills invade the high quality bar market," *New Steel*, Vol. 10, No. 7, p. 34.

[125]   ibid Robertson, S.

[126]   Paine Webber conference cosponsored by the American Metal market held on June 21-22, 1994 at Plaza Hotel, New York.

[127] Ritt, A., "Managing change in the world steel market," *New Steel*, Vol. 10, No. 8, August 1994, pp. 35-38.

[128] Ritt, A., "Managing change in the world steel market," *New Steel*, Vol. 10, No. 8, August 1994, pp. 35-38.

[129] Wang, Zhen Wu, paper presented at Steel Survival Strategies (SSS), organized by the American Metal Market and Paine Webber on June 21-22, 1994 at Plaza Hotel, New York.

[130] Ritt, A., "Managing change in the world steel market," *New Steel*. Vol. 10, No. 8, August 1994, p. 38.

[131] Brumer, W.L., "Improving efficiencies in Europe and Latin America," comments made at Steel Survival Strategies conference organized by the American Metal Market and Paine Webber, New York on June 21-22, 1994.

[132] Ritt, A., "Managing change in the world steel market," *New Steel*, Vol. 10, No. 8, August 1994, p. 38.

VII

Japanese Case Study

THE EVOLUTION AND UNIQUE CONTRIBUTION
OF THE MODERN JAPANESE STEEL INDUSTRY

The Japanese steel industry does not make the distinction between an integrated mill and a minimill; but it has adopted and utilizes the technologies of both the integrated mill and the minimill. As discussed in previous chapters, these technologies are:

a) the basic oxygen furnace (BOF),
b) the electric arc furnace (EAF) and
c) continuous casting, a procedure common to both technologies.

The importance of a case study of the Japanese steel industry is that the industry developed through technology transfer at a time when new steel technologies began to flourish. This was during the Meiji Restoration, which encompassed the reign of Emperor Mutsuhito (from 1868 to 1912). During the Meiji period, technologies being transferred to Japan had been developed within Western organizations whose structures often had no direct counterpart with their new setting in Japan.[133] Both physical and organizational technologies were important to Japan at this time, since Japanese steelmaking developed in response to the needs of a national economy undergoing an industrial revolution that was accomplished in a shorter period than in any other country of the world. The Japanese steel industry adopted those steelmaking technologies on the basis of an overriding interest in economic models that emphasized rational choice and rational calculation of costs and benefits.[134] In addition, Meiji Japan focused on the strategic competitive context of new technologies and on social contexts, especially access to information. Japanese steelmakers recognized the fact that access to information was a significant factor in accessing both physical and organizational technologies through international transfer.

The New Technologies

The modern Japanese steel industry has been characterized as having some of the best and most productive plants in the world and as having the most efficient organizations for assembling raw materials. Japan's success has been attributed, to a large extent, to being the product of a long-standing philosophy "to search out the best practice in the world and improve on it."[135] Thus, the Japanese steel industry initially obtained its technology from Germany and the US during the Meiji period, then made great strides forward in metallurgy. Japanese plant engineers of the Meiji period recognized the potential of Western technologies, and many industrialists scrapped their open hearth furnaces and installed new equipment such as the basic oxygen furnace and the electric-arc furnace.

During the Meiji Restoration and in particular during the 1870s, the first modern blast furnaces and mills were built near low-grade ore supplies at Kamaishi in northern Honshu. For some years the enterprise struggled, hindered by its remoteness from fuel supplies and other deficiencies. But in the late 1890s work commenced on what soon became the big coastal metallurgical plant at Yawata in northern Kyushu, its raw materials being supplied by the coal mines of Chikuho in the hinterland. Target output was 90,000 tons of steel, but by World War 1, Yawata accounted for 80 percent of the country's output. Similar location principles were followed at Muroran in 1909, where Ishikari coal and Kuchan ore were within easy reach. Other smaller works were built in the Hanshin industrial area, centered on Osaka and Kobe, and in Keihin or Tokyo Bay area, including two works at Kawasaki by 1918.[136]

From the 1930s, Japan experienced a resurgence in both steelmaking and steel use. From 1931 the economy began to shift more definitely from textiles to heavy industry, and demand for steel increased with the expansion in mining, chemical, engineering and war industries. In 1934, with government support, Yawata merged with six other steel corporations to form the Japan Iron and Steel Company. The merger and the demands of rearmament brought accelerated growth; in 1937 ingot production was 5.8 million tons, and in 1940, 7.5 million tons. Expansion involved more dependence on the importation of scrap, mainly from the United States, and pig iron from Manchuria. In addition, Japanese steelmakers' increased coal consumption meant that more and more coal had to be imported.[137]

By the late 1950s, the Japanese steel industry was aggressively obtaining technology from Austria, and it had deepened its operations in oxygen steelmaking. The steel industry's high productivity, combined with its relatively low capital and operations costs, justified further development and investment. The pace of development quickened, and increasing vessel size eventually made it worth closing existing melting shops in favor of newly-built converter plants.[138]

By the 1960s it became normal practice in Japan to construct additions to existing plants or to build new plants with oxygen converters, and by this time Japan was producing its own oxygen converters. In 1963 oxygen converter production costs were said to be 6-10 percent lower than the open hearth furnaces, and by 1968 as much as 30 percent lower.)[139] (Today, Japanese steel pricing is keenly competitive with steel pricing in Western Europe, North America and South America.[140]

During this latter time period, Japan adhered to the Austrian LD process, which it found to be extremely successful. However, technical progress in the industry was not confined to steelmaking itself, but extended to streamlining the entire production process. For example, the coke usage rate in Japan fell from 900 kg per ton in 1950 to 499 kg per ton in 1968, by which time it was 100-200 kg lower than Western European and US levels. By the mid 1970s, Japan had 22 blast furnaces with a volume greater than 2,000 cubic meters. At this time, the former Soviet Union countries had 17, the USA 1, and the United Kingdom had no blast furnaces of this capacity.[141]

Also, the cost of building a new plant in Japan was relatively low in comparison to the West. Although borrowing costs were relatively high for the Japanese, Japanese wages were lower, efficiency levels higher, and plant size was smaller. (This smaller plant size also aided efficiency by helping to reduce both internal transfer costs and heat loss.[142] The efficiencies achieved by the Japanese steel industry resulted in a belief commonly held throughout the international steel industry that every dollar invested in Japan Steel bought three times as much new capacity as a dollar invested in the US.[143] Although Western steel industry built new plants around this time, the Japanese steel industry, with its high levels of efficiency, was able to attract more investment than Europe or the US. By 1970 the Japanese steel industry was characterized by deep water docks and new high capacity blast furnaces, attractive three-converter oxygen steel shops, and huge-capacity blooming mills. If the reader will recall, the 15 questions posed in Chapter 2 of this study can be distilled into, How is capacity built? and How is demand sustained? In brief, Japan built its capacity by installing modern technologies; Japan sustained demand by focusing on providing its domestic shipbuilding and automotive industries with steel.

From the 1970s to the present day, the Japanese steel industry has remained competitive and built capacity by continuing to embrace new technologies. These technologies currently take the form of computer integrated manufacturing (CIM) techniques that have been commonly accepted and used throughout the steel industry. This CIM application owes its origin to the Purdue model, illustrated in Figure 7.1.

Figure 7.1
The Purdue Model

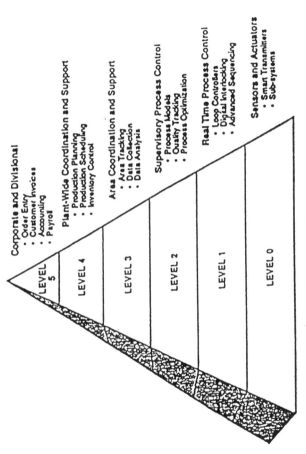

Corporate and Divisional
- Order Entry
- Customer Invoices
- Accounting
- Payroll

Plant-Wide Coordination and Support
- Production Planning
- Production Scheduling
- Inventory Control

Area Coordination and Support
- Area Tracking
- Data Collection
- Data Analysis

Supervisory Process Control
- Process Models
- Quality Tracking
- Process Optimization

Real Time Process Control
- Loop Controllers
- Digital Interlocking
- Advanced Sequencing

Sensors and Actuators
- Smart Transmitters
- Sub-systems

LEVEL 5
LEVEL 4
LEVEL 3
LEVEL 2
LEVEL 1
LEVEL 0

Source: Iron and Steel Engineer

Specifically, the Japanese steel industry now widely relies on process computers to achieve high levels of efficiency and product quality. Customers' continuing requirements for increasingly high quality steel products have spurred Japanese steel plants to use process computers to run their continuous production lines, and this increasingly powerful and flexible computer control has also helped Japanese plants to meet customers' demands for a greater variety of products. But a third objective for these advanced computer technologies has been to realize lower production costs. Consequently, the configuration and complexity of these process computer systems have become increasingly complex over time. They have evolved from standalone systems to centralized systems, and then from centralized to decentralized systems.

High reliability, ease of expansion and ease of maintenance have been essential characteristics of process control systems that steelmakers have installed in an effort to lower costs while meeting customers' increasingly stringent requirements.[144] Process control systems are complex, and must now include both distributed and centralized process computers linked by high-speed local area communication networks (LANs). These process control systems depend on the high-performance microprocessors and large memory capacities that are available today.[145] These complex, integrated systems rely on centralized information—that is, a single database—residing on a centralized computer. This information is then distributed to the decentralized process control computers. The architecture of a typical autonomous decentralized system is characterized by high fault tolerance and the ability to construct customized systems step by step; it can also maintain programs in an on-line system.[146] These combined computer and communication technologies have helped Japanese steelmakers stay on top of the changing requirements for plant controls.[147]

The modern Japanese steel industry has therefore achieved its competitive advantage in large part through the development and application of this through-process technology software. Figure 7.2 is a schematic of a typical layered software architecture used in the iron and steel industry.

Figure 7.2
Layered software architecture typically used in the modern
Japanese steel industry

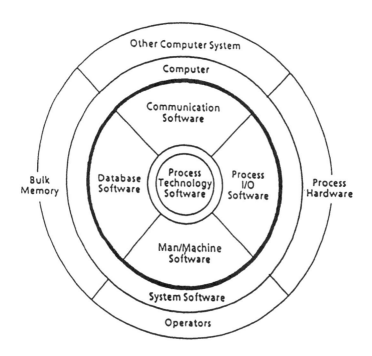

Source: Iron and Steel Engineer

Figure 7.2 illustrates the basic concept of layered software. To achieve a unified interface that includes all interface elements, a high-speed, real-time operating system manages and distributes information from the system's central database. Its access control is achieved by the use of unified interface parameters. A unified interface is defined by a function code—or program module name—and the data required by the application programs running on each input/output server. To ensure that the system is self-contained, not relying on anything else, it is important to obtain high portability of application programs. These applications execute prescribed processes without the help of other functional modules—in other words, they are stand-alone programs. To meet the needs imposed by this new generation of applications, an autonomous decentralized architecture was adopted. To ensure the high portability of such application programs, common functions were selected. Consequently, common functional units were designed together with high-quality software. In particular, it was important to select common functions and to unify capability needs in the design of application programs for similar process lines.

Further, a systems approach to achieve a common design of application programs and standard documents has been adopted. Rapid typing and a prototype method helped to confirm the key process functions in a small system prior to the total system development.[148]

Raw Materials Supply

Availability of raw materials has played a major role in the development of the Japanese steel industry. The island of Japan has never had significant deposits of either iron ore or coke. Japan had to rely heavily on the use of scrap. When in 1940 the world pig iron consumption/steel output ratio was 1:3, Japan's output ratio was only 1:1.9 or 1:2.0. This ratio remained more or less constant for almost ten years after the Second World War. However, as Japan embraced technological innovation and the use of oxygen converters, scrap became a less important raw material. From about 1968 on, the Japanese pig iron consumption/steel output ratio shifted from 1:1.87 to 1:1.45, at which point it was lower than that of the US. By 1968, the Japanese metal-making economy had matured, supplies of scrap in Japan increased, and the import of scrap decreased significantly. At about this time, scrap had become relatively high-priced in the world market, and so had electricity. This increased electricity cost slowed the replacement of open hearths by electric furnaces in Japan. Nevertheless, Japan's iron production increased from 5.2 million tons in 1955 to 72.2 million tons in 1991.

The large integrated mills in Japan, while undergoing the technical transformation discussed above, also had to import coking coal and iron ore on a scale unknown in any other industrialized country. In 1957, Japan was importing a combined total of 14.25 million tons of coke and iron ore; by 1971, this combined total was 272.2 million tons.[149]

To ensure themselves of sufficient supplies of both iron ore and coal, the Japanese sent economic missions abroad to purchase these raw materials. Iron ore was purchased under long-term contracts from several sources, including India, Labrador in Canada, Alaska in the US, Guinea in Africa, South Africa, Chile and Western Australia. The problem of ensuring a sufficient supply of coking coal proved more difficult. Coal was purchased primarily from Canada, particularly from the mines in Alberta and British Columbia, and from the iron ore mines in Utah and California. By the 1970s Australia became the main source of coal for Japanese steelmakers.[150]

STEELMAKING LOCATIONS IN JAPAN

During the Meiji Restoration, raw materials were brought into Japan at both the northern and southern "extremities" of the island as well as along the eastern coast. These import sites proved efficient and lowered assembly costs for the raw materials. It was easy for workers to get to their place of employment. These low assembly costs and close proximity of workers led to high levels of productivity, which in turn made Japan a competitive steel producer.

Today, Japan's import and industrial locations are very different. Competitive steel production today requires large, flat sites close to the big markets, in addition to ample supplies of raw materials such as cheap water and limestone flux. Finished steel is now moved by coastal vessels and is stored in warehouses until it is sold and shipped to its final destination. In fact, a leading theme of the Japanese steel industry in the postwar period has been the clustering of steel companies in Japan's central manufacturing belt.

Before the Meiji Restoration economic activity and population were concentrated in the eastern seaboard area from Tokyo through northern Kyushu. This area now forms an industrial/urban belt, perhaps the biggest in the world, exceeding in population even the 'megalopolis' of the northeastern seaboard of the United States. Within this eastern seaboard region are certain core areas or industrial nodes (see Maps 1 through 4 throughout this discussion), notably that of Kento, centered on Tokyo Bay; Tokai, whose center is Nagoya; Kinki, with Osaka/Kobe as the industrial core; and the Kita Kyushu-Fukuoka belt on the northern edge of the Kyushu island. Economic activity and growth have been concentrated here to a far grated degree than in Britain's so-called 'Axial belt' or the 'Golden Triangle' of the Common Market. As a result, outlying areas with a lower population density also have a much lower standard of living—the average income of workers in Tohoku and Hokuriku is about 20 percent less than that of a worker in the Kento region.[151] (Geographical concentration reflecting industrial development is represented in Map 1.)

Map 1 demonstrates that the steel market has helped to centralize Japan's heavy industries: first engineering, then shipbuilding, and later on, its ever growing motor industry. These central industrial belts were always more important than the steel finishing operations. Since 1932 the Keihin area had 42 percent of Japan's iron production and 17 percent of its ingots, but rolled 18.5 percent of the products. Yawata and its neighbors Tokata and Kokura, and, in the north, Muroran and Kamaishi, were all on the fringes of the industrial area.

Map 1
Geographical Distribution and Industrial Development in Japan

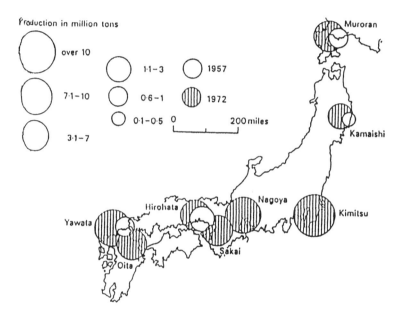

Source: Iron and Steel Works of The World

By 1941 Japan had constructed five other integrated works in the central industrial area, though their combined ingot capacity was only three quarters of Yawata's. Two of these, at Amagasaki and Funamachi in the Osaka-Kobe industrial belt, were of no more than 200,000 tons of steel capacity each. Finally, between 1937 and 1940 the Japan Iron and Steel Company built a new works at the northern shore of Hirohata (see Map 2 of the Inland Sea Coastline .

In 1935 the Japanese steel industry embarked upon a program of long-term planning. Sumitomo Metal Industries (founded in 1935) selected locations for its new steel plants based on a theory of centripetal drift. These new mills were to be concentrated along the farthest reaches of the coastline along the Inland Sea. Work began in 1940 and the first steel mill was completed in 1942, but full integration was not achieved until 1961. By that time, the Inland Sea had the greatest concentration of industrial capacity in the world, equal to that of the Ruhr Valley or the Chicago industrial area. (Sumitomo Metal Industries was acquired after it attained full integration, but retained its former name. [152]

The giant Japanese steelmaker Nippon Kokan (NKK) had long operated the two neighboring works of Kawasaki and Tsurumi along Tokyo Bay, and in 1956 started construction of a third one just to the north at Mizue. In 1960 NKK decided against constructing yet another Tokyo Bay area works at Funabachi, just east of Tokyo, instead building a plant in the Inland Sea area.

However, expansion in the Tokyo Bay area has remained attractive, and manufacturing has continued to grow steadily and rapidly in that area.[153] Both land and labor in the Tokyo Bay area are scarce and costly, but competition in the steel business is keen, and the area has strong attraction for expansion-minded management. Although NKK turned to the coastline along the Inland Sea after building its plant at Mizue, it is still engaged in increasing the capacity of its Tokyo Bay mills. NKK has a major raw materials terminal storage depot at Tokyo Bay as well as a preparation and forwarding operation on Oogishima island (an artificial island), offshore from the three mainland steel works (further reclamation was completed in 1974). NKK iron and steel plants in the Tokyo Bay area Produce slabs and blooms, which are shipped across the Inland Sea to the NKK finishing mills.

Other companies have also found the Tokyo Bay area desirable for steelmaking. In fact, Kayasaki Steel of Kobe was the first to build in Tokyo, when it began the Chiba works in 1951 on land that had been reclaimed at the north-eastern end of Tokyo Bay. By 1968 Chiba already had a capacity of six million tons. Today, it has a capacity of 25 million tons. [154]

Sumitomo's nearest integrated works is 400 km (248 miles) away from Tokyo, near Osaka, and although 85 percent of this mill's output leaves by water, companies still prefer to locate their plants nearer the prime industrial area. Beginning with pipe mills and a hot strip mill supplied from other works, Sumitomo now has a fully integrated plant at Kashima near the Kita Ura lagoon on the Pacific coast (see Map 3), fewer than 90 km (56 miles) northeast of the center of Tokyo; this works now has 50 million tons of steel capacity. [155] NKK has also built steel manufacturing plants on the Inland Sea, including a 50 million ton plant at Fukuyama that was completed in 1968. In 1959 Yamata moved into the Inland Sea area, and by 1965 had a fully integrated operation there with a steel plant with a capacity of 4.5 million tons.

Nagoya, the third largest city in Japan and the center of an industrial area devoted to auto manufacture—indeed, it is called "the Detroit of Japan"—had no important steel capacity until the late 1950s. Local interest and Fuji Steel set up Tokai Iron and Steel Company, the district's first integrated steelworks. Today, Nagoya is an established steel center in Japan.

Map 2
The Inland Sea Coastline

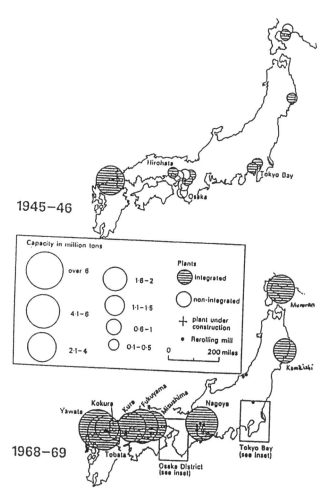

Source: Overseas Steel News

Map 3
The Tokyo Bay Area

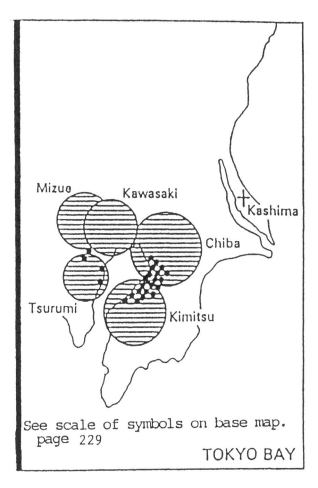

See scale of symbols on base map.
page 229

TOKYO BAY

Source: Iron and Steel Works of The World

Map 4
Osaka District

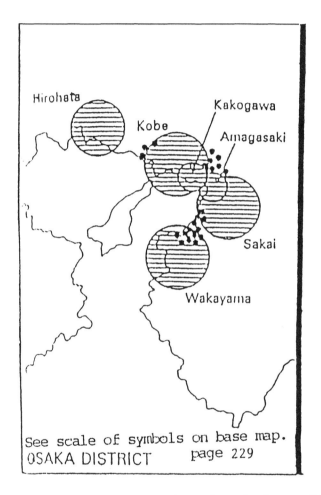

Source: Iron and Steel Works of The World

THREE KEY DEVELOPMENTAL CHARACTERISTICS OF THE JAPANESE STEEL INDUSTRY

Fifteen questions were initially posed in Chapter 2 of this study, then were refined to two basic questions about the development of the steel industry:

1. How is capacity built?
2. How is demand sustained?

We have seen that three prime physical characteristics drove the development of the Japanese iron and steel industry:

1. The active application of new technology at a time when many new technologies were proliferating throughout the world's iron and steel industry.
2. The development of the iron and steel industry along the eastern coastal region, facilitating importation, storage, and exportation of raw materials, namely iron ore and coke.
3. A strong domestic demand for steel, which resulted from the rapid development of the shipbuilding industry and, to a lesser extent, the automobile industry.

LESSONS OF EXPERIENCE FROM DEVELOPMENT OF THE JAPANESE STEEL INDUSTRY

From the discussion in this chapter, six basic developmental measures of the Japanese steel industry can be posited as relevant to the industrialized countries worldwide:

1. Assurance and capture of the domestic steel market
2. Continued modernization and rationalization
3. Emphasis on advanced and specialty steels
4. Diversification of business activities
5. Retention of work force loyalty
6. Governmental support for a long-range perspective.

Capturing and Maintaining the Domestic Market

Generally, a large domestic market for steel exists in all industrial countries. To ensure a healthy business base, a country's steel producers must gain and hold their domestic market.

In this sense, producers have a great advantage in that their mills are located near their strongest (domestic) customers. For example, Japan's largest-capacity steel mills have been located near automobile manufacturers and shipbuilding plants. The steel mills provide the carmakers with steel coils and the shipbuilding companies with many types of steel products—and they can provide these products at relatively low cost compared to the costs that overseas customers must bear. Proximity facilitates deliveries as well as information-gathering about customers, and it lets the mills provide their strongest customers with many specialized services. Furthermore, the customers also benefit because the steel industry is often an important buyer of the customers' goods and services. A strong domestic steel industry may thus easily gain and hold its domestic market by fully utilizing these advantages.

For example, auto manufacturers buy their steel on a "just-in-time" basis. They base their orders for steel coils on their preliminary production plans for the press lines, about two months in advance. With these orders in hand, the steel mills set up their preliminary production and operating schedules for each step of the manufacturing process. One month before the coils are required, the steelmakers finalize detailed production and delivery schedules according to the automaker's finalized production plan. The finished coils are shipped to the steel company's warehouses located nearest the customer's plant. From here the coils are delivered to the plant according to the plant's production schedule, and updated shipping information is reported daily to the steel mill.

This just-in-time process helps reduce inventory and increase savings for both the auto and steel companies. Further, the auto companies appreciate the steelmakers' efforts to work closely with them, and this close working relationship contributes significantly to the Japanese automakers' competitiveness in the world market.

Sustaining Competitiveness through Modernization and Rationalization

Although the steel industry is in the best position to gain and hold the domestic market, steel is traded internationally, so domestic steel prices must be internationally competitive. In this respect, steelmakers must constantly strive to modernize and rationalize their production facilities and operations.

The Japanese steel industry aggressively modernized its production facilities during its years of rapid economic growth. This modernization permitted increasingly rationalized operations and higher production volumes. However, after the first oil crisis of the 1970s, economic growth slowed and energy prices skyrocketed. These economic changes made it imperative that Japan's steel industry be further nationalized. With the stagnation in steel production, the Japanese steel industry took two main actions:

1. It concentrated production in the most modern and efficient facilities.
2. It used capital investments to rationalize production in ways that would save materials, energy, and manpower. Outstanding examples are the use of continuous casting and continuous annealing technologies as well as the conservation of energy, mainly in the form of heavy oil, and through recovery of waste heat and gases. Continued efforts to cut energy consumption after the oil crises had ended have resulted in a constant decline of energy consumed per ton of crude steel produced (see Figure 7.3)

Figure 7.3
Energy consumption per ton of crude steel in Japan

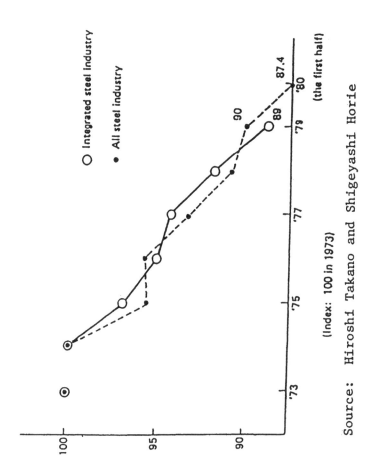

Developing Advanced and Specialty Steel

Advances in industrial infrastructures worldwide have gone hand-in-hand with increased demand for high-grade and specialty steels. For example, energy exploration and development companies have continually demanded steels increasingly capable of withstanding severe service conditions. Similarly, companies in the area of energy and manpower saving require specialized steels. Production of such steels requires advanced technologies that are currently available only in the most industrialized countries. And the steel industries in these countries must meet the requirements of both their domestic and foreign markets. Production of these specialized steels continually spurs advances in steelmaking technology and helps to continually revitalize a company's operations.

For example, the introduction of vacuum degassing facility permits large-volume production of high-grade steels. Steelmakers have vigorously added this and other 'out-of-furnace' refining technologies (including pretreatment of hot metal for desulphurization and ladle refining) to their production lines. Further, these additions have been made without disrupting the conventional production line of blast furnace, basic oxygen converter, and continuous casters (see Figure 7.4). Great improvements in steel quality have been achieved, for example, by reducing the sulphur content of steel used for manufacturing line pipe.

Technologies such as those just mentioned have permitted large-volume production of super-low-sulphur steel, often with sulphur content of less than 10 ppm (see Figure 7.5). Such an achievement was never thought possible in the past. Now, steel that can be used in an environment with high levels of hydrogen sulphide can be produced in large volumes.

Figure 7.4
Capacity of degassing (RH and DH) facilities in Japan

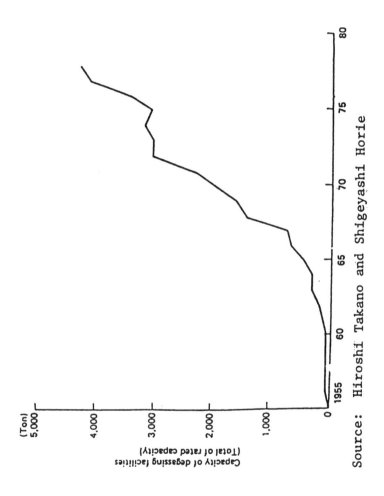

Source: Hiroshi Takano and Shigeyashi Horie

Figure 7.5
Change of average sulfur content in NKK's line pipe

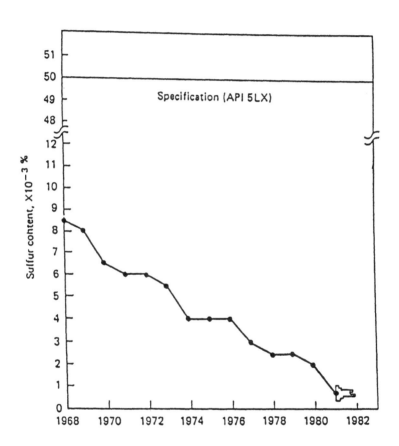

Source: N.K.K. Co. Ltd.

Diversifying Business Activities

However much customers may demand—and get—increasingly specialized and high-grade steels, it is not expected that industrialized countries will significantly increase their demands for steel in the near future. Steelmakers thus cannot expect that simply producing more sophisticated and specialized steels will bring new orders. Thus, steel companies may have to turn to other measures if they wish to maintain significant levels of growth. Japanese steel companies have expanded and revitalized their activities by entering steel-related industrial fields. In short, they are diversifying their business by utilizing existing technologies.

For example, one of NKK's current business divisions began as a shipbuilding company with its own steelmaking division. At present, this division has three shipyards with a total capacity of about one million gross tons per year, which makes it the fifth-largest in Japan's shipbuilding industry. NKK has entered the engineering and construction fields through utilization of both its steelmaking and shipbuilding technologies. And based on the steel fabrication and welding technologies at its shipbuilding division, NKK branched out into construction of pipelines and steel structures (such as bridges) many years ago. NKK's pipeline business, especially, has increased fairly steadily over time. With a view to extending into the field of energy development, including treatment of oil and natural gas, NKK utilized the steel and system control technologies it had developed in its steel making division to enter the business of constructing liquid natural gas (LNG) storage tanks, drilling facilities, and offshore platforms. NKK's eventual goal is to develop this sector into an integrated engineering and construction company in the energy-related field (see Figure 7.6).

In addition, this division uses technologies developed at NKK's steel division to construct and operate steel mills capable of engineering and constructing items such as iron and steelmaking equipment as well as pollution control facilities. The sales of this division have shown a steady increase (see Figure 7.7).

Figure 7.6
Plans for NKK's diversification into the engineering and
construction fields

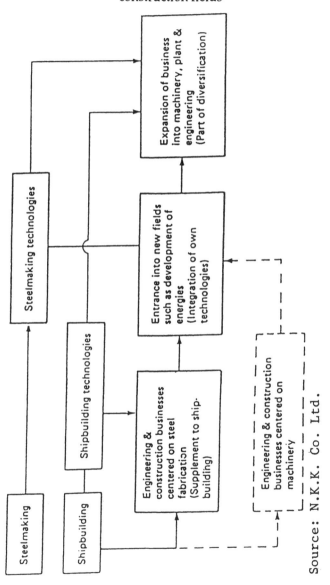

Source: N.K.K. Co. Ltd.

Figure 7.7
NKK's sales by division

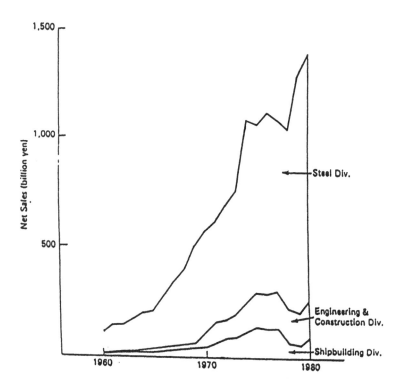

Source: N.K.K. Co. Ltd.

Retaining Work Force Loyalty

Japanese steelmakers strive to attract a steady stream of top-notch engineers by promoting research and development activities and by striving to maintain leadership positions in technology and science development. They are also making continuing efforts to improve the working environment for their labor forces. Intensification of pollution control measures and the automation of plant facilities have improved working conditions in plants. Today's working conditions are very different from the dusty, hot environments of conventional blast furnace shops.

Japanese steelmakers also actively strive to gain and improve employee morale. Japanese employment practices emphasizing lifelong employment as well as promotion based on seniority help to enhance loyalty to their employers. In addition, Japan's steel companies actively strive to promote mutual understanding between labor and management by constant dialogues about improving cooperation. Voluntary small group activities among blue collar workers (called "J-K"— Jishu Kanri, which translates to "Quality Circles," or "QC," and to "zero defect," or "ZD," management), have also been shown to enhance employees' goodwill and motivation.

Government Support

The Japanese government has directly or indirectly controlled the Japanese steel industry from the time of the Maiji Restoration to the end of the Second World War, and Japan's political structure since World War Two has remained highly conducive to government-guided industrial growth. By the end of the War, Japan's long tradition of government supervision of the economy had been capped by the recent experience of a government-directed war effort. Although the state-owned steel conglomerate Japan Steel Company (Nittetsu) was dissolved at the end of the War, the relationship between the government and the steel industry remained unusually close. The Liberal Democratic Party (LDP), with an abiding commitment to industrial growth, has held power throughout the postwar era. And the government body known as MITI has enjoyed wide-ranging influence over the Japanese steel industry during this period.

After the War, MITI officials often made the "descent from heaven" into leadership positions in the steel industry. Similarly, steel executives were heavily represented on many industry-government deliberative councils and associations whose views were solicited in the development of a consensus on the direction that government policy toward the steel industry should take. At one time MITI wielded the power to control imports and the import of technology, to provide financial assistance to industry, to regulate the allocation of raw materials, and to influence industry structure.

Indeed, MITI deserves much of the credit for the postwar reconstruction of the steel industry and its subsequent rapid expansion in the 1960s. In 1950 the Japanese Cabinet directed MITI to devise a comprehensive strategy for development of a steel industry that would be competitive on a worldwide scale. MITI implemented the First (1951-1955) and Second (1956-1960) Rationalization Programs, which emphasized capital investment for plant modernization and new plant construction. MITI controlled investment levels by regulating the import of machinery and technology and allocating domestic industry loans.[156] It provided direct and indirect assistance to the steel industry in the form of government loans, tax breaks, import protection, and improvements to Japan's infrastructure. The steel industry gained greater autonomy over its own development after 1960, but the government's continued provision of various forms of assistance has no doubt played a substantial role in the steel industry's spectacular ascent.

While MITI no longer enjoys many of these powers, the events of the "Yen Shock" period (from 1985 to 1988, when MITI intervened in a variety of ways to help the steelmakers surmount a crisis precipitated by a rapid shift in exchange rates) demonstrates that its influence in industry affairs remained substantial into the late 1980s.[157] (It is interesting to note that the Yen's continued appreciation since that time has not adversely affected the industries that rely on steel: shipbuilding, automobile manufacturing, and commercial construction.)

Availability of Capital:

One of the government's most important policy tools during the steel industry's period of most rapid growth was the use of its influence over the domestic banking system to ensure a flow of plentiful, low-cost capital. The Japanese steel industry financed its massive expansion during the 1960s, for the most part, with borrowed funds. During this time, the government held interest rates at artificially low levels, substantially reducing the cost of raising capital through bank loans. This naturally created an excessive demand for loans and led to development of a system for allocating credit among industrial sectors whose promotion was desired by the government. Japan's 13 city banks, which were the primary lenders to Japan's industrial corporations, were heavily dependent on the Bank of Japan (BOJ) for funds, and the BOJ's criterion for providing those funds was that the city banks lend in accordance with government priorities. In the 1960s, the steel industry was one of the government's leading industrial priorities.[153]

The government also provided the industry with direct loans and tax benefits. The general account budget of the Ministry of Finance lent governments funds to public financial institutions (such as the Japan Development Bank (JDB) and the Export-Import Bank of Japan), which in turn lent on favorable terms to Japanese industry. Government loans were also channeled through the Fiscal Investment and Loan Program (FILP), an entity within the Ministry of Finance. Such loans were significant not only for the sake of the capital but as a signal that MITI favored the recipient, and the company that received a JDB loan could easily raise whatever else it needed from private resources. In addition, the Long Term Credit Bank of Japan channeled a substantial amount of government funds into the steel industry for equipment acquisition and long-term working capital. While MITI's desire to provide tax benefits for the industry led it into recurrent conflicts with the Ministry of Finance, numerous tax measures favorable to the industry were implemented during the high growth period, including generous depreciation allowances and a variety of export-promoting tax measures.[159]

Encouragement of Technology Adoption:

One striking feature of the Japanese steel industry is its technological leadership, which has been aided by government interest in the steel industry. MITI, which from the 1950s through 1970 controlled the import of technology into Japan, played a major role in the Japanese industry's early adoption of the basic oxygen furnace (BOF), an Austrian invention that permitted a 20 to 40 percent reduction in unit costs from those of older open hearth furnaces. With the rapid expansion of the steel industry at this time, Japan was able to lead all other nations in adopting the BOF; by 1961, Japan had 20 BOFs in operation, while the US, with a much larger industry, had only 14. MITI has remained active in promoting the import of steelmaking technologies and, especially in the 1970s and 1980s, in funding research and development of new steelmaking techniques.[160]

At present, through its Agency for Industrial Science and Technology (AIST), MITI sponsors a number of joint R&D projects involving "a great deal of expense, risks, and long-range [long-term] period [of development]." These projects are typically conducted jointly by representatives of MITI, the leading steel firms, and Japanese universities.[161] MITI also has funded a new generation of joint R&D projects designed to enhance the energy efficiency of Japan's steel production. MITI makes annual subsidy grants to individual firms for R&D of "important technologies". It also recommends annual Japan Development Bank funding for R&D and pilot projects undertaken by individual steel firms seeking to improve energy efficiency and to develop methods for conversion from petroleum to alternative energy sources. MITI continually encourages Japanese steelmakers to conduct joint R&D with other firms and to share new technologies with each other.[162]

Government Support of Raw Materials Acquisition:

As mentioned earlier in this chapter, Japan's domestic iron ore and coal deposits are wholly inadequate to support its steel industry, and the government has traditionally assisted the

Japanese mills in acquiring essential raw materials from overseas.[163] Following the First Oil Shock in 1973, MITI, the Ministry of Finance and the Overseas Economic Planning Agency established the foreign currency loan system, which enabled Japanese steel firms to secure long-term, low interest loans for the development of overseas deposits of coal and ore (the Export-Import Bank of Japan provided the actual loans). Government loans were made to finance stockpiling of raw materials at overseas locations, particularly Australia. The Export-Import Bank also made substantial loans to the steel industry for spot imports of raw materials on an "urgent" basis.[164]

In order to discourage individual firms from bidding up the purchase price of raw materials, the government has favored the formation of raw materials purchasing consortia by Japanese firms. Under this system, one Japanese firm is designated to represent the entire industry in purchasing negotiations with overseas supplies. And MITI has repeatedly intervened directly in the scrap market, which is subject to particularly volatile price fluctuations, to prevent fluctuations from disrupting steelmaking operations.[165] During a 1987 scrap shortage, for example, MITI pressured integrated steelmakers to release their inventories of scrap and billet in order to stabilize domestic scrap prices for the electric-arc furnace mills producing steel products for the construction industry.

I shall next turn to the newly industrialized countries and developing countries to observe their steel industries, which are restricted to the production of common steel by concerted political action and strong governmental support. These influences have had varying degrees of success.

NOTES

[133] Takechi, K., *Basic Research into the Postal-Transport History of Early Meiji*, Tokyo: Yusankaku, 1978, pp. 15-17.

[134]   Stokaugh, R. and L.T. Wells, *Technology Crossing Borders: The Choice, Transfer, and Management of International Technology Flows*, Boston: Harvard Business School Press, 1984.

[135]   Cartwright, J., *Steel Times*, January 1970, p. 64

[136]   Okita, S., *IISI Tokyo Conference Report*, 1969, p. 51.

[137]   United Nations, *World Iron Ore Resources and Their Utilization*, 1950, p. 19.

[138]   Takeda, K. and S. Narita, "Developments in research on the LD and OG processes and their industrialization," *Journal of the Iron and Steel Institute*, May 1966, p. 417.

[139]   Stone, P.B., *Japan Surges Ahead*, European Coal and Steel Community (ECSC) Publication, 1969, pp. 191-192.

[140]   *The Steel Market in 1992*, Economic Commission for Europe, United Nations, New York, 1993, p. 45.

[141]   Tanake, S., "Iron ore industry problems as viewed by a consumer," *Business Review*, 1970, p. 36.

[142]   Iron and Steel Institute in Japan, 1963.

[143]   Hartke, V., *Iron and Steel Engineer*, January 1970, pp. 72-73.

[144]   Mori, K., "Autonomous controllability of decentralized systems aiming at fault tolerance," *Proceedings of the 8th IFAC World Congress*, Kyoto, 1981, pp. 129-134.

[145]   Torikoshi, H., et al., "Application and evaluation of autonomous decentralized system for iron and steel processes," *Kawasaki Steel Technical Report*, Vol. 20, No. 3, 1988, pp. 34-39.

[146]   Mori, K., et al, "On-line maintenance in autonomous decentralized loop network", *Proceedings of Compcon*, 1984, Arlington, Virginia.

[147]   Mori, K., et al., "Proposal of autonomous decentralized concept," *The Institute of Electrical Engineers of Japan*, Vol. 104, No. 12, 1984, pp. 303-310.

[148]   Mori, K., et al., "Application of autonomous decentralized system for iron and steelmaking process computer system," *The Hibachi Hyoron*, Vol. 70, No. 5, 1988, pp. 77-82.

[149]   *American Metal Bulletin*, January 1992, p. 6.

[150]   *Mining Journal*, Issue of March 8th 1968, pp. 178-179, and Issue of September 6, 1968, p. 169.

[151]   Allan, G.C., *Japan's Economic Expansion*, McMillan Press, London, 1965, pp. 40-41.

[152]   "Sumitomo's great leap forward," *Iron and Steel Engineer*, December 1969, p. 349.

153 *International Iron and Steel Institute* (IISI), Tokyo Conference Report 1969, p. 54.
154 *International Iron and Steel Institute* (IISI), Tokyo Conference Report 1993, pp. 114-120.
155 "Sumitomo's Great Leap Forward," *Iron and Steel Engineer*, December 1969, p. 349.
156 Johnson, C., *MITI and the Japanese Miracle*, Stanford, USA, Stanford University Press, 1982.
157 Kaplan, E., *Japan: The Government-Business Relationship*, US Department of Commerce, Washington, D.C., Feb. 1972.
158 Noguchi, Y., "The Government-Business Relationship in Japan," in Yamamura, et al., *Policy and Trade Issues of the Japanese Economy*, University of Washington Press, Seattle.
159 Hadley, E., *Japan's Export Competitiveness in Third World Markets*, Georgetown University, Washington, D.C., 1981, pp. 29-30.
160 Lynn, L.H., *How Japan Innovates: A Comparison with the U.S. in the case of Basic Oxygen Steelmaking*, Boulder, Colorado, USA: Westview Press, 1982.
161 Japan Steel Bulletin, September 1991, p. 17.
162 Organization for Economic Cooperation and Development (OECD), *Liberalization of International Capital Movement: Japan*, Paris, OECD, 1968, pp. 57-58.
163 US Trade Commission, *Steel Sheet and Strip Industry*, Washington, D.C., 1981, pp. 2-9.
164 Export-Import Bank of Japan, *Annual Reports* 1979 and 1981.
165 *Nihon Kogyo*, Feb. 10 and Sept. 17, 1975; *Japan Metal Bulletin*, Jan. 23, 1995; *Far East Iron and Steel Trade Report*, Dec. 1993 and Dec. 1994.

VIII

The Direction of Technology Transfer Within the Steel Industries in Newly Industrialized and Developing Countries

In response to a sharp worldwide increase in iron and steel consumption during the period of high economic growth in the 1970s, newly industrialized countries (NICs) such as Brazil, Mexico, Taiwan, and the Republic of Korea constructed integrated plants and minimills for ironmaking, steelmaking and rolling, and these countries have been steadily expanding their steelmaking capacity ever since. In addition , Mexico and Korea have been in the forefront of technological development, Mexico with the HYLSA reduction process and Korea with the Samsung Compact Stripping Process.

The two main reasons for the success of these NICs in the steel industry are:

1. Expanding domestic demand
2. Relatively cheap labor costs resulting in improved international competitiveness in common steel.

Less developed countries (LDCs) in contrast to NICs, often regard the steel industry as a key factor in their future economic growth, since increased steel consumption has historically been accompanied by economic growth. Their objective is typically to attain production capacity that will satisfy their domestic demand. As part of their overall development strategy, developing countries tend to develop their steel industries by using optimization criteria and seeking performance results that are often significantly different from those of the steel industries in more technologically advanced countries.

When considering future development of the steel industry in LDCs, the critical question is, Can LDCs and NICs find it worthwhile to establish and expand their domestic steelmaking capacity in the face of worldwide overcapacity, particularly in developed and industrialized countries? Of course, underlying this question is yet another: Why and how did the developed countries originally create such overcapacity when their domestic steel consumption was much lower than their installed capacity? The answer to both questions lies in the developed countries' vigorous and continual optimization, in their development of steel capacity through scrapping old steel facilities and plants, in reducing manpower requirements, and in increasing productivity while introducing newer, more innovative technologies. Developing countries are now following suit by seeking to optimizing their steel capacities. This goal is based on increasing domestic demands and on the economic objectives of self-reliance and self-sufficiency, reduction of foreign exchange and import costs, and establishment of a sound steelmaking technological base, which is expected to catalyze growth of engineering industries and to contribute significantly to the growing technical expertise of labor forces—both of which are expected to lead, in turn, to accelerated industrialization.

DIFFERENT ECONOMIC AND TECHNOLOGICAL DEVELOPMENT PARADIGMS IN NICs AND LDCs

NICs such as Brazil, Mexico, Taiwan, and the Republic of Korea have built both integrated plants and minimills. In general, NICs and LDCs do not as yet prefer one type of plant over another—they do not usually build integrated mills rather than minimills, and vice versa. Further, steel mills in both NICs and LDCs have freely adopted both integrated mill and minimill technologies. They have adopted such integrated mill technologies as the basic oxygen furnace (BOF), blast furnace (BF), and the open-hearth system (OHS). Likewise, they have adopted such minimill technologies as the electric arc furnace (EAF), continuous casting (CC), and ladle furnace technologies (LF).

NICs and LDCs have both identified the steel industry as vital to their continued economic development because of the view that increased steel consumption is always accompanied by economic growth. Many of these countries have been striving to attain a production capacity that can at least meet their own domestic demand.

The perspective is strikingly different from that of the developed countries. In developed countries, the social overhead capital is reaching a stage of maturity. The infrastructure of these countries is well developed and the level of construction activity is not considered a growth indicator, so infrastructure construction and maintenance is of less importance. In addition, the contribution of manufacturing to the Gross National Product (GNP) is gradually decreasing, and the emphasis is shifting toward knowledge-based industries such as ceramics, plastics, composites, and other advanced materials. These materials, in fact, provide intense competition to the steel industry in developed countries. There is no macroeconomic correlation between GNP and steel consumption in developed countries, so an increase in GNP does not necessarily change steel consumption. Moreover, it is generally agreed that the amount of steel required to support each additional unit of real GNP growth in developed countries will continue to decrease in the future.[166]

In my case study on Japan, I examined how the Japanese used technology transfer (i.e., they imported their steelmaking technology) to become a world leader in steel production and technology and continue to pursue mastery of flexible manufacturing systems, advanced steel products, and to encourage new demands for steel. (Flexible manufacturing systems are being achieved with next-generation technologies such as smelting reduction process, strip casting, thin-slab casting, and semi-solid processing controlled by artificial intelligence systems. For example, automated synchronized continuous processing is geared toward successful implementation of the flexible manufacturing system.[167]

On the other hand, NICs' demands for common steel products and for some higher grade steel (such as seamless pipe steel products, high-strength plates for shipbuilding, and cold-rolled sheets for automobiles) are directly linked to increases in GNP. In fact, NICs have focused so heavily on common steel that almost all these countries now produce common steels of similar qualities. Although NICs are also producing some higher grade steels such as fine steels, the quantities produced are too small to be worth exporting and, moreover, the grades are not yet of the same high qualities as are generally available on the world steel market. NICs are now focusing on producing high grade steels for their own domestic markets, while LDCs are increasing production capacity of common steel in order to meet their own domestic demands.[168]

The Importance of the Steel Industry to NICs' and LDCs' Economic Development

Now that NICs' and LDCs' striving towards steel capacity and product quality has been touched upon, an examination of their valuations of steel industry development to their economies is in order. NICs are currently experiencing a boomerang effect with respect to technology transfer. While developed countries have willingly transferred new technologies to NICs in an effort to maintain cooperative relations with them, this transfer has also allowed developed countries to take a leadership position in establishing a new development paradigm for the world's steel industry.

For example, in order to attain its leadership position in the steel industry, Japan paid an enormous amount of money to import technology during the period from 1951, when the First Rationalization Program was established, to 1979, when its technology trade volume equaled those of the US and Europe. In addition, Japan has invested more than any of the developed countries in research and development (R&D) efforts.[169] These efforts can be classified into three categories:

1. Assimilation and improvement of imported or existing technologies.
2. Development of composite material technologies.
3. Creation of innovative high technologies.

NICs are now actively developing their technology through the first R&D category, the assimilation and improvement of imported or existing technology. However, no NIC has been engaged in steel R&D activities for more than 30 years. These R&D activities usually started within a few national research institutions, then migrated into the hands of large private steelmaking firms when these began to recognize the importance of engaging in their own R&D. For example, large private steelmaking firms in the Republic of Korea only began doing their own R&D activities in the early 1980s.

In contrast to Japan, South Korea has been striving to develop its steelmaking capacity and quality only since the 1960s. In the late 1960s, South Korea suffered a comparative lack of integrated steelmaking capability[170]; the country's steel industry consisted largely of a few antiquated open-hearth furnaces as well as some rolling mills engaged in finishing operations—and these were largely dependent on imported semi-finished steel.

During the Second Five Year Plan (1966-1971), President Park Chung Hee declared that defense implications made development of a modern steel industry one of the country's highest priority. Under President Park's direction, the Pohang Iron and Steel Company (POSCO) was formed in 1968 (with government majority ownership) with the specific goal of modernizing Korea's steel industry. But POSCO immediately encountered a major obstacle when various foreign lending agencies refused to help finance the project on the grounds that it was not commercially feasible. The Korean government itself provided the necessary capital, using Japanese war reparations funds.[171]

Today, Korea produces enough steel products in the following areas to meet its domestic demand:
- sheets, coil and strips, bars and special steels for motor vehicle manufacture
- plates and sections of shipbuilding
- wire and wire products (wire rods).

However, Korea's technology has not yet developed sufficiently to allow it to take a leadership position in world steelmaking.

Although NICs have begun to develop composite materials technologies and other innovative high technologies, these efforts have not become widespread. These industries are embryonic and not yet competitive. However, these efforts should propel some NICs to leadership positions in some technological areas by the year 2000.[172]

The Impact of Technology on One Region's Competitiveness in the World Market

Despite the fact that they have not yet taken leadership positions in the world steel market, NICs currently have highly competitive technologies and the competitive edge in two areas in the steel processing: direct reduction (DR) and ladle metallurgy (LM). This section will examine DR's impact on development of the Latin American steel industry (encompassing both Central and South America) and how LM has played a key role in the increasing competitiveness of the Brazilian steel industry.

The DR Steelmaking Process

As stated in Chapter 2, direct reduction is the process whereby iron ore and coal are melted and formed into ingots that are used as feedstock in the making of common steel. In the NICs and LDCs, the relationship between economic development and per capita steel consumption has been studied extensively. Figure 8.1 shows this relationship for selected Latin American and industrialized countries.

Of course, the correlation between economic growth and steel consumption is not exact, and it should not be assumed that the two are inextricably linked. For example, the Eastern European countries typically have a very high per capita steel consumption in relation to their per capita GNP. However, experience has shown that as countries develop, their consumption increases significantly. As the above graph shows, if the Latin American economies continue to grow over the next several years, there will be a significant concomitant increase in their demand for steel. Gustavo Tobon Londono, President of the Latin American Iron and Steel Congress (ILAFA), recently stated that steel consumption in Latin America has been increasing by 10 percent per year over the last five years, and this trend is likely to continue for the next five years.[173]

Supporting this view, Dr. Donald Barnett of Economics Associates, Inc. (a leading steel industry consulting firm) has forecast that steel consumption in the developing world will increase 74 percent from 1985 to 2000, versus a mere 7 percent increase for industrialized countries over that same period.[174] The exact level of growth in Latin American steel consumption over the next 10 to 15 years is a matter of conjecture, but in any case it could be substantial.

Technology

Transfer

Figure 8.1
Per capita steel consumption vs. GNP

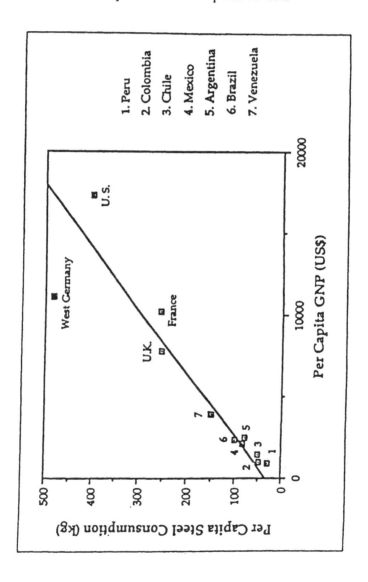

There are two compelling reasons to expect that most of this steel will be produced domestically. First, Latin American economic policies generally seek to conserve foreign exchange, so steel imports should decrease. Second, Latin America has abundant quantities of all the resources needed to produce steel: iron ore, energy (particularly natural gas), water, and labor. These resources are available in sufficient quantities and qualities, and at competitive prices, to produce steel efficiently.

OPTIONS FOR INCREASING STEEL CAPACITY

There are four possible process routes for providing the increased steelmaking capacity that Latin America requires:
- Coke oven/blast furnace/basic oxygen (CO/BF/BOF)
- New ironmaking (NIM) with computer-aided technologies
- Scrap-based electric arc furnace (EAF)
- Direct reduction/EAF (DR/EAF)

Each of these alternatives is discussed in detail below. Figure 8.2 shows iron and steel production from these processes for the period 1991-1994.

Coke oven/blast furnace/basic oxygen furnace-CO/BF/BOF

Approximately 59 percent of all the steel produced in Latin America is made using this process (used widely in integrated facilities). In addition, this process is clearly preferred to the coke oven/blast furnace/open hearth route (CO/BF/OH). The CO/BF/BOF process has revolutionized the steel industry throughout the world, but in Latin America its use has been limited by the following four factors, and it is highly unlikely that Latin American countries will be able to continue to meet their steel needs with this production route.

Figure 8.2

Steel production in Latin America
(Toneladas)

País	1991	1992	1993	1994
Argentina	2.972	2.680	2.885	3.300
Brasil	22.617	23.934	25.207	25.747
Chile	807	1.013	1.062	1.040
Colombia	652	657	687	702
Ecuador	20	70	27	22
México	7.964	8.459	9.200	10.172
Perú	404	343	417	485
Venezuela	3.304	3.489	3.389	3.411
América Latina	39.835	41.453	43.630	45.812

Fuente: ILAFA   *Cifras proyectadas
                                             LA REPÚBLICA

Source: La Republica, page 3, Tuesday, September 19, 1995.

Capital cost.

Due to the huge investment required for coke ovens, blast furnaces, power plants, environmental control equipment, and other facilities, the capital cost of an integrated facility is high, on the order of US$1,000 per annual ton (a.t.) of steel produced. Thus, for a plant of 3 million tons per year (t/y), the required investment is US$3,000 million. This capital outlay is a difficult hurdle for many Latin American countries to overcome.

Economy of scale.

The threshold at which an integrated facility achieves economy of scale is quite high, and it is generally not feasible to build an integrated plant that will produce less than 3 million t/y. Even if a single integrated plant could supply all of a single Latin American country's domestic steel needs, this would rule out construction of such a plant in all but two Latin American countries, Mexico and Brazil. Not only is this high production capacity too high to make it worth building integrated plants in Latin America, but integrated plants also tend to produce a narrow range of products. So, for producing the relatively small quantities of a large variety of steel products that are required in Latin America, the CO/BF/BOF route has significant limitations.

Lack of coking coal.

Latin America has few reserves of high quality coking coal, so it must be imported to any new integrated facilities; such imports would gradually deplete a country's foreign exchange reserves. Charcoal-based blast furnaces are a reasonable alternative for Latin America, but this solution could cause a significant environmental problem in the form of deforestation.

Environmental problems.

Coke ovens generate such high levels of pollution that industrialized countries are extremely reluctant to build new ones. NICs in Latin America are similarly reluctant, which hinders significant increases in CO/BF/BOF capacity. Although Brazil produces a substantial portion of its steel in charcoal-based blast furnaces, this approach will not be able to satisfy the country's increasing steel requirements. Concerns about deforestation are high and it will probably not be feasible to significantly increase charcoal-based blast furnace production.

New Ironmaking with Computer-aided Techniques (NIM)

Over the last fifteen years, firms around the world have attempted to develop technologies for producing liquid iron with non-coking coal. These efforts, which are intensifying, are driven by the need to avoid the capital costs and environmental problems of the CO/BF/BOF route. A number of promising technologies based on computer integrated manufacturing (CIM) and artificial intelligence (AI) are now in use, and the economics of this process are proving viable. These technologies generally entail lower capital investment costs than new CO/BF/BOF facilities. Indeed, the strong probability that the efficiencies of these technologies will eclipse the economies of scale of integrated facilities is yet another reason why many steel companies are averse to building new integrated facilities. In fact, the Latin American steel industry is now introducing these computer-based technologies with success.

Scrap-based Electric Arc Furnace (EAF)

The use of EAF steelmaking has increased considerably throughout the world in recent years, and this trend is continuing. Most EAF capacity is based on essentially a 100 percent scrap charge. In Latin America, approximately 35 percent of steel is produced via the EAF route, but only 60 percent of the charge is scrap.[175]

Scrap-based EAF steelmaking is the cheapest steelmaking route. The capital cost is on the low side of $400/a.t. as compared to $1,000/a.t. at an integrated facility. The EAF net energy consumption is about half that of an integrated plant, which results in a considerably lower operating cost. For example, 1994 data for Latin American countries show that, for similar products, operating costs for EAF-based minimills are about 10 percent lower than for integrated facilities.[176]

Projections indicate that the share of steel production captured by EAFs will continue to rise. Dr. Barnett forecasts that the EAF share worldwide will increase to 29 percent by 2000, up from 269 in 1987.[177] (These numbers assume no significant changes in technology.)

Availability and sources of charge scrap are therefore the keys to increased EAF production. Latin America cannot generate sufficient scrap to meet its own increased EAF materials requirements.[178] Importing scrap is a possibility, but many trends are pointing to decreased worldwide availability of high-quality scrap. The following factors further affect the viability of EAF production in Latin America:

Increase in continuous casting.

The percentage of continuously cast steel has increased tremendously in the last 18 years. Continuous casting has reduced the production of home scrap (scrap arising from steel production or finishing operations), which is the highest quality scrap, and which is favored for EAF production.

Scrap contamination.

Due to the increased use of high-strength low alloy (HSLA) and coated steels, contamination of ferrous scrap with metallic residuals is becoming a significant problem. A survey conducted in late 1988 by the consulting firm Arthur D. Little, Inc., found that 72 percent of integrated steelmakers and 76 percent of EAF steelmakers in the US and Canada believe that the residual and tramp elements of scrap are increasing at a significant rate.[179] Processes to reduce the metallic (particularly copper) content of scrap are under development, but even if these processes are successful, these treatments will add to the cost of high quality scrap. (Chapter 3 details the methods of reducing tramp elements in scrap.) Decreased scrap availability and costly scrap pretreatment will severely impact Latin American scrap importers, since mills in scrap-exporting countries will naturally use the best scrap, leaving only the remainder available for export.

Tighter quality specifications on steel products.

Rolling mills and other manufacturers are continuing to press their supplies for materials of higher and higher quality. Further, manufacturers are also expecting their suppliers to provide steel with fewer and fewer impurities. The Arthur D. Little survey[180] found that 100 percent of integrated steelmakers expect that by 1995 their customers will be looking for steel with "substantially" or "significantly" better properties—that is, with significantly lower levels of impurities. The most recent ILAFA conference was preoccupied with clean steels, clearly signaling the importance of clean steels to the entire industry.

Increase in scrap use.

Along with increased scrap use due to the growth in EAF steelmaking, BOF steelmakers are also purchasing and using larger percentages of scrap to increase their productivity and lower their costs. (Figure 8.3 shows the relationship between scrap purchased and steel produced.) This trend will continue to put pressure on the price of high quality scrap.

Thin slab casting (TSC).

Mexico, Brazil, Argentina, Venezuela, Colombia, Chile and Peru are now using TSC technology. TSC requires high quality scrap feedstock, and it produces flat products at a comparatively lower price than conventional technology. The plant size ranges between 500,000 to 1,000,000 tons per year. Although the worldwide steel industry is putting increased pressure on the scrap market (see Chapter 3), and suppliers are being pressed to provide greater quantities and higher qualities of scrap, sufficient quantities of scrap to accommodate the TSC process are still available.

Figure 8.3
Scrap purchased/steel produced

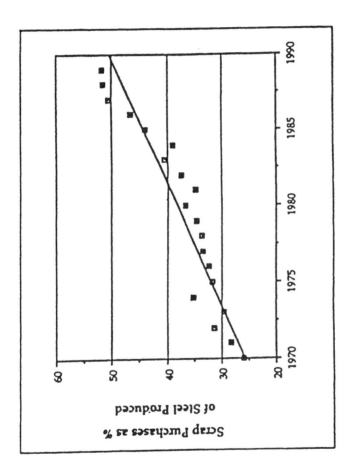

Fig. 8.3   Scrap purchased/steel produced

However, the net effect of the growth in EAF steelmaking will lead to a substantial increase in scrap purchasing. Dr. Barnett forecasts that even without the introduction of TSC, purchased scrap requirements worldwide will increase by 56 percent by the year 2000, whereas overall steel production will increase by 19 percent.[181] Increased production by Latin American steelmakers is expected to create sharp demands in both scrap and direct reduction (in the form of hot briquette iron—BRI) markets over the next 10 to 15 years.

Direct Reduction/Electric Arc Furnace (DR/EAF)

Since the three processes discussed above will not meet the needs of Latin American steel producers, the DR/EAF steelmaking route must play a major role in Latin American steelmaking. Production and consumption of DR/EAF products in Latin America has been increasing for many years. Latin American DR production has increased steadily over the last nine years (see Figure 8.4) with over 95 percent of DR products now being used by captive steel mills. (At captive plants, the DRI produced at a DR plant is channeled to an adjacent steel mill.) In 1994, approximately 12 million tons of steel were produced by the DR/EAF route in Latin America, with Mexico, Venezuela, and Argentina also relying on DR/EAF for a large part of their steel production.[182]

Coal-based DR is possible, and coal-based plants in Brazil and Peru produced a total of 90,000 tons of DRI in 1988 (total capacity of these plants is 165,000 t/y). However, this route has several limitations. First, this process requires coal of very high quality. The lack of high quality coal has led to marginal plant performance in Brazil and Peru. Second, this process has significant technical limitations, and the maximum unit capacity of any coal-based DR plant is about 150,000 t/y. This low production ceiling results in poor economies of scale compared to natural gas-based DR plants. Finally, the DRI produced by coal-based plants often has low metallization and high fines content.

Figure 8.4
Latin American DRI production

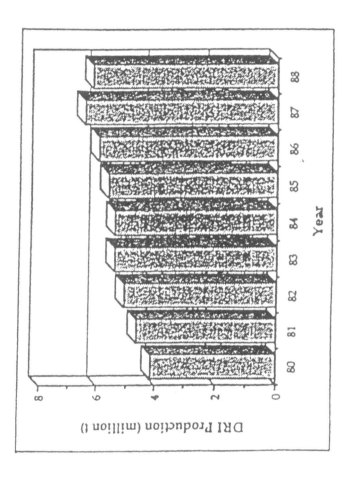

Figure 8.4   Latin American DRI production

Gas-based DR therefore appears to be the best choice for Latin America, since it has the following advantages:
- Latin American countries are rich in steelmaking materials and resources such as iron ore, natural gas, water, and labor. Domestic steel production will improve the countries' economies, since the money used to manufacture and to purchase steel products will remain within each country. Even if some of the resources must be purchased from other Latin American countries, the money will stay within the region, fostering regional development.
- The value of the available domestic scrap will be maximized, since it can easily be used as a "sweetener" to dilute scrap residuals in high quality DRI production. DRI can be used in two ways: in conjunction with poor quality scrap to produce common steel products, or in conjunction with high quality scrap to produce higher quality products. Either way, the value of the domestic scrap is maximized.
- The use of DRI will allow EAF steelmakers to move into production of the highest grades of steel, including steels of extra deep drawing quality, as the market demands. It would be very difficult economically to make this move if the steelmakers were dependent on imported scrap. Also, DRI will allow the development of thin slab casting technology, which may benefit Latin American steelmakers by allowing them to produce relatively small volumes of flat products economically.
- The gas-based DR/EAF route is economic in the production range of 400,000 t/y and up. These size plants fit in very well with the current and projected steel needs of many Latin American countries.
- Gas-based DR is a proven technology, producing over 13 million tons of DRI in 1988.
- Two types of DR plants are feasible in Latin America: captive and merchant. Captive plants are suitable for production of steel destined for larger countries. Steel needs of the smaller Latin American countries could be

met by merchant plants producing hot-briquetted DRI for several regional steel mills.

Ladle Metallurgy Processes

Various types of ladle metallurgy processes are available for treating liquid steel as shown in Figure 8.5.

The utility of each LM process depends on the final application to which the finished steel will be put. Apart from reducing the content of residual elements, LM can also fulfill certain other production objectives—each of which alone could often justify its utilization. These objectives include:

- Homogenization and better control of bath temperature and composition.
- Better control of morphologies of inclusions.
- Manufacture of high alloyed steels.
- Increased yield of additives.
- Better synchronization of primary steelmaking and casting processes.
- Increased productivity due to performing part of the refining operation during ladle treatment rather than in the primary furnace.

For example, the use of ladle furnace treatment (one type of LM) can increase productivity in electric melting shops and can reduce the temperature required by BOF shops. These gains can reduce refractory consumption in converters and can allow steelmakers to use a greater proportion of scrap in the charge. Concomitant gains in alloy addition yields and improved composition control make it economically viable to employ light treatment for tonnage treatment of steel.

However, there is as yet no single process that would make it possible to perform in one procedure all the available ladle treatment functions. Steelmakers must currently choose among alternative LM processes.

For example, steelmakers producing ultra-clean steels currently combine various LM and pretreatment processes which are listed in Figures 8.7 and 8.8.

Figure 8.5
Usual ladle metallurgy processes

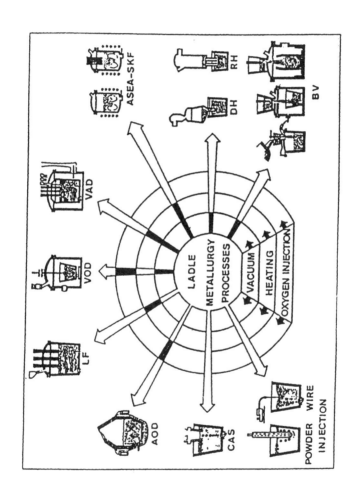

Figure 8.5   Usual Ladle Metallurgy Processes

Figure 8.6
Ladle treatments (model reactor)

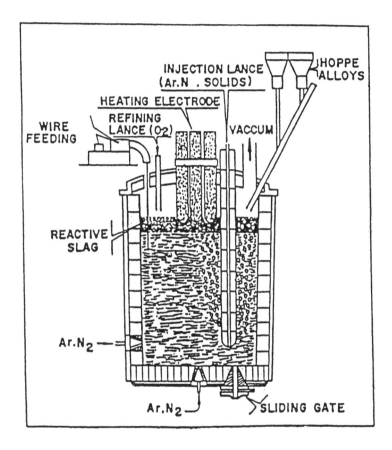

Figure 8.6 Ladle Treatments (Model Reactor)

Figure 8.7
The NSR System (NSC) for producing clean steel

	PRETREATMENT		BOF	NSR				PRODUCTS			
	TDS	KR		VSC	P	LF	RH	CHEMICAL COMPOSITION (PPM)			
	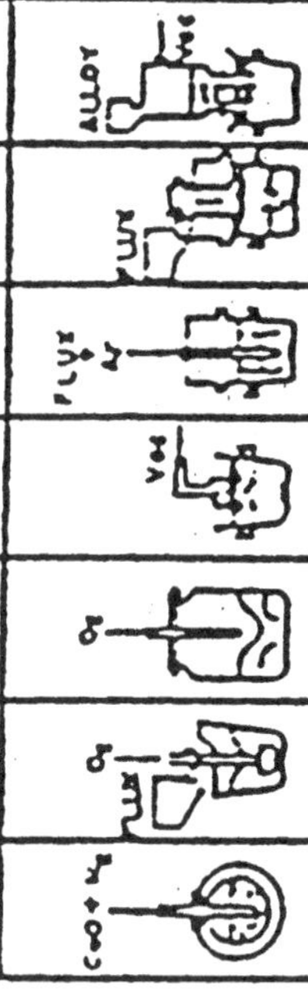							[P]	[S]	[N]	[O]
I	O	O	O	O	(O)	O	O	50	10	1.5	15
II	O	—	O	O	(O)	O	O	120	10	1.5	15
III	O	—	O	O	O	—	O	120	20	1.5	—
IV	O	—	O	O	—	—	O	120	50	1.5	—
V	O	—	O	(O)	—	—	O	150	50	1.5	—

Figure 8.7 The NSR System (NSC) for Producing Clean Steel

Figure 8.8
Reduction of impurities through combination of process

	ELEMENT	C	N	O	P	S	H
PROCESS							
Hot Metal Pretreatment			0		0	0	
Converter		0	0	0	0		
Ladle	Powder Injection			0		0	
Metallurgy	Vacuum	0	0	0	0		0

0 Effective   0 Decisive

In particular, BOF shops manufacturing ultra-clean steel at low cost must pretreat pig iron and converters with combined blowing, then must also perform ladle treatment.

Other processes incorporate additional resources in producing specialty steels. For example, the RH process combined with oxygen injection gave rise to the RH-OB process, which is used to manufacture stainless steel and very low carbon steel.

On the other hand, some processes are, in effect, simplified versions of other processes, the object of the simplified process being reduction of investment costs. For instance, the ladle furnace procedure developed at the beginning of 1970s was derived from the original Fink/VAD and ASEA/SKF processes. This newer process simply eliminated the vacuum system.

Continued advances in LM techniques have produced formidable results in the manufacture of ultra-clear steels. The quantities of residual elements in tonnage steelmaking have continually decreased over the last several years, and this trend is expected to continue.

The number of LM units in operation throughout the world have steadily increased.[183] The Brazilian steel industry, in particular, has been at the forefront of this trend. Brazil has made important achievements meriting particular treatment and which exemplify the ways that NICs and the developing countries have conformed to worldwide steelmaking trends.

Ladle Metallurgy In Brazil

In Brazil, the use of LM technology was launched in 1969, when an ASEA-SKF unit came into operation in Acos Villares. (At about the same time, Mannesmann, a reputable supplier of state-of-the-art technology, had already introduced a system of gas bubbling through a porous plug for bath homogenization.) Although companies only really started using LM on a large scale in 1980[184], LM use continues to increase in both electric steelmaking and BOF shops. From the operating results, it appears that the Brazilian steel industry has mastered LM technologies.

Ladle Furnace (LF) Technologies

Ladle furnace (LF) is the most widely used process in the Brazilian steel industry, and it is also the one which has shown the greatest potential for further growth. The first LF units to be installed in Brazil were those at Acos Villares in 1969 and at Acos Finos Piratini in 1973. These early units used a vacuum system and produced special steels for forging and rolling. From 1980 onwards, LF application was expanded to the manufacture of plain carbon steels as well as these special steels. Newer LF units are much simpler in design, and they dispense with the vacuum system. Some have no electromagnetic stirring: bath agitation is performed by argon bubbling through a porous plug.

In principle, ladles were used in electric steelmaking shops, but they were later applied in BOF shops as well. Steel treated by this process is used to achieve the following:
- Degassing and decarburization (in units with vacuum).
- Synchronization of primary steelmaking with continuous casting.
- Improved yields of alloy additions.
- Desulphurization.
- Reduction of tramp elements and other inclusions.

- Improved control over composition and temperature of steel.
- Increased productivity.

LF technology for the production of high-quality steel is readily available at competitive prices, and it can be easily implemented by a steelmaking facility. LM technology is thus enjoying increasing application in Brazil, other NICs, and LDCs and in all major steelworks of the world. LM processes are considered to be an important metallurgical tool in the modern steel industry.

TECHNOLOGICAL PROSPECTS FOR NICs AND LDCs

The LDCs' and NICs' struggles to be competitive in the world steel industry tend to lead them towards optimization criteria and to seek performance results that are often significantly different than those sought by already developed countries.

The Brazilian Experience

Today, the Brazilian steel industry is the sixth largest in the world with an installed capacity of about 27 million tons of steel per year. Brazil makes a full range of steel products, including flat, non-flat, carbon, stainless, and special alloy steels to meet the needs of the country's sophisticated industrial base and growing domestic economy, as well as for export markets.

Indeed, the Brazilian steel industry's prospects for growth are currently among the best in the world. Despite having one of the highest capital costs per ton of installed steel capacity, no major steel producing country (with the possible exception of South Korea) has lower steel production costs than Brazil. The Brazilian steel industry is clearly competitive internationally. With low labor costs per ton of steel produced and continuously improved productivity per man-hour, Brazilian steel producers should be able to maintain their competitive edge in cost even though wages are expected to increase continually (thanks largely to use of sophisticated management techniques and application of newer technologies, both proven and emerging).

Brazil's raw steel output is expected to be 25.5 million tons in 1989, up from 24.7 million tons in 1988. Exports, meanwhile, are expected to remain steady: about 11 million tons of semi-finished and finished steel in 1989, up from 10.9 million tons in 1988 (slab exports accounted for about 5 million tons in 1989). Brazil's largest producer of slabs, Cia Siderugica de Tubarao (CST), exported about 3 million slabs in 1989. Usiminas, also a large slab producer, exported about 0.4 million tons of slabs during the same period, including exports to Lone Star Steel and California Steel in the United States.

However, the combined effects of the 1977-1979 oil shock of rising interest rates on international loans and debts have been severe and long-lasting. Between 1980 and 1983, domestic economic depression lowered Brazil's per capita steel consumption by about 30 percent, and total domestic apparent consumption dropped by 40 percent. Total domestic apparent consumption gradually recovered in 1987 and even surpassed the 1980 levels, but per capita steel consumption still remained 20 percent below 1980 levels—at about 25 percent of US per capita steel consumption. The Brazilian steel industry was thus confronted with debt crisis and negative growth, particularly when its expansion to meet projected increased domestic steel demand was taken into account. Thus, the only choice remaining to the Brazilian steel industry—if it wanted to remain viable—was to export, which it did in hope of eventually achieving a share of the world export market consistent with its share of world steel production.

Domestic factors.

The decline in Brazil's domestic steel market and a slow economic recovery also slowed the steel industry's recovery. Brazil was also faced with several half-completed projects that it could not easily afford to complete, but which could not be canceled. Likewise, the industry was burdened with superfluous equipment that it could not easily discard. Neither could the completion of ACOMINAS and CST's two new greenfield plants be stopped. While the second National Plan called for the establishment of 50 million tons annual capacity by the year 2000, the project expansion had to be curtailed to a 30 percent increase of the installed capacity during the same period.

Thus, the Brazilian steel industry was forced to concentrate more on fulfilling optimization plans rather than on direct expansion plans. SIDERBRAS, the state-owned steel group, is now engaged in a project designed to boost the productivity levels of the completed integrated plants of COSIPA, USIMINAS and CSR, and it is engaged in further optimizing the steel product mix and applying environmental control measures.

The Indian Experience

Crude steel production in India during 1988 was 14.2 million tons; of this about 11 million tons were produced in the major integrated steel plants and the remaining 3.2 million tons in the mini steel plants based on the electric-arc furnace route using steel scrap and DRI sponge.

The first major integrated steel plant in India was set up in 1910-1911 by the Tata Iron and Steel Co. Ltd. (TISCO). This plant is still in use. It currently has a capacity of 2.2 million tons of crude steel per year; future expansion plans call for an increase to 3 million tons. TISCO is the only major integrated private sector steel plant in India, although there are also some semi-integrated steel plants in the private sector. All other major integrated steel plants are state-owned, including the new complex at Visakakpatnam, which is nearing completion. The Indian minimill industry belongs wholly to the private sector.

The technologies used in India's integrated steel plants vary widely, and India's plants were built at various times. As India lacked the funds to build its own plants, it was forced to rely on money available at various intervals from foreign financial aid agencies. India also lacked sufficient domestic steel expertise to develop its own technologies and plants, and so purchased its technologies from a variety of overseas technical collaborators who also often offered attractive aid packages.

However, India currently suffers with outmoded plants, low production efficiencies, and low production levels of poor quality products. Most Indian plants utilize a low proportion of sinter in the blast furnace burden (ranging from 30 to 40 percent); only one plant utilizes up to 62 percent sinter burden. Owing to high ash coke and adverse $A1O/SiO$ ratio in Indian iron ores, the coke consumption rate at Indian plants ranges from 680 to 1080 kgs/ton of iron. The production of the average Indian blast furnace is also low, with different plants ranging from 0.6 to 1.1 tons/cu.m/day. In fact, steel production in general is very low, with different steel plants ranging from 30 tons to 75 tons per man-year. The average energy consumed per ton of crude steel is also quite high, with plants using from 10 to 15.5 (G cal) million kilo calories. Forty-two percent of the total Indian crude steel capacity is still based on basic OH process. But LD oxygen steelmaking production is being expanded: the average number of heats ranges from 5,000 to 7,000 per year. The proportion of continuously cast steel produced in integrated steel plants is likewise low: a mere 12 percent—27 percent if the minimills are taken into account.

India's generally poor productivity, high energy consumption, and low yields lead to high steel production costs. Integrated steel plants have begun a massive modernization program to upgrade their production technologies and productivity levels, and to lower their operational and production costs. However, India's current steelmaking situation is dismal, and the country's overall optimization is one of the world's lowest. Crude steel production in India in 1988 totaled a mere 14.2 million tons; of this about 11 million tons were produced in major integrated steel plants while the remaining 3.2 million tons were produced in minimills using the EAF route with steel scrap and DRI sponge in charge.

What exactly are the reasons behind the poor state of the Indian steel industry? One of the most fundamental reasons, as touched on above, is that the Indian steel industry owes its very existence to "tied" technical and financial packages offered by foreign countries such as the former Soviet Union, the UK, and FRG. (For example, the steel plants at Bhilai and Bokaro were set up with Soviet collaboration, while those at Durgapur and

Rourkela were set up with British and FRG collaboration, respectively.) While these packages were initially quite affordable, they have often served to tie India to further reliance on the donor nations. The technologies offered by these "donor" nations have not always been the most modern or up-to-date. India has not been free to choose the optimum steel plant designs and equipment for its own industrial development and it has often suffered severe limitations in adapting and utilizing the donor technologies with its own natural, labor, and economic resources. (In contrast, steel plants in South Korea, Taiwan (ROC), and Malaysia were often able to select much more modern and efficient technologies. These countries' technology purchases—from Japan, for example—have yielded optimization characteristics and performance results that surpass the Indian steel industry's, both qualitatively and quantitatively.)

Since India's steel technology was purchased from multiple donors, each plant's facilities are different from one another. Further, no Indian plant incorporates the latest design or technologies. In particular, technology that was installed in the 1960s is the most obsolete. One glaring example is the jumbo slabbing mill at the Bokaro steel plant that was installed by the Russians in the 1970s. By the time of this installation, continuous slab casting was a proven technology, and plants in many nations were using it. However, a continuous slab caster has only been slated for the installation at Bokaro during this decade - almost a quarter century after Bokaro could have put this technology into production. Furthermore, Bokaro's jumbo slabbing mill is reportedly unable to cold-roll strip below 0.3 to 0.4 mm thick. The Bokaro plant has made up for this deficiency by installing separate cold-rolling mill stands from Wean-United (in the United States) to achieve 0.15 to 0.2 mm thickness required for tin plate production. Similarly, the Bhilai steel plant installed Soviet-built jumbo basic open hearth steelmaking furnaces of up to 500 tons capacity at the same time that, in Japan and elsewhere, LD oxygen steelmaking/BOF furnaces were being set up.

The performance norms of some Indian integrated steel plants are very low when compared with current international practice. With these outmoded, inefficient, and low-capacity technologies, it is little wonder that labor productivity in the Indian steel industry has consistently been one of the lowest in the world, as shown in Figure 8.9.

Figure 8.9
Steel plant productivity in tons of steel ingot produced per man-year

Years	Bhilai	Bokaro	Durgapur	Rourkela	IISCO	TISCO
1982-83	72	71	39	44	34	64
1983-84	63	63	34	42	28	64
1984-85	69	60	31	43	22	68
1985-86	68	65	37	46	30	68
1986-87	68	61	39	48	29	74

The Chinese Experience

The Chinese steel industry's growth in recent decades is a classic example of self-reliance combined with a judicious selection of foreign collaboration untied to foreign aid limitations. Starting almost from scratch after World War II, the Chinese steel industry has grown from 8 million tons per year output in 1958 to about 60 million tons in 1988-1989.

China adopted the BOF/LD oxygen steelmaking practice soon after the Rourkela steel plant in India put up its 40-ton BOF/LD vessels in 1950s. The first BOF/LD oxygen steelmaking shop set up at Shoude Iron and Steel Co., consisted of three 30-ton converters rated to produce 0.6 million tons of steel per year. Today, the same shop in China, still using the same converters, is producing 1.88 million tons of steel annually. (In contrast, the three 40-ton BOF/LD oxygen steelmaking converter shop at Rourkela was designed to produce 750,000 tons of steel per year; it is currently producing 500,000 tons of steel/year and the maximum the shop has ever achieved was 811,000 tons during 1965-1966.

The Experience of the Former COMECON Countries

The situation in the former CMEA (COMECON) countries is no different from that in India. Almost all the steel plants in the COMECON countries were built with Soviet collaboration. Thus, no universal optimization characteristics can be globally applied to the burgeoning steel industries in developing countries in which the Japanese steel industry has played a very valuable role, particularly in the case of South Korea, Brazil and China.

CONCLUSION

It is appropriate to stress that the steel industry's establishment and sustained growth in developing countries should not be left to the vagaries of bilateral financing and technical collaboration, but should be subjected to critical technical and economic evaluation by independent experts and industry sources. Developing countries have historically been plagued by and still struggle with obsolete technologies and technologies that do not match their resource mixes or development needs, and that have very little chance of significantly boosting their domestic economies or of allowing them to establish a prominent position in the world market.

Yet another typical illustration of this state of affairs is the installation of large continuous bloom casters in a steel plant. The continuously cast bloom is rolled in a billet steel rolling mill, and the final products are RCC rods, bars, and rounds that must be rolled from the billets in a merchant mill. A continuous billet caster would have been ideal for this plant, as it would have eliminated the capital costs of bloom and billet steel rolling as well as the even heavier capital cost of a continuous bloom caster. In this instance, the bilateral donor/technical collaborator simply did not have continuous billet caster technology to offer.

Such examples are legion throughout LDCs. Purchases often tie developing countries to donor nations' financial packages and technologies. Developing countries' selection of technologies and steelmaking equipment often tends to be based on non-technical factors—in other words, the developing nation must often take whatever the donor nation has to offer. For example, a leading developing country installed its first BOF/LD oxygen steelmaking plant in the late eighties. BOF/LD oxygen steel making technologies had been a proven technology since the early sixties, but this country has remained tied to BOH steel melting technology for those two decades because that is all its donor nation would sell. The history of the steel industry in developing countries is replete with such examples of empirical rather than optimized growth.

Developing countries must strive to optimize their steel industries, encouraging development and acquisition of the most appropriate technologies and the most efficient equipment and plant layout. That developing countries have not always done so in the past does not mean that such trends and history should repeat themselves in the future.

In short, developing countries' decisions regarding their steel industries should be based on sound technical and economic criteria designed to optimize their own domestic demands and opportunities instead of on political considerations. The steel industry in any nation is highly capital-intensive, and it is inextricably linked with a country's own economic and, often, political well being. Developing countries striving to attain self-direction and perhaps a world leadership position cannot afford to make any other decision.

NOTES

[166]   "Report on a Dynamic Analysis of the Steel Industry," *Nomura Research Institute*, Tokyo, 1983.
[167]   Adachi, Y.H., *Technology Development Policies Towards 21st Century*, Tostuko-Kai, Tokyo, October 1989.

[168] Choi, H.S., "Study on the Future Prospect and Development Strategy of the Steel Industry," *Journal of Korean Institute of Metals*, Vol. 22, No. 10, Seoul, 1984.

[169] ibid.

[170] "The industry suffered from poor integration, inadequate scale economies and superannuated equipment, and was unable to satisfy more than about one-fourth of South Korea's domestic steel demand." *Korean Development Bank (KDB)*, Industry in Korea 1976, pp. 50-53; *Korea News Review*, November 1983, p. 13.

[171] "In 1973 the World Bank refused to loan money to the POSCO project, considering it impractical." *Wall Street Journal*, May 13, 1981.

[172] Choi, H.S., "Direction for the Development of Iron and Steel Technology in the Newly Industrialized Countries," *Proceedings of the Sixth International Iron and Steel Congress*, Nagoya, Japan, ISIJ 1990, p. 43.

[173] Londono, G.T., "Growth in the Iron and Steel Industry in Latin America," *Proceedings of the Latin American Iron and Steel Congress*, ILAFA - 36, held in Cartagena, Colombia, September 17 to 20, 1995.

[174] Barnett, D.F., "US Profits, Capabilities and Resources," presented at *Steel Survival Strategies III*, New York, NY, June 21, 1988, pp. 23-24.

[175] Ziniga, L.J.A., "Trends in steel technology," presented at the ILAFA Congress-35 held in Santiago, Chile, September 20-23, 1994.

[176] Soares, R.C., "Technology and marketing positioning," presented at ILAFA Congress-36 held in Cartagena, Colombia, September 17-20, 1995.

[177] Barnett, D.F., "US Profits, Capabilities and Resources," presented at *Steel Survival Strategies III*, New York, NY, June 21, 1988, p. 24.

[178] Machado, O., "Raw materials," under the heading of "Competitivity of the Latin American steel industry," ILAFA Congress-36, Cartagena, Colombia, September 17-20, 1995.

[179] Blanchard, A. and Grander, F. Jr., *Ferrous Scrap Quality: The Steelmakers' Point of View*, Arthur D. Little, Inc., Cambridge, MA, March 1989.

[180] ibid.

[181]   Barnett, D.F., "US Profits, Capabilities and Resources," presented at *Steel Survival Strategies III*, New York, NY, June 21, 1988, pp. 23-24.

[182]   Mendoza, C., "Direct Reduction - General Overview," paper presented at the Latin American Iron and Steel Congress, ILAFA 36, held in Cartagena, Colombia on September 17-20, 1995.

[183]   Tivelius, B. et al., Elaboration de l'acier secondaire: Procedes actuels, In: Conference on Inclusions and Residuals in Steels: Effects on Fabrication and Service Behavior, Ottawa, Canada, March 1985.

[184]   Pimenta, J.L.R., Metalurgia da panela: objectivos e situaca do Brasil, *Metalurgia ABM*, 40(323) 1984.

IX

Future Research

This study began with an identification of the central technologies used by steel minimills to produce high-quality steel products from scrap iron. The rationale for this identification was to create a context within which international technology transfer could be examined.

A BRIEF REVIEW

Central to the creation of this context was the delineation of 15 central questions. These were then distilled into two crucial questions that are inextricably linked with two critical variables: capacity and demand. Specifically, the two crucial questions that evolved from the original fifteen are:

1. How is capacity built?
2. How is demand sustained?

An analytical framework was then derived by viewing these two issues in a two-step function in the context of:
- Independent variables
- Dependent variables.

The independent variables were identified as technological processes (Mildrex, HYL, and the Nucor continuous strip process) or feedstocks. Price was identified as the dependent variable, and it is the critical variable that has controlled the emergence of the steel minimill industry, which combines the three-step process of the electric-arc furnace (EAF), the ladle process, and continuous casting.

Even though the proprietary technological processes are statistically independent, four hypotheses were generated through the interplay of the independent and dependent variables. The hypotheses were centered around the miniaturization of the industry and the global competition that emerged toward the end of the 1980s. This global competition was based primarily on pricing of steel products but also on efficient organizational structures for corporate and political governance. In a nutshell, these hypotheses stated that the steel minimill industry responded to global competition through competitive pricing. This new competitiveness reconfigured the steel minimill industry. The challenges posed by this industry transformation are as follows:

1. How does international technology transfer facilitate and foster development of the steel minimill industry?
2. Within the technology transfer matrix, how do the supplier and the recipient of technology generate the expansion of the steel minimill industry?

A VIEW TO FUTURE STUDIES

The case study in Chapter 7 examines how Japan used technology transfer to rapidly develop its steel industry during the Meiji period. Japan, whose national economy was undergoing a rapid revolution during this period, relied almost exclusively on technologies purchased from Western organizations to develop its steelmaking capacity. Japan based its management practices on rational economic models, the efficient use of information technology (though this term was no coined until later), and organizations designed specifically to respond to cost competitiveness. the analytical schema used to discuss the Japanese steel industry's preeminence in utilizing new technologies, raw materials supply, and geographical location explains the continued modernization and rationalization of its steel industry.

Yet further work in this area could be undertaken. Japan's continuing efforts to modernize and rationalize its steel industry remain interesting. Specifically, further studies could examine the shifting dynamics of the automobile industry, the shipbuilding industry, and Japan's continued quest for alternative feedstocks and feedstock technologies. For example, as automobiles have become more compact, research and development efforts have created new materials in the form of plastic-steel mixtures that are extremely durable and much lighter than steel. (Likewise, technological advances have yielded steels with decreased tensilities and carbon contents.) And although automobiles have become smaller, oceangoing ships have grown larger while decreasing their dead-weight tonnage. The technological synergies which have given rise to this market shift would be an intriguing subject of further research.

On the other hand, Chapter 8 showed that the newly industrialized countries (NICs) and the less-developed countries (LDCs)—in contrast to Japan's example of economic growth—are preoccupied with finding substitutes for scrap, the principal feedstock of the minimill steel industry. It appears that the NICs and LDCs are not yet ready to follow Japan's lead, not yet ready to assimilate imported technologies or to develop new product line. Rather, they are focusing on using their existing natural resources and refining their technological processes (for example, manipulating pressure and temperature) to obtain higher yields from iron ore. Chapter 8 describes how two dominant steelmaking processes—the Mildrex process and the HYL process—have been effective in producing higher yields for LDCs and have helped to establish hot-briquetted iron (HBI) as a valuable commodity. Future research and development into new technological processes might produce methods of extracting even higher yields from ores. these technical developments would then open up exciting new avenues of inquiry. For example, are these processes evolutionary in nature, merely refinements to existing technologies? Or are they revolutionary developments that should be considered in the context of Schumpeter's perspective of creative destruction or in the context of the quantum leap, a current theory of strategic thinking. Another intriguing way of approaching such research would be to seek to validate either the Schumpeterian perspective or the incremental nature of technological developments in the steel industry.

This discussion in Chapter 6 describes a bivariate relationship between the suppliers and recipients of technology. The lessons to be drawn from this discussion are:

1. International technology transfer is based on continuous and close collaboration among equipment manufacturers, their suppliers, and mill operators. The industry recognizes that cooperation makes technology transfer possible and that minimill products can only remain competitive if the collaboration continues. Further, the sharing of proprietary knowledge generates improvements in steel products.

2. Examination of this close collaboration through a knowledge-based framework yielded an understanding of the extent of the technology being transferred, the effort required for the transfer, and the ability of the organization adopting the technology to be an active partner in the transfer process and to adapt to the change required by the new technology.

The theoretical basis of these two lessons was laid in Chapter 4, which identified the four technology transfer variables: the nature of the technology being transferred, the method of transfer, the character of the organization involved, and the environment (society) in which the transfer takes place. But it must be remembered that no researcher's treatment of these variables can be value-neutral—studies of technology transfer have proven this again and again. However, this study' has attempted to avoid this common problem by studying technology transfer through stock and flow variables. This methodology, derived from engineering control theory, has been proven and formalized within the field of systems dynamics.

STOCK AND FLOW VARIABLES—AN INTERACTIVE MODEL OF TECHNOLOGY TRANSFER

The use of stock and flow variables can form the foundation upon which an interactive model of technology transfer can be built. Such a model can help to determine the effectiveness of technology transfer, since the model can use negative and positive feedback loops to establish linkages and inter-dependencies within the transfer process; the feedback loops will then show quantitative linkages among the three flow variables.

Further, a systemic approach such as this has the advantage of incorporating exogenous variables such as the form of corporate organization between the supplier and receiver of the technology (e.g., a joint venture or other partnership strategy), the role of competition within the industry in which the technology is being transferred, the degree to which private enterprise exists in both the supplier's and recipient's countries, and the extent to which the industry is regulated. Stock and flow variables can offer a greater understanding of the mix and sequencing of these variables as well as the speed of their deployment. It seems intuitively obvious that such a model would also uncover phenomena such as private ownership within a climate of limited competition, corporatization without private sector entry, and privatization without effective regulation. These situations, as shown in Chapter 6, are relevant to the field of international technology transfer.

The modality of technology transfer observed in Chapter 6 was premised upon appropriability theory, market imperfections, and transaction cost (that is, the market's creation of conditionals for technology transfer). Continuous improvements within the minimill industry have led to ever-greater productivity and flexibility of production lines. An exciting avenue of research would be to determine how structural changes in the minimill industry facilitate this transfer of technological improvements.

This study has suggested that there are three dimensions to the process of technology transfer: the supplier, the recipient, and the changes occurring within the industry. There have been many studies on the supplier/recipient framework. However, to date, the dimension of change has not been incorporated into these studies.

Changes in technology transfer also have three components: the nature of the change, the degree of the change, and the scope of the change. These changes affect the way the industry is transformed, causing its re-engineering and streamlining. Other studies should be carried out to capture the dimensions of the changes that have already occurred in the industry as well as the changes that are expected to occur.

THE PATHFINDING NATURE OF THIS STUDY

An ideal model of technology transfer would perhaps model both the development of technological innovations and their spread throughout the industry. This model would provide a realistic and accurate representation of the technology, of the firm as the institution in which innovations are generated and adopted, and of the selection of different environments in which the firms operate. These three variables—technology, the firm, and the selection environment—are analytically separable but also intimately intertwined.

The foundation for any transfer of technology is the unit of the firm. The firm's response to information and uncertainty within its environment forms the basis of its ability to adopt transferred technology—or to disseminate the technology to be transferred. Chapter 6 developed a knowledge-based framework for technology transfer. This framework described the extent of the technology being transferred, the effort required for the transfer, and the ability of the adopting organization to adapt to changes necessitated by the technology and to interact in the transfer process. Indeed, the knowledge to be transferred itself often poses a difficult hurdle for the transfer process: since innovation escapes the neoclassical assumption of perfect information, it creates more information as well as more uncertainty.

Chapter 6 also showed that the more radical an innovation, the more information about it will be available. However, it has been shown that information about a new technology becomes more complete and more reliable as the technology is adopted and individuals and organizations learn how to use it more effectively. Further research into this phenomenon could help to determine ways in which difficult aspects of a new technology can best be communicated to new users or what mechanisms could help to ensure reliability of technological information. Future research would do well to focus on the completeness of the information for transfer.

In a related point, it is possible to view trajectories of technological development as simply the disaggregated decision rules that firms adopt—and change from time to time - concerning the characteristics of their products and processes. technological decision rules are characterized by stability over the short term, but evidence also shows that they may also be common to a very large number of firms or to whole industrial sectors.

This study has attempted to demonstrate the need for a systemic approach to the study of technology transfer, and it has done so with stock and flow variables. These variables are powerful analytical tools and they are a strong basis upon which an interactive model of technology transfer can be developed. No previous studies have used this method of assessing technology transfer. However, technology transfer should be viewed from the three dimensions, mentioned above, in which technological change is central to the transfer. As this study is analytical in nature, it should provide a fresh and meaningful path into future research on technology transfer in general.

Notwithstanding, this study does have its limitations. Minimill technologies are within the private domain and are proprietary in nature, so there is a paucity of reliable data available about them. Further, steel firms share technologies among themselves but do not make them publicly available. This limited information has, in turn, limited the possible depth and scope of quantitative analyses possible in this study. The use of interviews and questionnaires could overcome these constraints. Interviews can readily become the subjects of case studies (which subsequent studies could examine) and the knowledge thus gained could become the empirical foundation of future systemic models.

The model developed in this study has thus offered some perspective on technology transfer, but both model and perspective must be further developed. Although this study includes two case studies, I have not written them at a firm-specific level, a worthwhile approach that the questionnaires would have made possible. Questionnaires, in all likelihood, would also have made possible comparisons among countries of different levels of development. This type of information would provide valuable insights that would help public policy makers to develop regulations and other structures to foster technology transfer and to encourage continuous productivity improvements within firms. With this type of information, researchers and policy makers alike would also be more able to anticipate the effects of these policy measures.

In sum, this study breaks new ground. The central questions of capacity and demand have been examined through dependent and independent variables in an effort to demonstrate the responsiveness of demand and capacity to product pricing and to the spread of technology.

In closing, future research efforts would find a focus on recent advances in the mixing and sequencing of technology from the steel and the polymer industries to be especially worthwhile. Steel-polymer blends, as mentioned above, have permitted the two disparate market trends of smaller, lighter automobiles and of larger and more capacious ships. These blends make lighter steel possible and offer more flexible product avenues than have been possible before. While technology transfer formerly favored transferring methods of improving steel manufacture and on incremental improvements in steel qualities and products, the future of technology transfer within the steel industry should be focused more on transferring methods of improving steel properties. It should therefore be intuitively obvious that the mingling of these two previously separate areas of technology, steel and plastics, is one of the most important future directions for technology transfer within the steel industry.

Glossary

Abbreviations, Coined Words and Symbols

Alloys
: Metallic substances added to steel to enhance properties such as machinability or heat resistance.

Bar
: A shaped steel product available in many configurations, including rounds, squares, ovals, hexagons, and rectangles.

BOF/BOP
: (Basic Oxygen Furnace/Process) A steelmaking process that involves blowing high-purity oxygen onto the surface of a bath of molten pig iron. It has been the dominant steelmaking process in the United States since the 1970s.

Beam blanks
: Special shapes that are subsequently rolled into structural shapes, mainly I-beams.

Billet
: A square or rectangular semifinished piece of steel that is later rolled into a finished product, such as a bar.

Bloom
: A square or rectangular semifinished piece of steel (larger than a billet) that is rolled into a finished product, such as an I-beam or other shape.

241

Carbon steel	Steel whose properties depend mainly on its carbon content and microstructure (as opposed, for example, to alloy steels, which depend on alloying elements for their enhanced properties). Carbon steel accounts for the largest percentage of steel produced world-wide.
Coke	Material used in blast furnaces, formed by baking coal in the absence of air. Cokemaking is the largest source of pollution in the steelmaking process.
Cold-rolled/ cold-formed products	Flat-rolled products that are not heated immediately prior to rolling/forming. Cold reduction results in a product that is thinner, smoother, and has a higher strength-to-weight ratio.
Continuous caster	A machine that converts a heat of molten steel to semifinished shapes. The continuous casting process is more efficient and generally yields a higher quality product than the traditional ingot casting method does.
EAF	(Electric Arc Furnace) A device that passes a strong electric current through steel scrap, thereby melting it (because of scrap's high heat resistance) to be cast into steel shapes. Minimills and specialty mills use EAFs, as do some integrated mills.
Hot end	The melting, refining, and casting facilities of a steel mill.

Hot-rolled products	Flat-rolled products that are reduced to final thickness by heating and rolling at elevated temperatures (usually at a range of 815 to 1,205 degrees Celsius).
I-beams	Structural steel products shaped like the letter "I". Used in construction of bridges, buildings, and ships and for other construction purposes.
Iron	A common mineral found in the earth's surface in the form of iron mixed with rock, earth, or sand.
Ingot	A large steel shape, formed when molten steel is poured (teemed) into an ingot mold to solidify. The ingot is later reheated and rolled into a semifinished steel shape such as a billet, bloom or slab.
Integrated mills	Mills that follow all six steps of steelmaking (ore processing, cokemaking, ironmaking, steelmaking, rolling, and treating). Generally, integrated mills are substantially larger than specialty mills or minimills.
Ladle metallurgy	The practice of further steel refinement, performed in a ladle after partial refining of a heat in a steelmaking furnace.
Long products	Steel products that are not flat rolled.
Minimills	Mills that usually bypass the first three steps of steelmaking (ore processing, cokemaking, and ironmaking) and use scrap as the primary raw material in electric arc furnaces. Minimills occupy a growing share of the US steel industry.

Near-net-casting	Process of casting steel in a semifinished shape that requires only minimal physical alteration to produce finished products.
Open-hearth furnace	A reverberatory, regenerative steelmaking furnace that has largely been replaced by the BOF. It was the dominant process of steelmaking in the United States until the 1970s.
Pig iron	A metallic product of the blast furnace that is not usefully malleable. Contains over 90 percent iron and over 2 percent carbon.
Rationalization	Company efforts to improve ;its competitive position, usually in response to imbalance between capacity and production and poor financial performance. Rationalization typically includes sizable workforce reductions, plant closure, and modernization of remaining facilities.
Reconstituted mill	A mill whose financial structure has been substantially restructured, usually through bankruptcy or sale.
Rolling mill	Equipment that reduces and transforms the shape of semifinished or intermediate steel products by passing the material between rolls through a gap that is smaller than the entering material.
Secondary steelmaking	See "Ladle metallurgy".
Semifinished steel	Steel shapes such as billets, blooms, or slabs that are later rolled into finished products.

Specialty steels   Steel, such as stainless, heat-resisting, and tool steel, produced in volumes to meet specialized needs.

Steel   Alloy of iron and carbon, malleable as first cast, and containing by weight 2 percent or less of carbon. Many contain other elements, but iron must predominate over each of the other elements.

Structural shapes   Rolled flange-shapes having at least one dimension of their cross-section 76 mm or greater. Used mainly for construction purposes.

Tolerance   The expected deviation from industry-set dimensional specifications.

VRAS   Voluntary restraint agreement

Bibliography

Achilladelis, B., A.B. Robertson, and P. Jervis, *Project SAPPHO: A Study of Success and Failure in Industrial Innovation,* 2 vols., London: Centre for the Study of Industrial Innovation, 1971.

Adachi, Y.H., *Technology Development Policies towards 21st Century,* Tostuko-Kai, Tokyo, October 1989.

Adamson, R.E., "Functional Fixedness as Related to Problem Solving: A Repetition of Three Experiments," *Journal of Experimental Psychology* 44 (1952).

Adamson, R.E. and D.W. Taylor, "Functional Fixedness as Related to Elapsed Time and to Set," *Journal of Experimental Psychology* 47 (1954).

Agiletta, M. and R. Boyer, "Pôles de Compétitivité, Strategie Industrielle et Politique Macro-economique," *Working Paper CEPREMAP* No. 8223, Paris, 1983.

Ahlström, G., *Engineers and Industrial Growth,* London: Croom Helm, 1982.

Allan, G.C., *Japan's Economic Expansion,* McMillan Press, London, 1965.

Allen, Robert C., "Collective Intervention," *Journal of Economic Behavior and Organization* 4, No. 1, March 1983.

Allen, Thomas J., *Managing the Flow of Technology,* Cambridge, MA: MIT Press, 1977.

Allen, T.J., D.B. Hyman and D.L. Pickney, "Transferring Technology to the Small Manufacturing Firm: A Study of technology transfer on Three Countries," *Research Policy* 12, No. 4, August 1983.

Allen, T.J. and D.G. Marquis, "Positive and Negative Biasing Sets: The Effects of Prior Experience on Research Performance," *IEEE Transactions on Engineering Management* EM-11, No. 4, December 1964.

247

American Metal Bulletin, January 1992.

American Metal Market Co Metal Statistics: The Purchasing Guide of the Metal Industries, New York: AMM, various years.

Anderson, D.F., "Worldwide Political and Economic Change - Effect on the Iron and Steel Industry," *Ironmaking Conference Proceedings*, 1992.

Anderson, P. and M.L. Tushman, "Technological Discontinuaties and Dominant Designs: A Cyclical Model of Technological Change," *Administrative Science Quarterly* 35, 1990.

Anderson, W.A. and J. T. Arnold, "A Line-Narrowing Experiment," *Physical Review* 94, No. 2, April 15, 1954.

Ando, A. and A. Auerbach, "The Corporate Cost of Capital in Japan and the US: A Comparison," *Research Working Paper No. 1762*, Cambridge: National Bureau of Economic Research.

Annual Reports of NKK, 1987-1993, Tokyo, Japan.

Annual Reports of Usinor Sacilor, 1994, Paris, France.

Antonelli, C., *Cambiamento Tecnologico e Teoria dell' Impresa*, Torino: Loescher Editore, 1982.

Arocena, J., "La Création d'Enterprise," *La Documentation Française*, 1983.

Arrow, Kenneth J., "The Economic Implications of Learning by Doing," *Review of Economic Studies* 29, June 1962.

Avery, C.M., *Organizational Communications in Technology Transfer between a Research and Development Consortium and its Shareholders*, Doctoral Dissertation, 1989, College of Communications, University of Texas, Austin.

Aylen, J. "Plant Size and Efficiency in the Steel Industry: An International Comparison," *National Institute Economic Review* 100, May 1982.

Axelrod, Robert, *The Evolution of Cooperation*, New York: Basic Books, 1984.

Bailey, R.E., "The Development of a Practical Planning Framework for International Technology Transfer," in Technology Transfer in a Global Economy, *Proceedings of the Technology Transfer Society's 15th Annual Meeting*, Dayton, Ohio, June 1990.

Baker, W.J., *A History of the Marconi Company*, New York: St. Martin's Press, 1971.

Barnett, D.F., "US Profits, Capabilities and Resources," presented at *Steel Survival Strategies III*, New York, NY, June 21, 1988.

Barnett, D.F. and L. Schorsch, *Steel: Upheaval in a Basic Industry*, Cambridge, MA: Ballinger, 1983.

Barnette, H., *Address at the International Iron and Steel Institute Conference*, October 1994.

Bauer, M. and E. Cohen, *Qui Gouverne les Groupes Industriels?*, Paris: Editions du Seuil, 1981.

Beer, J.J., *The Emergence of the German Dye Industry*, Harmondsworth: Penguin, 1959.

Ben-David, J., *Fundamental Research and the Universities*, Paris: Organization for Economic Cooperation and Development, 1968.

Birat, J.P., "Manufacture of flat products for 21st century," *Ironmaking and steelmaking*, 14, 1987, No. 2.

Blanchard, A. and Grander, F. Jr., *Ferrous Scrap Quality: The Steelmakers' Point of View*, Arthur D.Little, Inc., Cambridge,MA, March 1989.

Boyle, K., "Technology Transfer between Universities and the UK Offshore Industry," *IEEE Transactions on Engineering Management*, (February 1986), Vol. EM-33, No. 1, pp. 33-42.

Brumer, W.L., "Improving efficiencies in Europe and Latin America," comments made at Steel Survival Strategies conference organized by the American Metal Market and Paine Webber, New York on June 21-22, 1994.

Buchner, A.R., Das symposium "Endabmessungsnables Giessen" der AIME, *Stahl u. Eisen* 109, 1989, No. 24.

Buer, T.K., "Investigation of Consistent Make or Buy Patterns of Selected Process Machinery in Selected US Manufacturing Industries," PhD dissertation, *Sloan School of Management*, MIT, Cambridge, MA, 1982.

Burns, T. and G. Stalken, *The Management of Innovation*, London: Tavistock Publications, 1966.

Carlsson, B., "Technical Change and Productivity in Swedish Industry in the Post-War Period," Stockholm: *The Industrial Institute for Economic and Social Research*, Research Report No. 8, 1980.

Carter, C., ed. *Industrial Policy and Innovation*, London: Heinemann, 1981.

Cartwright, J., *Steel Times*, January 1970.

Caves, R. and M. Uekasa, *Industrial Organization in Japan*, Washington, DC: Brookings Institution, 1976.

Cawson, A., P. Holmes and A. Stevens, *The Interaction between Firms and the State in France: The Telecommunications and Consumer Electronics Sectors*, Cambridge: Trinity Hall, England, December 10-13, 1985, Mimeo.

Centre d'Economie Industrielle, *Quelques Réflexions à Propos des Mécanismes de Trasnfert Etat-Industrie Mis en Oeuvre en France et en Allemagne*, Centre d'Economie Industrielle, Les Milles, n.d. Mimeo.

Centre for Metals Production, "Electric Arc Furnace Steelmaking: The Energy Efficient Way to Melt Steel," *CMP Tech Commentary*, Vol. 1, No. 3, 1988.

"Chemicals & Additives '83: A Modern Plastics Special Report," *Modern Plastics* 60, No. 9, September 1983.

Choi, H.S., "Study on the future Prospect and Development Strategy of the Steel Industry," *Journal of Korean Institute of Metals*, Vol. 22, No. 10, 1984.

Choi, H.S., "Direction for the Development of Iron and Steel Technology in the Newly Industrialized Countries," *Proceedings of the Sixth International Iron and Steel Congress*, Nagoya, Japan, ISIJ 1990.

Clark, K.B., "The Interaction of Design Hierarchies and Market Concepts in Technological Evolution," *Research Policy* 14.

Clarke, R.W., "Innovation in Liquid Propellant Rocket Technology," PhD Dissertation, *Stanford University*, Stanford, CA, 1968.

Cockerill, A., *The Steel Industry: International Comparison of Industrial Structure and Performance*, Cambridge, England: Cambridge University Press, 1974.

Cohen, H., S. Keller and D. Streeter, "The Transfer of Technology from Research to Development," *Research and Management*, Vol. 22.

Cohen, M. and M. Bauer, *Les Grandes Manoeuvres Industrielles*, Paris: Pierre Belfond, 1985.

Collins, E., *Corporation Income Tax Treatment of Investment and Innovation Activities in Six Countries*, Washington, DC: National Science Foundation, 1981.

Collins, E., ed. *Tax Policy and Investment in Innovation*, Washington, DC: National Science Foundation.

Collins, H.M., "Tacit Knowledge and Scientific Networks," in *Science in Context: Readings in the Sociology of Science*, eds. B. Barnes and D. Edge, Cambridge, MA: MIT Press, 1982.

Collis, D.J., "A Resource-based Analysis of global Competition: The Case of the Bearing Industry," *Strategic Management Journal*, 12, Summer Special Issue.

Commerce Clearing House, "National Cooperative Research Act of 1984 (Act of October 11, 1984, Public Law 98-462)," Trade Regulations Reports.

Commissariat Général du Plan, Aides à l'Industrie, 1982, Mimeo.

Committee on Science, Engineering and Public Policy, *Frontiers in Science and Technology: A Selected Outlook*, New York: W.H. Freeman, 1983.

"Construction Equipment: Ten Years of Change," *Engineering New Record* 21, February 1963.

"Consumption of Iron and Steel Products: *Evolution of the Specific Consumption of Steel*," Economic Commission for Europe, United Nations Publication, New York, 1984.

Cordero, Raymond, Serjeantson and Richard, (eds.), *Iron and Steel Works of the World*, 18th edition, London: Metal Bulletin Books Limited, 1993.

Corey, E.R., *The Development of Markets for New Materials: A Study of Building New End-Product Markets for Aluminium, Fibrous and the Plastics*, Boston: Division of Research, Graduate School of Business Administration, Harvard University, 1956.

Council of Economic Advisers—1981 Annual Report, in *Economic Report of the President*, transmitted to the Congress, together with the Annual Report of the Council of Economic Advisers, 21-213, Washington, DC: US Government Printing Office, 1981.

Dahlman, C.J. and L.E. Westphal, "The Meaning of Technology Mastery in Relation to Transfer of Technology," in the *Annals of the American Academy of Political and Social Science*, 1981.

Daly, A. and D.T. Jones, "The Machine Tool Industry in Britain, Germany and the United States," *National Institute Economic Review* 92, May 1980.

Darmon, J., *Le Grande Dérangement: La Guerre du Téléphone*, France: J.-C. Lattès, 1985.

Darnall, R.J., "Prospects for the US Steel Industry," *Financial Times Conference on the World Steel Industry*, held in London, England on March 5, 1995.

David, P.A., "Standards for the Economics of Standardization in the Information Age," in Dasgupta, P. and P. Stoneman (eds.), *Economic Policy and Technological Performance*, Cambridge, England: Cambridge University Press, 1987.

Demuki, N. and S. Sugiura, "Development of Reactor Steelmaking Process," *Proceedings of the Sixth International Iron and Steel Congress*, Nagoya, Japan, ISIJ 1990, Vol. 4.

Devine, M.D., T.E. James, Jr. and T.I. Adams, "Government Supported Industry, University Research Centers: Issues for Successful Technology Transfer," *Journal of Technology Transfer*, Vol. 12, 1987.

Dewar, R. and J. Dutton, "The Adoption of Radical and Incremental Innovations: An Empirical Analysis," *Management Science*, Vol. 32, 1986.

Dickson, K., "The Influence of Ministry of Defence Funding on Semiconductor Research and Development in the United Kingdom," *Research Policy* 12, April 19

Dimancescu, D. and J. Botkin, *The New Alliance: America's R&D Consortia*, Cambridge, MA: Ballinger Publishing, 1986.

Dore, R., *A Case Study of Technology Forecasting in Japan — The Next Generation Base Technologies Development Programme*, London: The Technical Change Centre, 1981.

Dosi, G., "Technological Paradigms and Technological Trajectories," *Research Policy* 11, June

Duncker, Karl, "On Problem Solving," trans. Lynne S. Lees, *Psychological Monographs* 58, No. 5, 1945.

Dunning, J.H. and R.D. Pearce, *The World's Largest Industrial Enterprises, 1962-1983*, New York: St. Martins, 1985.

Dupuy, F. and J.-C. Theonig, *Sociologie de l'Administration Française*, Paris: Armand Colin, 1983.

Earle, E.M., "Adam Smith, Alexander Hamilton, Friederich Liske: The Economic Foundations of Military Power," in P. Paretz, ed., *Makers of Modern Strategy*, Princeton: Princeton University Press, 1986.

Encaoua, D., P. Geroski and R. Miller, "Price Dynamics and Industrial Structure: A Theoretical and Economic Analysis," Paris: Organization for Economic Cooperation and Development (Economic and Statistics Department Working Paper No. 10), July 1983, Mimeo.

Enos, J.L., *Petroleum Progress and Profits: A History of Process Innovation*, Cambridge, MA: MIT Press, 1962.

Ergas, H., "Biases in the Measurement of Real Output under Conditions of Rapid Technological Change," *Organization for Economic Cooperation and Development* (Expert Group on the Economic Impact of Information Technologies, Working Party on Information, Computer and Communications Policy,) Paris, 1979.

Ergas, H., "The Inter-Industry Flow of Technology," *Organization for Economic cooperation and Development* (Workshop on Technological Indicators and the Measurement of Performance in International Trade,) Paris, September 1983.

Ergas, H., *Telecommunications Policy in France*, 1983, Mimeo.

Ergas, H., "Corporate Strategies in Transition," in A. Jacquemin, ed., *European Industry: Public Policy and Corporate Strategy*, Oxford, Oxford University Press, 1984.

Ergas, H., "Why Do Some Countries Innovate More Than Others?" *Centre for European Policy Studies Paper No. 5, Brussels, 1984.*

Ess, T.J., "The Hot Strip Mill Generation II," *Association of Iron and Steel Engineers*, Pittsburgh, 1970.

Ettlie, J.E., "The Commercialization of Federally Sponsored Technological Innovations," *Research Policy* II, June 1982.

Ettlie, J., W. Bridges and R. O'Keefe, "Organizational Strategy and Structural Differences for Radical versus Incremental Innovation," *Management Science*, Vol. 30, Mp. 6, June 1984.

Export-Import Bank of Japan, *Annual Reports* 1979-1981.

Farrell, J. and C. Shapiro, "Dynamic Competition with Switching Costs," *Rand Journal of Economics* 19, 1988.

Floud, R., "Technical Education 1850-1914: Speculation on Human Capital Formation," *Centre for Economic Policy Research*, London: April 1984, Mimeo.

Forman, P., *Industrial Support and Political Alignments of the German Physicists in the Weimar Republic*, Minerva, January 1974.

Fortune Magazine, "Steel: It's a Brand New Industry," December 1960.

Fox, J.R., *Arming America: How the US Buys Weapons*, Cambridge, MA: Harvard University Press, 1974.

Foxall, G.R., F.S. Murphy and J.D. Tierney, "Market Development in Practice: A Case Study of User-Initiated Product Innovation," *Journal of Marketing Management* 1, 1985.

Freeman, C., *The Economics of Industrial Innovation*, Harmondsworth, England: Penguin Books, 1974.

Freeman, R.B., *The Market for College Trained Manpower*, Cambridge, MA: Harvard University Press, 1971.

Freeman, R.B., *The Overeducated American*, New York: Academic Press, 1976.

Fritz, E. V. Pawliske, etc. "Scrap Melting with Effective Use of Fine Coal in 5-ton Test Converters," *Proceedings of the Sixth International Iron and Steel Congress*, Nagoya, Japan, ISIJ 1990, Vol. 4.

Furokawa, T., "Linking the Blast Furnace to the Electric Arc Furnace," *New Steel*, Vol. 10, No. 7, July 1994.

Gansler, J.S., *The Defense Industry*, Cambridge, MA: MIT Press, 1980.

Garvey, R., "Minimill Round Table Discussion," *New Steel*, Vol. 10, No. 4, 1994.

Garvey, R., "The 1993 Steel Survival Strategies (SSS) Forum," sponsored by *American Metal Market and Paine Webber's World Steel Dynamics*, June 1993.

Gaskins, D.W. Jr., "Dynamic Limit Pricing: Optimal Pricing under Threat of Entry," *Journal of Economic Theory* 3, September 1971.

Geiger, G.H., "Minimills, Technology and People," *ASM Metals Congress*, Detroit: September 19, 1984.

Geneva Steel Installiert Stranggiessanlage, *Stahl u. Eisen* 110, 1990.

George, K.D. and T.S. Ward, *The Structure of Industry in the EEC: An International Comparison*, Cambridge, England: Cambridge University Press, 1975.

Geroski, P.A., "Do Dominant Firms Decline?" *University of Southampton* Discussion Paper in Economics and Econometrics No. 8509, August 1985, Mimeo.

Glover, I. and P. Lawrence, "Engineering the Miracle," *New Society* 30, September 1976.

Glover, R.W., "Apprenticeship in America: An Assessment," *Proceedings of the Industrial Relations Research Association*, December 1974.

Godkin, L., "Problems and Practicalities of Technology Transfer: A Survey of the Literature," *International Journal of Technology Management*, Vol. 3, No. 5, 1988.

Golding, A.M., "The Semiconductor Industry in Britain and the United States: A Case Study in Innovation, Growth and the Diffusion of Technology," PhD. dissertation, University of Sussex, England, 1971.

Gönenç, R., "Electronisation et Réorganisation Verticales dans l'Industrie," Thèse de Troisième Cycle, Université de Paris, Nanterre, 1984.

Gönenç, R., "Changing Investment Structure and Capital Markets," in H. Ergas, ed., *A European Future in High Technology?*, Brussels: Centre for European Policy Studies, 1986.

Gönenç, R. and Y. Lecler, "L'Electronisation Industrielle au Japon," *Sciences Sociales du Japon Contemporain No 2*, Paris: Centre National de la Recherche Scientifique, Centre due Documentation Sciences Humaines, 1982, Mimeo.

Graham, T., *Proceedings at the Annual Conference of Chief Executive Officers of the Steel Industry*, held in New York by Paine Webber in June 1994.

Griliches, Z. and J. Schmookler, "Comment: Inventing and Maximizing," *American Economic Review* 53, No. 10, September 1963.

Grjebline, A., *L'ete d'Urgence*, Paris: Flammarion, 1983.

Hadley, E., *Japan's Export Competitiveness in Third World Markets*, Georgetown University, Washington, DC, 1981.

Hall, P., *Great Planning Disasters*, Berkeley, CA: University of California Press, 1980.

Hartke, V., *Iron and Steel Engineer*, January 1970.

Hatzichronoglou, T., "International Trade in High Technology Products: Europe's Competitive Position," in H. Ergas, ed., *A European Future in High Technology?*, Brussels: Centre for European Policy Studies, 1986.

Hayes, R.H. and S.C. Wheelwright, *Restoring Our Competitive Edge: Competing Through Manufacturing*, New York: Wiley, 1984.

Hecksher, E.F., *An Economic History of Sweden*, Cambridge, MA: Harvard University Press, 1984.

Henderson, P.D., "Two British Errors: Their Probable Size and some Possible Lessons," *Oxford Economic Papers* 29, July 1977.

Henderson, W.O., *The Rise of German Industrial Power 1834-1914*, Berkeley, CA: University of California.

Hess, G.W., "Minis Move Closer to Maxi Status," *Iron Age*, October 1992.

Hess, G.W., "Big Steel is Still Spending More Than $1 billion a Year," *Iron Age*, Vol. 9, No. 9, September 1993.

Hess, G.W., "A New Steelmaker Built in the Image of Nucor," *New Steel*, Vol. 9, No. 11, November 1993.

Hess, G.W., "Reclaiming Zinc from Electric-Furnace Dust," *New Steel*, Vol. 9, No. 12, December 1993.

Hildebrand, K.G., "Labour and capital in the Scandinavian countries in the nineteenth and twentieth centuries," in P. Mathias and M.M. Postan, (eds.) *The Cambridge Economic History of Europe: The Industrial Economies—Capital, Labour and Enterprise: Britain, France, Germany and Scandinavia*, Cambridge, England: Cambridge University Press, 1978.

Hirata, T., H. Ishida, etc., "Scrap Melting Process in a Steelmaking converter using Initially Charged Coke," *Proceedings of the Sixth International Iron and Steel Congress*, Nagoya, Japan, ISIJ 1990, Vol. 4.

Hitch, C.J. and R.N. McKean, *The Economics of Defense in the Nuclear Age*, Cambridge, MA: Rand Corporation and Harvard University Press, 1960.

Hodenheimer, A.J., *Major Reforms of the Swedish Education System 1950-1975*, Washington, DC: World Bank Staff Working Paper No. 290, 1978.

Hoeffer, E., "The Ups and Downs of Recycling Coated Scrap," *New Steel*, Vol. 10, No. 9, September 1994.

Hofer, P., F. Oeters, H. G. Geck, P. Patel, H.J. Selenz, "Scrap Melting with Cost-Effective Energies," *Proceedings of the Sixth International Iron and Steel Congress*, Nagoya, Japan, ISIJ 1990, Vol. 4.

Hogan, W.T., *Economic History of the Iron and Steel Industry in the United States*, vols. 1-5, Lexington Books, 1971.

Hogan, W.T., *Steel Capacities in Industrialized Countries*, Lexington Books, 1991.

Hogwood, B.W. and B.G. Peters, *The Pathology of Public Policy*, Oxford: Clarendon Press, 1985.

Hollander, S., *The Sources of Increased Efficiency: A Study of Du Pont Rayon Plants*, Cambridge, MA: MIT Press, 1965.

"How 'Silicon Spies' Get Away with Copying", *Business Week* 2633, 21 April 1980.

Huettner, D., *Plant Size, Technological Change and Investment Requirements*, New York: Praeger Publishers, 1974.

Imai, K., I. Nonaka and H. Takeuchi, *Managing the New Product Development Process: How Japanese Companies Learn and Unlearn*, Tokyo: Institute of Business Research Discussion Paper No. 118, Hitotsubashi University, March 29, 1984, Mimeo.

"*Impact of Developments in Scrap Reclamation and Preparation on the World Steel Industry*," ECA Steel Series 1993, United Nations, Geneva.

"*Impact of the Growing Use of Scrap in Western Industrialized Countries*," *Impact of Developments in Scrap Reclamation and Preparation on the World Steel Industry*, ECA Steel Series 1993, United Nations, Geneva.

IMS America, Semi-annual Audit of Laboratory Tests, Hospital Labs. January-June 1977; July-December 1977, Ambler, Penn: IMS America, n.d.

Ingham, J.N., "And the Earth Shifted," The Revolutionary World of Iron and Steel, 1985-1920," in *Making Iron and Steel*, Columbus, Ohio: Ohio University Press, 1991.

Institute for Defense Analyses, *The Effects of Patent and Antitrust Laws, Regulations and Practices on Innovation*, 3 vols., Arlington, VA: National Technical Information Service, 1976.

International Iron and Steel Institute (IISI) Bulletin, 1972.

International Iron and Steel Institute (IISI) Bulletin, 1993.

International Iron and Steel Institute (IISI), Tokyo Conference Report, 1969.

International Iron and steel Institute (IISI), Tokyo Conference Report, 1993.

Iron and Steel Institute in Japan, 1963.

Isenson, R.S., "Project Hindsight: An Empirical Study of the Sources of Ideas Utilized in Operational Weapon Systems," in *Factors in the Transfer of Technology*, ed. W.H. Gruber and D.G. Marquis, Cambridge, MA: MIT Press, 1969.

Itami, H., *Mobilizing Invisible Assets*, Cambridge, MA: Harvard University Press, 1987.

Jacobson, J.E., "Future Winners in World Steel: Minimills, Dofasco, China," *New Steel*, Vol. 10, No. 1, January 1994.

Jacobson, J.E., "Staying Alive in a Volatile Market," *New Steel*, Vol. 11, No. 7, July 1995.

Jacobson, J., "Old Steel and New Steel," *Iron Age,*, Vol. 9, No. 9, September 1993.

Japan Steel Bulletin, September 1991.

Jewkes, J., D. Sawers, R. Stillerman, *The Sources of Invention*, 2nd ed., New York: Norton, 1969.

Johnson, C., *MITI and the Japanese Miracle*, Stanford, CA, USA: Stanford University Press, 1982.

Johnson, P.S., *Cooperative Research in Industry: An Economic Study*, New York: Wiley, 1973.

Jones, I. and H. Hollenstein, *Trainee Wages and Training Deficiencies: An Economic Analysis of a 'British Problem'*, London: National Institute of Economic and Social Research Industry Series, No. 12, June 12, 1983, Mimeo.

Juhasz, A.A., Jr., "The Pattern of Innovation Exhibited in the Development of the Tractor Shove," SM thesis, *Sloan School of Management*, MIT, Cambridge, MA, 1975.

Kamien, M.I. and N. L. Schwartz, "Market Structure and Innovation: A Survey," *Journal of Economic Literature* 13, No. 1, March 1975.

Kamien, M.I. and N.L. Schwartz, *Market Structure and Innovation*, Cambridge, England: Cambridge University Press, 1982.

Kantrow, A.M., "The Strategy-Technology Connection," in *The Management of Technological Innovation*, Cambridge, MA: Harvard Business Review, 1982.

Kaplan, E., *Japan: The Government-Business Relationship*, US Department of Commerce, Washington, DC, February 1972.

Katz, B. and A. Phillips, "The Computer Industry," in R. Nelson, ed., *Government and Technical Progress*, New York: Pergamon Press, 1982.

Katz, M.L. and C. Shapiro, "Network Externalities, Competition, and Compatibility," *American Economic Review* 75, 1985.

Katzenstein, P.J., *Corporatism and Change: Austria, Switzerland, and the Politics of Industry*, Ithaca, NY: Cornell University Press, 1985.

Katzenstein, P.J., *Small States in World Markets: Industrial Policy in Europe*, Ithaca, NY: Cornell University Press, 1985.

Keeling, B., "The World Steel Industry," *The Economist Intelligence Unit, Structure and Prospects* in the 1990s, July 1992.

Kingston, W., *Innovation: The Creative Impulse in Human Progress*, London: John Calder, 1977.

Kitti, C., "Patent Invalidity Studies: A Survey," *National Science Foundation*, Division of Policy Research Analysis, Washington, DC, January 1976.

Klein, B., J. Kaufman and S. Morgenstern, "Determination of Serum Calcium by Automated Atomic Absorption Spectroscopy," in *Automation in Analytical Chemistry: Technicon Symposia*, Vol. 1, New York: Mediad, 1967.

Knight, K.E., "A Study of Technological Innovation: The Evolution of Digital Computers," PhD dissertation, Carnegie Institute of Technology, Pittsburgh, Penn., 1963.

Kodama, Fumio, "Technological Diversification of Japanese Industry," *Science 233*, No. 4762, 18 July 1986.

Kondo, H., N. Tamur, etc. "Application of Scrap-Melting Practice to Q-BOP and K-BOP," *Proceedings of the Sixth International Iron and Steel Congress*, Nagoya, Japan, ISIJ 1990, Vol. 4.

Kono, T., *Strategy and Structure of Japanese Enterprises*, London: MacMillan, 1984.

Konsynski, B.R. and I. Cash, Jr., "IS Redraws Competitive Boundaries," *Harvard Business Review*, March-April 1985.

Korean Development Bank (KDB), Industry in Korea 1976.

Korea News Review, November 1983.

Kotch, J.A., "Neighborhood Steelmaking: a Look at the Miniplants," *Iron and Steel Engineer Year Book*, 1991.

Kredietbank, "Mini Steelworks: Pygmies among Giants," *Weekly Bulletin*, March 27, 1981.

Kreps, D.M. and A.M. Spence, "Modelling the Role of History in Industrial Organization and Competition," in Feiwel, ed., *Issues in Contemporary Microeconomics and Welfare Analysis*, Cambridge, England: Cambridge University Press, 1985.

Kuster, T., "Wanted: Raw Residual Scrap," *New Steel*, Vol. 10, No. 4, April 1994.

Kuznets, S., "Inventive Activity: Problems of Definition and Measurement," in *The Rate and Direction of Inventive Activity: Economic and Social Factors*, a Report of the National Bureau of Economic Research, Princeton, NJ: Princeton University Press, 1962.

Laboratorio di Politica Industriale, *Materiali de Discussione*, Bologna: Laboratorio di Politica Industriale, November 1982, Mimeo.

Ladd, Hon. D., Commissioner of Patents, Statements before the Patents, Trademarks, and Copyrights Subcommittee of the Judiciary Committee, US Senate, September 4, 1962, re: S2225. Quoted in Elmer J. Gorn, *Economic Value of Patents, Practice and Invention Management*, New York: Reinhold, 1964.

Lafay, F., "Spécialization Française: Des Handicaps Structurels," *Revue d'Economie Politique*, (95)5, 1985.

Lankford, W.T., *The Making, Shaping and Treating of Steel*, Herbick and Held Publication, 10th ed., 1985.

Launer, H. and W. Ochel, "Industrielle Strukturenpassung: Das Japanische Model," Ifo-Schelldienst, September 26, 1985.

Lavington, S., *Early British Computers: The Story of Vintage Computers and the People Who Built Them*, Manchester: The Digital Press, 1980.

Laycock, C., G. Winfield, "Scrap and the Consumer," *Ironmaking and Steelmaking* 3, 1976, No. 6.

Leamer, E.E., *Sources of International Comparative Advantage: Theory and Evidence*, Cambridge, MA: MIT Press, 1984.

Lehmann, W.G., "Innovation in Electron Microscopes and Accessories," SM thesis, *Sloan School of Management*, MIT, Cambridge, MA, 1975.

Le Monde, "M. Jean-Jacques Duby quitte le CNRS," 6 February 1986.

Le Monde, "Le rapport hannoun soligue la forte concentration et la faible efficacité des aides publiques à l'industrie," 27 September 1979.

Levin, R.C., "A New Look at the Patent System," *American Economic Review* 76, No. 2, 1 May 1986.

Levin, R.C. and R.R. Nelson, "Survey Research on R&D Appropriability and Technological Opportunity, Part I: Appropriability," *Working Paper, Yale University*, New Haven, CN, July 1984.

Levitt, T., *The Marketing Imagination*, New York: Free Press, 1983.

Levonian, M., "*Steel Minimills and the Spatial Characteristics of Steel Demand*," MIT PhD thesis, December 1985.

Liebenau, J., "Innovation in Pharmaceuticals: Industrial R&D in the Early Twentieth Century," *Research Policy* 14, August 1985.

Lionetta, W.G., Jr., "Sources of Innovation within the Pultrusion Industry," SM thesis, *Sloan School of Management*, MIT, Cambridge, MA, 1977.

Lipsey, R.E. and I.B. Kravis, *The Competitive Position of US Manufacturing Firms*, Cambridge, MA: National Bureau of Economic Research Working Paper No. 1557, February 1985.

Londono, G.T., "Growth in the Iron and Steel Industry in Latin America," *Proceedings of the Latin American Iron and Steel Congress*, ILAFA-36 held in Cartagena, Colombia, September 17-20, 1995.

Lovatt, M., "United States Mills Play Safe," *Metal Bulletin Monthly*, March 1991.

Lucas, B. and S. Freedman, *Technology Choice and change in Developing Countries*, Dublin: Tycooly International Publishing, 1983.

Luchins, A.S., "Mechanization in Problem-solving: The Effect of Einstellung," *Psychological Monographs* 54, 1942.

Lynn, L.H., *How Japan Innovates: A Comparison with the US in the case of Basic Oxygen Steelmaking*, Boulder, Colorado: Westview Press, 1982.

Machado, O., "Raw Materials," under the heading of "Competitivity of the Latin American Steel Industry," ILAFA Congress-36 held in Cartagena, Colombia, September 17-29, 1995.

MacLaurin, W.R., *Invention and Innovation in the Radio Industry*, New York: MacMillan, 1949.

Mahon, J., "Trade Secrets and Patents Compared," *Journal of the Patent Office Society* 50, No. 8, August 1968.

Malerba, F., "Demand Structure and Technological Change: The Case of the European Semiconductor Industry," *Research Policy* 14, October 1985.

Mansfield, E., *The Economics of Technological Change*, New York: Norton, 1968.

Mansfield, E., et al., "Society and Private Rates of Return from Industrial Innovation," *Quarterly Journal of Economics* 91, No. 2, May 1977.

Marcus, P. and K. Kirsis, *Economics of the Minimill: World Steel Dynamics Core Report*, New York: Paine Webber, June 1994.

Marcus, P. and K. Kirsis, *Economics of the Minimill: World Steel Dynamics Core Report X*, New York: Paine Webber, 1984.

Marples, D., "The Decisions of Engineering Design," *IRE Transactions on Engineering Management*, June 1961.

Marx, Karl, *"Capital" A Critique of Political Economy*, 1867, Vol. 1 (Model Library Edition, ed. Ernest Untermann), New York: Random House, 1936.

Materials Advisory Board, Division of Engineering, National Research Council, *Report of the Ad Hoc Committee on Principles of Research-Engineering Interaction*, Publication MAB-222-M, Washington, DC: National Academy of Sciences, National Research Council, July 1966.

Maurice, M., F. Sellier, et al., *Politique d'Education et Organisation Industrielle en France et en Allemagne*, Paris: Presses Universitaires de France.

Mauss, M., "The Gift: Forms and Functions of Exchange in Archaic Societies," trans. I. Cunnison, Quotation from the Havamal, with selections from other poems in the Edda, xiv, Glencoe, Ill: Free Press, 1954.

McCardle, K.F., "Information Requisition and the Adoption of New Technology," *Management Science*, 1983, Vol. 31, No. 1.

McKenna, M., "Steelmakers' Focus on Survival Strategies," *Iron Age*, Vol. 9, No. 8, August 1993.

McManus, G.J., "Re-engineering the Steel Industry," *New Steel*, Vol. 10, No. 1, January 1994.

McManus, G.J., "Thin Slab Steel, DC Furnaces, Direct-Reduced Iron," *New Steel*, Vol. 10, No. 9, September 1994.

McManus, G.J., "A DC Furnace with Four Electrodes," *New Steel*, Vol. 10, No. 9, September 1994.

Meadows, D.L., "Accuracy of Technical Estimates in Industrial Research Planning: Data Appendix," *MIT Sloan School of Management* Working Paper No. 301-67, Cambridge, MA, December 1967.

Mendoza, C., "Direct Reduction—General Overview," Paper presented at the Latin American Iron and Steel Congress, ILAFA-36 held in Cartagena, Colombia, September 17-20, 1995.

Merton, R.K., *The Sociology of Science: Theoretical and Empirical Investigation*, ed. N.W. Storer, Chicago: University of Chicago Press, 1973.

Meyer-Krahmer, F., G. Gielow and U. Kuntze, "Impacts of Government Incentives Towards Industrial Innovation," *Research Policy* 12, June 1983.

Mietz, J., M. Bruhl, F. Oeters, "Stand der Verfahrenstechnik fur das Einschmelzen von Schrott mit Fossiler Energie," *Stahl u. Eisen* 100, 1990, Np. 7.

Milward, A.S. and S.B. Saul, *The Development of the Economies of Continental Europe 1850-1914*, Cambridge, MA: Harvard University Press, 1977.

Minimill Round Table Discussion held on February 16, 1994, in Nappa, CA, attended by John Correnti, President of Nucor Corp., Thomas Boklund, President and CEO of Oregon Steel SMA, Bob Higgins, Publisher of New Steel, with Bryan Berry, editor of New Steel as moderator.

Mining Journal, Issues of March 8th and September 6th, 1968.

Mitchell, J.P., "New Directions for Apprenticeship Policy," *Worklife* January 1977, Washington, DC: US Department of Labor.

Miyoshi, S., Address on the Japanese steel industry at the conference organized by the International Iron and Steel Institute held in Paris, France in October 1993.

Moffat, B.S., "The Growing Internationalisation of Steel," *Financial Times Conference on the World Steel Industry*, London, England, March 6-7, 1995.

Mori, K., "Autonomous Controllability of Decentralized Systems Aiming at Fault Tolerance," *Proceedings of the 8th IFAC World Congress*, Koyoto, 1981.

Mori, K., et al., "On-line Maintenance in Autonomous Decentralized Loop Network," *Proceedings of Compcon*, 1984, Arlington, Virginia.

Mori, K., et al., "Proposal of autonomous decentralized Concept," *The Institute of Electrical Engineers of Japan*, Vol. 104, No. 12, 1984.

Mori, K., et al., "Application of autonomous Decentralized System for Iron and Steelmaking Process Computer system," *The Hibachi Hyoron*, Vol. 70, No. 5, 1988.

Mowery, D.C., "Innovation, Market Structure, and Government Policy in the American Semiconductor Electronics Industry: A Survey," *Research Policy* 12, August 1983.

Mowery, D.C., "Economic Theory and Government Technology Policy," *Policy Sciences* 12, August 1983.

Mueller, D., "Persistent Performance Among Large Corporations," Brussels: Centre for European Policy Studies, November 1985, Mimeo.

Murray, C., *Losing Ground: American Social Policy 1950-1980*, New York: Basic Books, 1984.

Nakamura, T., *The Postwar Japanese Economy—Ots Development and Structure*, Tokyo: University of Tokyo Press, 1981.

Nakayama, S., (J. Dusenbury, trans.) *Academic and Scientific Traditions in China, Japan and the West*, Tokyo: University of Tokyo Press, 1984.

National Academy of Engineering, "The Competitive Status of the US Auto Industry," *Committee on Technology and International Economic and Trade Issues, Automobile Panel*, Washington, DC: National Academy Press, 1982.

National Manpower Council, *A Policy for Skilled Manpower*, New York: Columbia University Press, 1954.

National Science Board, *Science Indicators—The 1985 Report*, Washington, DC: National Science Foundation, 1986.

National Science Foundation, *Science and Engineering Personnel: A National Overview*, Washington, DC: National Science Foundation, 1985.

Nelson, R.R., "The Role of Knowledge in R&D Efficiency," *Quarterly Journal of Economics* 97, No. 3, August 1982.

Nelson, R.R., *High-Technology Policies: A Five Nation Comparison*, Washington, DC: American Enterprise Institute, 1984.

Nelson, R.R., ed., *Government and Technical Progress: Cross-Industry analysis*, New York: Pergamon Press, 1982.

Nelson, R.R. and S.G. Winter, *An Evolutionary Theory of Economic Change*, Cambridge, MA: Harvard University Press, 1982.

Nemeth, E.L., "Mini-Midi Mills—US, Canada, and Mexico," *Iron and Steel Engineer* 61, No. 6, June 1984.

Newell, A. and R.F. Sproul, "Computer Networks: Prospects for Scientists," *Science* 215, No. 4534, 12 February 1982.

New Steel, Vol. 10, No. 9, September 1994.

Nihon Kogyo, February 10 and September 17, 1975; *Japan Metal Bulletin*, January 23, 1995; *Far East Iron and Steel Trade Report*, December 1993 and December 1994.

Nijhawan, B.R., "Global Scenario of World Steel Industry Growth Particularly up to 1985," paper presented in Paris, France, on the steel industry in the 1980s, OECD Publication, February 1980, document No. 5

Nippon Steel Annual Report 1993.

Noble, D.F., *America by Design*, Oxford: Oxford University Press, 1977.

Noguchi, Y., "The Government-Business Relationship in Japan," in Yamamura et al., *Policy and Trade Issues of the Japanese Economy*, Seattle: University of Washington Press.

Nomura Research Institute, *Characteristics of Japan's Import and Export Structures*, Tokyo: Nomura Research Institute, 1983.

Nonaka, I., T. Kagono and S. Sakamoto, *Evolutionary Strategy and Structure — A New Perspective on Japanese Management*, Tokyo: Institute of Business Research Discussion Paper No. 111, Hitotsubashi University, March 1983, Mimeo.

Nove, A., *The Economics of Feasible Socialism*, London: George Allen & Unwin, 1983.

Office of Technology Assessment, "Technology Transfer to the Middle East," Washington, DC: US Congress, 1984.

Ohlsson, L.A., *Engineering Trade Specialization of Sweden and Other Industrial Countries*, Amsterdam: North-Holland Publishing Co.

Okita, S., *IISI Tokyo Conference Report*, 1969, p. 51.

Olson, M., *The Logic of Collective Action: Public Goods and the Theory of Groups*, Cambridge, MA: Harvard University Press, 1965.

Organization for Economic Cooperation and Development (OECD), *Liberalization of International Capital Movement: Japan*, Paris: OECD, 1968.

Organization for Economic Cooperation and Development (OECD), *Policies for Apprenticeship*, Paris: OECD, 1979.

Organization for Economic Cooperation and Development (OECD), *Industry and University: New Forms of Cooperation and Communication*, Paris: OECD, 1984.

Organization for Economic Cooperation and Development (OECD), *Mergers and Takeovers*, Paris: OECD, 1984.

Organization for Economic Cooperation and Development (OECD), *Changes in Working Patterns and the Impact on Education and Training: Human Resources Policies and Strategies in Germany*, Paris: OECD, 1986.

Organization for Economic Cooperation and Development (OECD), *North/South Technology Transfer: The Adjustment Ahead*, Paris: OECD, 1986.

Ozawa, K., F. Umezawa, et al., "Development of Scrap Melting Process and Behavior of Scrap Melting," *Proceedings of the Sixth International Iron and Steel Congress*, Nagoya, Japan, ISIJ 1990, Vol. 4.

Paine Webber cosponsored conference with the American Metal Market held on June 21-22, 1994 at Plaza Hotel, New York.

Pakes, A. and M. Schankerman, "An Exploration into the Determinants of Research Intensity," in *R&D, Patents and Productivity*, ed., Z. Grilliches, Chicago: University of Chicago Press, 1987.

Park, C.W. and V.P. Lessig, "Familiarity and Its Impact on Consumer Decision Biases and Heuristics," *Journal of Consumer Research* 8, No. 2, September 1981.

Patuzzi, A., K. Antilinger, H. Grabner, W. Krieger, "Comparative Study of Modern Scrap Melting Processes," *Proceedings of the Sixth International Iron and Steel Congress*, Nagoya, Japan, ISIJ 1990, Vol. 4.

Pavitt, K., "Sectoral Patterns of Technical Change: Towards a Taxonomy and a Theory," *Research Policy* 13, No. 6, December 1984.

Peck, M.J., "Inventions in the Postwar American Aluminium Industry," in *The Rate and Direction of Inventive Activity: Economic and Social Factors*, a report of the National Bureau of Economic Research, Princeton, NJ: Princeton University Press, 1962.

Peck, M. and R. Wilson, "Innovation, Imitation, and Comparative Advantage," in H. Giersch, ed., *Emerging Technologies: Consequences for Economic Growth, Structural Change and Employment*, Tubingen: J.C.B. Mohr, 1991.

Penson, S., "In-line Strip for Italian Minimill," *Metal Bulletin Monthly*, March 1991.

Perry, B.W., et al., *A Field Evaluation of the Du Pont Automatic Clinical Analyzer*, Wilmington, Del.: Du Pont, n.d.; 2nd printing, January 1978.

Peters, A.T., *Ferrous Production Metallurgy*, New York: John Wiley and Sons, 1982.

Peterson, T. and F.J. Comes, "An Electronics Dream That's Shorting Out," *Business Week*, March 4, 1985.

Pflaum, D.A., "Residual Problems and the Scrap Industry," in Residual and Unspecified Elements in Steel, ASTM STP 1042, A.S. Melilli and E.G. Mosbett, eds., *American Society for Testing and Materials*, Philadelphia, 1989.

Phillips, A., *Technology and Market Structures: A Study of the Aircraft Industry*, New York: Health Lexington Books, 1971.

Pickens, S.H., "Pultrusion—The Accent on the Long Pull," *Plastics Engineering* 31, No. 7, July 1975.

Pimenta, J.L.R., "Metalurgia da panela: objectivos e situaca do Brasil," *Metalurgia ABM*, 40(323) 1984.

Porter, H.E., ed., *Competition in Global Industries*, Boston, MA: Harvard Business School Press, 1986.

Prahalad, G. and Y. Dox, *The Multinational Mission: Balancing Local Demands and Global Vision*, New York: Free Press, 1987.

Prais, S.J., *Productivity and Industrial Structure*, Cambridge: Cambridge University Press, 1981.

Prais, S.J. and K. Wagner, *Schooling Standards in Britain and Germany: Some Summary Comparisons Bearing on Economic Efficiency*, London: National Institute Discussion Paper No. 60, 1983.

Prais, S.J. and K. Wagner, "Some Practical Aspects of Human Capital Investment: Training Standards in Five Occupations in Britain and Germany," *National Institute Economic Review*, August 1983.

Pratten, C.F., *Economies of Scale in Manufacturing Industry*, Cambridge: Cambridge University Press, 1971.

Pratten, C.F., *A Comparison of the Performance of Swedish and UK Companies*, Cambridge: Cambridge University Press, 1976.

Proceedings of the European World Steel Conference of the International Iron and Steel Institute, Paris, France, October 1993.

"Production, Processing and Usage of Steel, *Evolution of the Specific Consumption of Steel,*" Economic Commission for Europe, United Nations Publication, New York, 1984.

Rautel, C.S. and R.J. Liedtke, "Automated Enzymic Measurement of Total Cholesterol in Serum," *Clinical Chemistry* 24, No. 1, January 1978.

Rauch, J.A., ed., *The Kline Guide to the Plastics Industry*, Fairfield, NJ: Charles H. Cline, 1978.

Regan, D.T. and R. Fazio, "On the Consistency Between Attitudes and Behavior: Look to the Method of Attitude Formation," *Journal of Experimental Social Psychology* 13, No. 1, January 1977.

"Report on a Dynamic Analysis of the Steel Industry," *Nomura Research Institute*, Tokyo, Japan, 1983.

Riche, R.W., D.E. Hecker and J.U. Bergen, "High Technology Today and Tomorrow: A Small Slice of the Employment Pie," *Monthly Labor Review*, November 1983.

Ritt, A., "Managing Change in the World Steel Market," *New Steel*, Vol. 10, No. 8, August 1994.

Roberts, E.B., "Exploratory and Normative Technological Forecasting: A Critical Appraisal," *Technological Forecasting* 1, 1969.

Roberts, J.H. and G.L. Urban, "New Consumer Durable Brand Choice: Modeling Multiattribute Utility, Risk and Dynamics," *MIT Sloan School of Management* Working Paper No. 1636-85, Cambridge, MA, 1985.

Robertson, S., "Minimill Priorities: Thin-slab Steel DC Furnaces, Direct-reduced Iron," *New Steel*, Vol. 10, No. 9, 1994.

Robertson, S., "New Minimills Invade the High Quality Bar Market," *New Steel*, Vol. 10, No. 7, 1994.

Robson, M., J. Townsend and K. Pavitt,, "Sectoral Patterns of Production and use of Innovations in the UK: 1945-1983," *Centre for Science, Technology and Energy Policy* (Economic and Social Research Council), May 30, 1985, Mimeo.

Roger, E.M. and F.F. Shoemaker, *Communication of Innovations: A Cross-Cultural Approach*, 2nd ed., New York: Free Press, 1971.

Rosenberg, N., *Perspectives on Technology*, Cambridge: Cambridge University Press, 1976.

Rosenberg, N. and L.E. Birdzell, Jr., *How the West Grew Rich: The Economic Transformation of the Industrial World*, New York: Basic Books, 1986.

Rosenberg, R.S., "Technological Innovation in Firms and Industries: An Assessment of the State of the Art," in *Technological Innovation: A Critical Review of Current Knowledge*, eds., P. Kelly and M. Kranzberg, San Francisco: San Francisco Press, 1978.

Rotemberg, J.J. and G. Saloner, *A Supergame-Theoretic Model of Business Cycles and Price Wars During Booms*, Cambridge, MA: MIT Working Paper No. 349, July 1984, Mimeo.

Rothwell, R., et al., "SAPPHO Updated—Project SAPPHO Phase II," *Research Policy* 3, 1974.

Rothwell, R. and W. Zegveld, *Innovation and the Small and Medium Sized Firm*, Hingham, MA: Kluwer-Nijhof, 1981.

Rothwell, R. and W. Zegveld, *Industrial Innovation and Public Policy*, Westport, Conn: Greenwood Press, 1981.

Russell, C. and W. Vaughan, *Steel Production: Process Products and Residuals*, Baltimore, MD: The Johns Hopkins University Press, 1976.

Ryan, P., "Job Training, Employment Practices and the Large Enterprise: The Case of Costly Transferable Skills, in O. Osterman, ed., *Internal Labor Markets*, Cambridge, MA: MIT Press, 1984.

Samire, S. and K. Roth, 'The Influence of Global marketing Standardization on Performance," *Journal of Marketing*, 56 (2), 1992.

Saxonhouse, G.R., "What is All This About 'Industrial Targeting' in Japan?" *World Economy*, September 1984.

Schelling, T.C., *Choice and Consequence*, Cambridge, MA: Harvard University Press, 1984.

Scherer, F.M., Inter-industry Technology Flows in the United States," *Research Policy* 11, August 1982.

Scherer, F.M., *Innovation and Growth: Schumpeterian Perspectives*, Cambridge, MA: MIT Press, 1984.

Scherer, F.M., et al., *Patents and the Corporation*, 2nd ed., Boston: James Galvin and Associates, 1959.

Scherer, F.M. and D. Ravenscraft, "Growth Diversification: Entrepreneurial Behavior in Large-scale United States Enterprises," *Zeitschrift fur Nationalokonomi*, Suppl. 4, 1984.

Schmalensee, R., "Product Differentiation Advantages of Pioneering Brands," *American Economic Review* 72, June 1982.

Schmookler, J., "Changes in Industry and in the State of Knowledge as Determinants of Industrial Innovation," in *The Rate and Direction of Inventive Activity: Economic and Social Factors*, A report of the National Bureau of Economic Research, Princeton, NJ: Princeton University Press, 1962.

Schon, D.A., *Technology and Change*, New York: Delacorte Press, 1967.

Schroter, L., "Steel Works Now!: The Conflicting Character of Modernization," paper presented to the International Institute of Management Conference, Berlin, Germany, 1982.

Schumpeter, J.A., *Capitalism, Socialism and Democracy*, 3rd ed., New York: Harper & Row, 1950.

Science and Technology Agency, (Japan), 1985, White Paper on Science and Technology 1986, Tokyo: Foreign Press Center of Japan.

"Scrap Magnet," *New Steel*, Vol. 10, No. 6;, June 1994.

Shapley, D., "Electronics Industry Takes to 'Potting' Its Products for Market," *Science* 202, No. 4370, 24 November 1978.

Shaw, B., "Appropriation and Transfer of Innovation Benefit in UK Medical Equipment Industry," *Technovation* 4, No. 1, February 1986.

Shimshoni, D., "Aspects of Scientific Entrepreneurship," PhD. dissertation, Harvard University, Cambridge, MA, 1966.

Shinshara, M., *Structural Changes in Japan's Economic Development*, Tokyo: Konokuniya, 1970.

Shonfield, A., *Modern Capitalism*, Oxford: Oxford University Press, 1965.

Sitting, M., *PoliAcetyl Resins*, Houston, Tex.: Gulf Publishing Company, 1983.

Skinner, W. and D. Rogers, *Manufacturing Policy in the Electronics Industry: A Casebook of Major Production Problems*, 3rd ed., Homewood, Ill.: Richard D. Irwin, 1968.

Smith, Adam, *An Inquiry into the Nature and Causes of the Wealth of Nations*, (1776; 5th ed. 1789), New York: Random House, 1937.

Smithson, L.H., *Overview of the Clinical Laboratory Market*, Menlo Park, CA: Stanford Research Institute, n.d.

Soares, R.C., "Technology and Marketing Positioning," presented at ILAFA Congress-36 held in Cartagena, Colombia, September 17-20, 1995.

Solow, R., "Technical Change and the Aggregate Production Function," *Review of Economics and Statistics* 39, No. 3, August 1957.

Spital, F.C., "The Role of the Manufacturer in the Innovation Process for Analytical Instruments," PhD. dissertation, Sloan School of Management, MIT, Cambridge, MA, 1978.

Steffen, R., 16 OBM/Q-BOP-Lizenznehmer-Konferenz, *Stahl u. Eisen* 110, 1990, No. 5.

Stevens, B., "Labour Markets, Education and Industrial Structure," in H. Ergass, ed., *A European Future in High Technology?* Brussels: Centre for European Policy Studies, 1986.

Stigler, G.J., *The Organization of Industry*, Homewood, Ill.: Richard D. Irwin, 1968.

Stokaugh, R. and L.T. Wells, *Technology Crossing Borders: The Choice, Transfer, and Management of International Technology Flows*, Boston: Harvard Business School Press, 1984.

Stone, P.B., *Japan Surges Ahead*, European Coal and Steel Community (ECSC) Publication, 1969.

"Sumitomo's Great Leap Forward," *Iron and Steel Engineer*, December 1969.

Summers, L.H.N. Birdall, et al, "Strategies for Rapid Accumulation," *The East Asian Miracle: Economic Growth and Public Policy*, Oxford University Press, pp. 191-258.

Suzuki, K., "An Empirical Analysis of the Interdependence of R&D Investment and Market Structure in Japan," Tokyo: Research Institute of Capital Formation, The Japan Development Bank Staff Paper No. 4, October 1985, Mimeo.

Tachibanki, T., "Labour Mobility and Job Tenure," in M. Ac, ed., *The Economic Analysis of the Japanese Firm*, Amsterdam: North-Holland, 1984.

Takechi, K., *Basic Research into the Postal-Transport History of Early Meiji*, Tokyo: Yusankaku, 1978.

Takeda, K. and S. Narita, "Developments in Research on the LD and OG Processes and their Industrialization," *Journal of the Iron and Steel Institute*, May 1966.

Tanake, S., "Iron Ore Industry Problems as Viewed by a Consumer," *Business Review* 1970.

Teoh, L.L., "Electric arc furnace technology: Recent developments and future trends," *Ironmaking and Steelmaking*, 16(5) 1989.

Teubal, M. and E. Steinmueller, "Government policy, innovation and economic growth," *Research Policy* 11, October 1992.

Tilton, J.E., *International Diffusion of Technology: The Case of Semiconductors*, Washington, DC: Brookings Institution, 1971.

Tivelius, B, et al., Elaboration de l'acier secondaire: Procedes actuels, In: Conference on Inclusions and Residuals in Steels: Effects on Fabrication and Service Behavior, Ottawa, Canada, March 1985.

Torgenson, W.S., *Theory and Methods of Scaling*, New York: Wiley, 1958.

Torikoshi, H., et al, "Application and evaluation of autonomous decentralized system for iron and steel processes," *Kawasaki Steel Technical Report*, Vol. 20, No. 3, 1988.

Tyre, M.J., "Managing the introduction of new process technology: international differences in a multi-plant network," *Research Policy* 22, 1991.

Uena, H., "Conception and evaluation of Japanese industrial policy," *Japanese Economic Studies*, Winter (1976-77), 1977.

United Nations, "Strategy for energy use in the iron and steel industry," *Economic Commission for Europe*, ICE/STEEL/41, UN, Geneva, April 1984.

United Nations, *World Iron Ore Resources and Their Utilization*, 1950.

United Nations, The Steel Market in 1992, Economic Commission for Europe, New York, 1993.

US Trade Commission, *Steel Sheet and Strip Industry*, Washington, DC: 1981.

Urban, G.L. and J. R. Hauser, *Design and Marketing of New Products*, Englewood Cliffs, NJ: Prentice-Hall, 1980.

Urban, G.L. and E. von Hippel, "Lead user analyses for the development of new industrial products," MIT Sloan School of Management Working Paper No. 1797-86, Cambridge, MA, June 1986.

Utterback, J.M., "The Process of Inovation: A Study of the Organization and Development of Ideas for New Scientific Instruments," *IEEE Transactions on Engineering Management*, Vol. EM-18, No. 4, November 1971, pp. 124-131.

Utterback, J.M. and W. Abernathy, "A dynamic model of process and product innovation," *Omega, the International Journal of Management Science* 3, No. 6, 1975.

Vernon, R., "International investment and international trade in the product cycle," *Quarterly Journal of Economics* 80, May 1966.

Vernon, B., *Big Business and the State: Changing Relations in Western Europe*, London: MacMillan, 1974.

Vernon, R., "The product cycle hypothesis in a new international environment," *Oxford Bulletin of Economics and Statistics* 41, November 1979.

von Hippel, E., "Appropriability of Innovation benefit as a predictor of the source of innovation," *Research Policy* 11, No. 2, April 1982.

von Hippel, E. and S.N. Finkelstein, "Analysis of innovation in automated clinical chemistry analyzers," *Science and Public Policy* 6, No. 1, February 1979.

Wall Street Journal, May 13, 1981.

Webbink, D.M., *The semiconductor Industry*, Washington, DC: Government Printing Office, 1977.

Weinberg, A.M., *Reflections on Big Science*, Oxford: Pergamon Press, 1967.

White, W., "Effective transfer of technology from research to development," *Research Management*, 1990, Vol. 20.

Williams, W.F., "The American steel industry in the 90s: Can it meet the challenges?" *Iron and Steel Engineer*, November 1991.

Williamson, O.E., "Innovation and market structure," *Journal of Political Economy* 73, No. 1, February 1965.

Wilson, R.A., "The Sale of Technology Through Licensing," PhD. dissertation, Yale University, New Haven, Conn., 1975.

Worswick, G.D., ed., *Education and Economic Performance*, Aldershot, England: Gower Publishing Company, 1985.

Writson, W.B., *The Twilight of Sovereignty*, New York: Charles Scribner & Sons, 1992.

Wu, Whang Zhen, Paper presented at Steel Survival Strategies (SSS), organized by the American Metal Market and Paine Webber on June 21-22 at Plaza Hotel, New York.

Yorsz, W., "A study of the innovative process in the semiconductor industry," SM thesis, Sloan School of Management, MIT, Cambridge, MA, 1976.

Young, S. and A. Lowe, *Intervention in the Mixed Economy*, London: Croom Helm, 1974.

Zimmermann, W., et al., "Statistische einstazoptimierung bei einem electrolichtbogenofen," *Stahl u Eisen* 103, No. 18, 1983.

Ziniga, L.J.A., "Trends in steel technology," presented at the ILAFA Congress-35 held in Santiago, Chile, September 20-23, 1944.

Zucherman, A., "Mix reviews for ISO 9000," *New Steel*, Vol. 10, No. 2, February 1994.

Index

Acme Metals, 124
Administrative environmental
variables, 81
AGC (automatic gauge control)
systems, 100
Alloy design, aim of, 8
Alloys, 241
Anecdotal normative approach to
technology transfer, 77-
78
Appropriability models of
technology transfer, 76
Arab world, scrap in, 47-48
Automated systems, 33
Automatic gauge control (AGC)
systems, 100

Baghouse dust, zinc in, 136
Bar, 241
Bar mills, 114
Basic-oxygen process (BOF), 4, 5-
6
Beam blanks, 241
Bethlehem Steel, 110
Bibliography, 247-275
Billet, 241

Blast oxygen furnace, placing
more scrap in, 132
Bloom, 241
Blooming and slabbing mills, 97
BOF (basic-oxygen process), 4, 5-6
BOF/BOP, 241
Boron, 8
Brazil, ladle metallurgy processes
in, 222
Brazilian steel industry, 223-225

CAD/CAM control systems, 24-
25
Canada, 140
Capital requirements, 85-86
Capital (or "old") scrap, 28
Carbon content, 8
Carbon steel, 242
Carbon steel scrap, 30
Cast iron scrap, 30
Casting, continuous, see
Continuous casting
China, 75
technology transfer to, 156-
157
Chinese steel industry, 228-229
Circulating scrap, 27

Cleanness
    of scrap, 30
    of steel, 25
Coal based ironmaking, 132-133
Coated sheets and plates, 102
Coke, 242
Coke oven/blast furnace/basic
        oxygen furnace
        (CO/BF/BOF) process,
        207
Cold-rolled/cold-formed
        products, 242
Cold-rolling strip
    reversing mills for, 102
    tandem mills for, 101-102
Compact strip production (CSP)
        mills, 122, 123, 124-125
Competition, global, 22
Conservation of natural
        environmental
        equilibrium, 33-34
Continuous billet mills, 97
Continuous casters, 242
    described, 12-13
Continuous casting, 6-7
    increase in, 211
    literature review, 93-96
Continuous strip production
        (CSP) technology, 21
Corex plant, 132-133
Corporate hierarchies, 18
CSP (compact strip production)
        mills, 122, 123, 124-125
CSP (continuous strip production
        technology, 21
Cultural environmental variables,
        81

De-zincing, thermal, 135

Decarburization, 90-91
Degassing, 91
Deoxidation, 91-92
Desulphurization, 91
Developing countries, production
        shift toward, 74
Direct reduced iron (DRI), 20-21
Direct reduction
    in Latin America, 205-217
    minimills based on, 15
Direct reduction/electric arc
        furnace (DR/EAF), 214-
        217
Dissemination models of
        technology transfer, 76-
        77
Dominant players, 70-71
DRI (direct reduced iron), 20-21
Dynamic taxonomy of technology
        transfer, 82-85

EAF, *see* Electric arc furnaces
Eastern Europe, 138
EC, *see* European Community
Economic development
    steel industry and, 202-204
    world-wide, 72
Economic environmental
        variables, 80-81
Economic transactions, 18
Electric arc furnaces (EAF), 4, 5-6,
        39-40, 242
    described, 12
    scrap and, 142-143
    scrap-based, 210-214
Electric oxygen furnace (EOF)
        process, 16
Electroslag remelting process, 89
Employment costs, 119-120

Energy consumption, 61
  by Japanese steel industry, 184
Energy intensity, steel industry and, 64
Entry and exit, 120-122
Entry induction, 67-69
Environmental equilibrium, natural, conservation of, 33-34
Environmental variables, 78, 80-81
EOF (electric oxygen furnace) process, 16
Europe, technology transfer to, 157
European community (EC)
  scrap in, 45
  scrap resources in, 55
Exit and entry, 120-122

Ferrous scrap reclamation industry, 34-35
Flow variables, 82, 237
Four-high heavy plate mills, 99-100
France, 140

Gallatin Steel, 125
Geographic variety, 70
Global competition, 22
Globalization effect, 72-76
Glossary, 241-245
Gross national product (GNP), 201-202, 206

HBI (hot briquette iron), 21
HCI (high carbon iron), 21
Heavy-section mills, 97-98

High carbon iron (HCI), 21
Home scrap, 28
Hot briquette iron (HBI), 21
Hot end, 242
Hot-rolled products, 243
Hot-rolled strip production, 50
Hot-strip mills, 6-7, 114, 115
HYL process, 21

I-beams, 243
ICM (integrated compact mill), 155-156
In-line mills, 114
In-line strip mills, 123-124
Indian steel industry, 225-228
Infrastructural environmental variables, 81
Ingot, 243
Injection, 90
Instrip production process (ISP), 155
Integrated compact mill (ICM), 155-156
Integrated mills, 3-4, 243
  capacities of, 109
  compared with minimills, 107-126
  employment costs, 119
  entry and exit, 121-122
  future of technology for, 116
  geographic locations of, 109-110
  product types, 108
  productivity of, 116, 117-118
  raw materials for, 112-113
  technology of, 113, 114-115
Inter industry technology transfer, 149-154

International technology transfer,
        129-159
Ipsco minimill, 122-124
Iron, 243
Iron-bearing waste, 27
Iron carbide, post combustion of,
        133-135
Iron-ore systems, scrap systems
        compared with, 62
Iron ores, 26
    in steelmaking, 63
Ironmaking processes
    coal based, 132-133
    in commercial production,
        153
    under development, 154
    new, with computer-aided
        techniques, 210
ISP (instrip production process),
        155

Japan, 75, 145-146
    capacity of degassing
        facilities in, 186
    Inland Sea coasting, 178
    Osaka district, 180
    scrap in, 44
    scrap resources in, 56
    Tokyo Bay area, 179
Japanese steel industry
    case study of, 165-195
    characteristics of, 181-190
    energy consumption by, 184
    evolution of, 165-173
    government support of, 191-
        195
    layered software architecture
        in, 170, 171
    locations for, 173-180

    maps of, 175, 178-180
    MITI and, 192-195
    new technologies in, 166-172
    raw materials supply in, 172-
        173
    work force loyalty in, 191

Kawasaki Steel, 150-151
Knowledge architecture, 131-143
Knowledge-based framework of
        technology transfer, 129-
        130
Korea, 75

Ladle furnace technologies, 222-
        223
Ladle furnaces, 5-6
Ladle metallurgy, 243
Ladle metallurgy processes, 217-
        222
    in Brazil, 222
Ladle refining furnaces, 12
Latin America, 138
    direct reduction in, 204-217
    increasing steel capacity in,
        207-217
    scrap in, 46
    steel production in, 208
    technology transfer to, 157
Less developed countries (LDCs),
        199-202
Literature review of technology
        transfer in steel
        industry, 67-103
    dominant players, 70-71
    dynamic taxonomy of
        technology transfer, 82-
        86
    entry induction, 67-69

environmental variables, 78, 80-81
globalization effect, 72-76
organizational variables, 78, 80
public sector initiatives, 86
steel minimill industry, 87
technological processing of raw materials, 88-93
technological progress, 71-72
technology transfer models, 76-78
technology variables, 79
transfer variables, 79
Long products, 243

Market direction, 144-149
Market expansion, 85
Markets, 18, 22
Medium-section mills, 98
Metallurgical processing, 92-93
Mexico, 158
Mildrex process, 20-21
Mill scrap, 27
Mills
integrated, *see* Integrated mills
minimills, *see* Minimills
rolling, 96-103, 244
Miniaturization of steel industry, 22
Minimill-like plants, 109
Minimills, 3-4, 151-152, 243, *see also* Steel minimill industry
based on direct reduction, 15
capacities of, 108-109
compared with integrated mills, 107-126

conventional, 17
employment costs, 119-120
entry and exit, 120-121
future of technology for, 116
geographic locations of, 111
product types, 107
productivity of, 116-117, 118
raw materials for, 111-113
technology of, 113-116
MITI and Japanese steel industry, 192-195
Miyoshi, Shunkichi, 144
Multilayer perceptrons, 7-8

Natural environmental equilibrium, conservation of, 33-34
Near-net-casting, 244
Network externalities, 68
Networking, 68
Neural networks, 7-9
Neurons, 8
Newly industrialized countries (NICs), 199-204
Nippon Kokan (NKK), 176-177
change of average sulfur content in line pipe of, 187
diversification of, 188, 189
sales by division, 190
Nippon Steel, 150
NKK, *see* Nippon Kokan
Non-oxidizable elements, 25
Nonscrap waste, 27
North Star mills, 142
NSR System (NSC) for producing clean steel, 220
Nuclear energy, 86
Nucor process, 21

"Old" (or capital) scrap, 28
Open-hearth furnaces, 4-5, 6, 39, 244
Organizational restructuring, adapting through, 137-141
Organizational variables, 78, 80
Oxygen converters, 50
    scrap use in, 51, 53

Pellets, 112
Perceptrons, multilayer, 7-8
Pig iron, 108, 244
Political environmental variables, 81
Post combustion of iron carbide, 133-135
Prices, 20
    scrap, 51
Primary metals, steelmaking, *see* Steelmaking primary metals
Process scrap, 28
Production sequence for steel products, 14
Production shift toward developing countries, 74
Productivity
    of integrated mills, 116-118
    of minimills, 116-117, 118
Public sector initiatives, 86
Purchased scrap, 28
Purdue model, 169

Quality
    scrap, 27-31
    steel product, 23-25
Quality variables, 8

Rathbone, Allan M., 129
Rationalization, 244
Raw materials, 26
    for integrated mills, 112-113
    for minimills, 111-112
    for steel minimill industry, 87
    supply of, in Japanese steel industry, 172-173
    technological processing of, 88-93
R&D (research and development), 22
Rebar, 118
Reclamation industry, ferrous scrap, 34-35
Reconstituted mill, 244
Refining, 92
Research and development (R&D), 22
Residual elements, 25
Reversing mills for cold-rolled strip, 102
Revert scrap, 28
Rod mills, 114
Rolling mills, 96-102, 244

Scrap, 26
    in Arab world, 47-48
    cleanness of, 30
    electric arc furnaces and, 141-142
    in European Community, 45
    in Japan, 44
    in Latin American countries, 46
    in oxygen converter use, 51, 53

placing more, in blast oxygen furnace, 132
in steelmaking, 63
tin-coated, 137
in United States, 41-43
world trade in, 49
zinc in, 134-135
Scrap-based electric arc furnace, 210-214
Scrap capacity, 21
Scrap contamination, 211
Scrap impurities, 135
Scrap market, 39-64
Scrap pathways in steel industry, 32
Scrap prices, 51
Scrap purchased, steel produced and, 213
Scrap quality, 27-31
Scrap quality classification systems, 28-31
Scrap quality control, statistical, 31
Scrap reclamation industry, ferrous, 34-35
Scrap recycling, flow diagram of, 60
Scrap resources, 58
in European Community, 55
in Japan, 56
in United States, 54
in world, 57
Scrap supply, increased, 40
Scrap systems, iron-ore systems compared with, 62
Scrap utilization, 23
maximizing, 33-36
Secondary steelmaking, 244
Semifinished steel, 244

Sheets, 108
Shredders, 35
Sinter, 112
Small-section mills, 98
Social institutions, 18
Societal variables, 78, 80-81
Software architecture, layered, in Japanese steel industry, 171, 172
South Korea, 203-204
Specialty steels, 245
in Japan, 185
Statistical scrap quality control, 31
Steel, 245
clean, NSR System (NSC) for producing, 220
cleanness of, 25
shaping, 93
Steel capacity, increasing, in Latin America, 207-217
Steel consumption, apparent, 72, 73
Steel Dynamics, 124
Steel gas, 61
Steel industry
Brazilian, 223-225
Chinese, 228-229
continuous casting in, *see* Continuous casting
economic development and, 202-204
energy intensity and, 64
Indian, 225-228
Japanese, *see* Japanese steel industry
literature review of technology transfer in, *see* Literature

review of technology
transfer in steel industry
miniaturization of, 22
resurgence of, 3-9
scrap pathways in, 32
technology transfer in, 18-31
in United States, 75
Steel-making technology and
strategy, 5-7
Steel minimill industry, 3
central technologies of, 12-17
dependent and independent
variables in models of,
20-21
hypotheses for, 22
literature review, 87
model of, 20
overview of, 11-36
raw materials for, 87
Steel minimills, *see* Minimills
Steel production
in Latin America, 208
scrap purchased and, 213
Steel products
production sequence for, 14
quality of, 23-25
Steel technology, modern, 31, 33-
36
Steelmaking
iron ore, scrap, and primary
metals in, 63
technology transfer and, 4-5
Steelmaking primary metals, 63
world trends for, 59
Stirring, 90
Stock variables, 82, 237
Strategic variety, 71
Strength variables, 8
Strip mills, 6-7

truncated, 7
Structural shapes, 245
Sumitomo Metal Industries, 176,
177
Synthetic slags, 89

Tandem mills for cold-rolling
strip, 101-102
Technological processing of raw
materials, 88-93
Technological progress, 71-76
Technology transfer
brief review of, 233-234
central questions in, 19-20
challenges of, 155-156
to China, 156-157
direction of, 199-230
dynamic taxonomy of, 82-87
to Europe, 157
future research in, 233-240
inter industry, 149-154
interaction of main elements
in process of, 84
interdependent variables in
process of, 83
international, 129-159
knowledge-based framework
of, 129-131
to Latin America, 157
literature review of, *see* Literature
review of technology
transfer in steel industry
models of, 76-78
in steel industry, 18-31
steelmaking and, 4-5
Technology trends, 122-126
Technology variables, 79
Temperature control, 92
Thermal de-zincing, 135

Thin slab casters, 6-7
Thin slab casting (TSC), 212, 214
Tin-coated scrap, 137
Tippins/Samsung process (TSP)
       mills, 122, 125-126, 156
Tolerance, 245
Tramp elements, 25, 31
Transfer method, 131
Transfer risks, 82
Transfer scope, 131
Transfer variables, 79
Truncated strip mills, 7
TSC (thin slab casting), 212, 214
TSP (Tippins/Samsung process)
       mills, 122, 125-126, 156
Tundish cars, 13

United States, 139
    scrap in, 41-43
    scrap resources in, 54
    steel industry in, 75
Usinor Sacilor, 140, 141

Vacuum-arc furnaces, 88
Vacuum degassing, 91
Vacuum processes, 89
Voest-Alpine, 149
VRAS, 245

Western Europe, 138
Wire rod mills, 99
Wire-strip mills, 100-101
Withdrawal, speed of, 94
World, scrap resources in, 57
World trade in scrap, 49
World trends for steelmaking
       primary metals, 59
World-wide economic
       development, 72
WorldClass Steel, 126

Zinc
    in baghouse dust, 136
    in scrap, 134-135

VITA

Shastri Moonan holds the following academic degrees:

Ph.D. from the Fletcher School of Law and Diplomacy.
B.Sc. (Economics) from the University of the West Indies.
M.S. (Management) from the Massachusetts Institute of Technology.
M.A.L.D. from the Fletcher School of Law and Diplomacy.

Professional Qualifications: Barrister-at-Law from the Honourable Society of Lincoln's Inn, London, England.

He has been engaged in extensive commercial activities.

T - #0030 - 230425 - C0 - 216/138/16 [18] - CB - 9780815329978 - Gloss Lamination